Ruminations of a Gadfly

Deena Khatkhate is a former director of research at the Reserve Bank of India, a former assistant director at the International Monetary Fund, and a former senior consultant for the United Nations and the World Bank. After early retirement from the IMF, he served as managing editor of the reputed academic journal *World Development* (earlier published by the Pergamon Press and now, the Elsevier). Dr. Khatkhate is the author of numerous articles on economic development and monetary policy, which have appeared from time to time in leading academic journals such as *The Quarterly Journal of Economics, The Review of Economics and Statistics, Economic and Political Weekly, The Journal of Post-Keynesian Economics,* and *Oxford Economic Papers.*

Dr. Khatkhate lives in Chevy Chase, Maryland, USA.

RUMINATIONS OF A GADFLY

Persons, Places, Perceptions

DEENA KHATKHATE

ACADEMIC FOUNDATION
NEW DELHI

www.academicfoundation.com

First published in 2008
by

ACADEMIC FOUNDATION
4772-73 / 23 Bharat Ram Road, (23 Ansari Road),
Darya Ganj, New Delhi - 110 002 (India).
Phones : 23245001 / 02 / 03 / 04.
Fax : +91-11-23245005.
E-mail : academic@vsnl.com
www. academicfoundation.com

Cataloging in Publication Data--DK
Courtesy: D.K. Agencies (P) Ltd. <docinfo@dkagencies.com>

Khatkhate, Deena.
Ruminations of a gadfly / Deena Khatkhate.
p. cm. Essays exploring societal changes in India and abroad; most previously published. Includes index.

ISBN 13: 9788171886579
ISBN 10: 8171886574

1. Social change--India. 2. Social change--United States. 3. Social change--Cross-cultural studies. 4. Celebrities--India. 5. Communism. I. Title.

DDC 303.409 54 22

Typeset by Italics India, New Delhi.
Printed and bound in India.

To

Three Graces

Shanta, Amala, Anya (Andy)

who made my life worth living

Contents

PART V

TIME'S SWEET REVENGE

Preface

FRIENDS may wonder why I have chosen to bring out this unusual book of my unusual writings rather than my academic papers published in economic journals of international repute during my professional career as economist of more than four decades. In 1980, Vijay Joshi, Fellow at Merton College, Oxford, lined up Basil Blackwell to publish a collection of my economic writings. Then again, Manu Shroff who, after a distinguished career in the Government of India and the World Bank, became editor of *The Economic Times*, offered to edit all my economic writings for a volume and find a suitable publisher. But when I went over my articles written over a long time span, I felt that they had served their purpose, provoking comment, controversy, and debate; to hark back to them would not contribute further to the academic and scholarly discourse.

I have made an exception to that self-imposed rule in bringing out this volume, containing several of my non-economic reflections on the world around me—good and bad, profound and profane, conviviality and conflicts, hypocrisy and honesty, and approbation and opprobrium. The leitmotif behind this has been to recapture my passion, idealism, and social awareness in my early youth, when I was involved in the student union movement with a political orientation and organisations for the uplift of workers in the city of Bombay—as it was named then—though the experience was disillusioning. This disposition of mine spurred me on to give vent to my innate restlessness and the devil-take-the-hindmost sort of outlook on life. It did, of course, interfere in the smooth conduct of my official life. I often wrote, generally under a *nom de plume*, articles on politically incorrect issues or on 'things not done' in a placid, hierarchical, ersatz official life.

A colleague, who later rose to a prominent position in the Government of India, gave me a sobriquet—"angry and excitable young man"—rather a corny expression, whether out of affinity of a friend or derogation of a non-friend. But it was not anger or excitability any more than my aversion to things *de rigueur* and conformism. My belief system evolved out of my early experiences and the attitude towards life formed by these led me to write on aspects of life that agitated any educated, socially conscious member of society. I did not model myself on anyone until I came to know in the 1990s late Asok Mitra, a distinguished member of the Indian Civil Service, well-known demographer and art critic who, in his hallowed career often stood for his convictions even at the risk of demotion. He wrote profusely on a variety of problems without fear or favour. His life touched deep chords in me, as would be evident in my tribute to him included in this volume.

My early retirement from the International Monetary Fund in 1987 made me a free bird soaring high in the intellectual space with abandon. I requested Krishna Raj, then editor of the *Economic and Political Weekly*, with whom I had a long personal and professional association, if I could write a regular column, "Potomac Musings". In this column, I wanted to look at America from the eyes of an Indian national, look at India and the world from the eyes of an Indian emigrant to a developed land, and open a window to reprise the god of ideology I once worshipped and then discarded. Krishna Raj was a little hesitant. He knew well enough that I would be saying things in this freewheeling column that might run counter to his ideological beliefs. After a few articles were published, his reticence made way to enthusiasm in the face of the readers' reactions and also because Krishna Raj himself was in a 'change mode' ideologically. Around the same time, I was invited by Dilip Padgaonkar, Swaminathan Aiyar and late Dilip Mukherji of *The Times of India* to write a fortnightly column. I jumped at this opportunity. Soon after, Ashok V. Desai of the *Business Standard* persuaded me to write a column, "Gadflight", a precursor of this book, so to say. Only recently, I published a few articles in *E-Social Sciences*, an online journal of Padma Prakash, on the editorial board of which I am a member. For inclusion in this volume, I have drawn on all these journals but largely the *Economic and Political Weekly,* in addition to some unpublished articles in the belief that they still remain relevant and of enduring interest to the inquiring readers.

My thanks are to the editors of the *Economic and Political Weekly, The Times of India, Business Standard* and *World Development* for permitting me to reproduce the articles published in their journals. I express my appreciation of Arthur Monteiro who did an excellent job in preparing this manuscript and its format for publication and of Ms. Southamini Borlo and Chet Ninoo-Quarcoo of the World Bank-IMF library for helping me with references.

Making of a gadfly

> "There is no commandment which may not be broken; neither those and I say unto you, nor those laid down by the prophets."
>
> —*Jorge Luis Borges*

I never believed in planning how I would live my life. My coming to the International Monetary Fund had been as unpremeditated as my leaving it, or what I have done thereafter. By happenstance, I read an article by H.C. Coomb, former distinguished governor of the Reserve Bank of Australia, in which he aired his thoughts on retirement. A day after his last day in office, Coomb looked out through the window of his drawing room, not knowing what he would do next. He saw the green grass, chirping birds and the blue sky, all of which reminded him of how much he had missed in life, having been confined to a rigid regimen for his livelihood, where one could not be master of one's destiny. He could paint, he could organise art museums, he could write. He thought then that retirement was not the end but could well be the beginning of a new phase of his life.

I was in the same frame of mind on my last day in the Fund. Sitting alone at a corner of its cafeteria I recalled my eighteen years in the Fund with both nostalgia and relief. Being a free spirit I had been a little stifled by the culture in the Fund, which can be characterised as "What I do not know is not knowledge, debate is dissent, and to be different is to be similar." My contrived and cultivated caution often gave way during my career in the Fund. Towards the end of my active duty I wrote an introduction to a special number of *World Development*, an academic journal, in which I slipped in some ideas that did not quite adhere to the party line.

Though I euphemistically described the article as The Editor's Perspective, which the impish editor of the Fund's Staff News, a house magazine, thought to be a subterfuge to save my skin, it provoked a remark from the clearance office that "it mocks at the Fund." Somewhat earlier, I had written a little naughty piece on Sri Lanka, which I had visited in course of my work, using the legend of the Buddha's death-and-rebirth cycle as a metaphor for Sri Lanka's polity. Though the Buddhist philosophy could not have even remotely been connected with the Fund's stabilisation policy, permission to publish was denied. These two episodes determined the course of my life beyond the Fund: they told me to do the things I was doing in the Fund differently, to ruminate as a gadfly on issues that would come to my mind, and to write as a libertine.

My first outstation was the managing editorship of *World Development*. While in the Fund, I had suggested as a member of the editorial board of the Fund's Staff Papers, introduction of a referral process for the selection of articles. I applied the referee system rigorously in my new incarnation. It undoubtedly enhanced the status of the journal, mainly because academics put a great premium on refereed journals, and I felt rewarded when four of the contributors to it were given tenure at their universities on the basis of their published articles, among which those appearing in *World Development* figured prominently. At the same time, I came to understand better the scepticism with which my suggestion on refereeing had been greeted in the Fund, since the actual experience of it showed that it was not always infallible. To my dismay, reviewers who were distinguished in their own fields gave diametrically opposite verdicts and reviewers who saw their own theories contradicted in manuscripts rejected them.

I was inducted, not by design, into the World Bank where I wrote in the same areas as I did in the Fund. The assignment was a background paper for the 1989 *World Development Report* on the financial sector, carrying very broad terms of reference. Not being bound by any bureaucratic rules, I made it a freewheeling effort, putting forth my ideas on financial liberalisation with a degree of freedom I could never have dreamed of either in the Fund or in the Reserve Bank of India, where I had started my career. Somehow it passed muster in the Bank, though it received flak from a Harvard professor, who reviewed it in a learned journal. The professor took the Bank to task for allowing upstarts like me and my co-author Yoon Je Cho (who had a brief stint in the Fund after this paper was out before becoming a senior counsellor to the Finance Minister of Korea) to intellectually seduce the Bank. This experience brought home to me how these two Bretton Woods twins, a street apart, operate unlike twins in matters intellectual.

By some quirk of fate I became a commentator on economic policy issues in *The Times of India*. The time was most propitious, as India was on a new track of economic reform. There was a strong belief in India that Indian policymakers were hostages to the blandishments of the Fund and the World Bank. Being fully convinced that the Fund recipe of fiscal and monetary retrenchment was the only way to bring about economic salvation for India, I rationalised the Fund's advice. Seeing the byline indicating my past association with the Fund, I was branded as a mercenary. Curiously enough, the Fund's daily news-sheet cited another paragraph of the same column which stated, "Not that the sanctimonious attitude of the international bureaucracy, involved in negotiations, does not grate your nerves nor are the conditions always carefully thought through" as very critical of the Fund. I had thus the unique honour of being at the same time both an apologist for the Fund and an apostate!

The gadfly in me surfaced in another of my activities. I had some literary pretensions that I had not been able to vent while bound by the institutional ethos. I vividly remember when a senior official in the Fund, while commenting on one of my internal advisory reports, called my prose as suited to a political tract. Not quite amused, I wrote back tongue in cheek that apparently the wise man had neither written at any time a political tract nor an article on economics. My insouciance later found full reflection in 'Potomac Musings' that appeared in the *Economic and Political Weekly*. It was an experiment where I tried to make serious points in a light-hearted fashion, giving full rein to my impulses, rational or irrational. In one piece, entitled "Craving for a Philosopher's Stone", I wrote that

> Even when all his diagnosis and prognosis have been proven wrong, the economist can still be trusted to provide an ex-post facto rationalisation for every new economic event. A case in point is the economists' continuously shifting positions on what constitutes an appropriate international exchange rate system.

In another piece, "Waiting for Godot", I lampooned forecasters, including those in the Fund engaged on its *World Economic Outlook*, saying that economists and forecasters had become astrologers and that they felt little embarrassment when they went wrong times without number. At times I wondered whether I could have committed such a sacrilege while in the Fund.

In 1993, during the Fund-Bank Annual Meetings, I was asked by the then Finance Minister, Dr. Manmohan Singh, to write a report on Indian financial reform. I agreed to it as a labour of love and was assured of full freedom to say what I wanted to say, with access to all confidential material and officials. The only condition I stipulated was that the report should be published with minimum delay, for public discussion and debate. I thought it was a lifetime opportunity to encapsulate in one report all that I had come to believe about the Indian banking system and monetary policy. In less than a month the report was ready. It was then fully discussed with the Finance Ministry officials and the Finance Minister and agreed for release after a month. Although the report was candid, well documented, and comprehensive, it was eventually pigeonholed for reasons never explained to me. As Ashok V. Desai wrote, "the job of an economic adviser is to tell as it is and advise as he sees right." But I learnt to my cost that advice can only be taken if it helps the political survival of bureaucrats who excel in playing the game of snakes-and-ladders. Nevertheless, this episode gave me some satisfaction that I lived up to my reputation as a free spirit. If my former Fund colleagues had known what I had written in the report, they would have thought that I had at last matured with age!

Age seems to have matured the Fund, too. A cognoscente can discern that it has been talking prose lately without knowing it, like Moliere's hero. Now devaluation has been devalued and is no longer frequently resorted to in the Fund's adjustment programmes. Also, there is a charming humility in the acknowledgement that it is difficult to know how exchange rates are determined, whether by current account position or capital flows: a certain openness is seen in recognising that the Fund misjudged the balance of payments of Mexico in 1995 and the subsequent Asian financial crises. The Fund has become more transparent and can turn the light inward, as the Fund's excellent evaluation reports since 2001 bear out. There is growing realisation amongst the Fund's staff that what one does not know could also be knowledge. I have come to believe that life after the Fund is one of gay abandon intellectually.

Part I

Americana

1

Bearable lightness of being

AMERICA is a melting pot of cultures, races and histories. There is no one distinct trait that American society can call its own, except the drawling accent of the Southerner, the swagger of the billionaire, the hoop-la of the political conventions, the hyperbole of the football game, the vulgarity of Hollywood's glitter and the picturesqueness of American English. The world's nomads stream into this rich man's land with hope and the heavy baggage of their beliefs, traditions and the preachers' mind-set. Hope is for a new life of material comfort and relief from the meanness of human existence. But the baggage they carry in the early years is heavy and overpowering. They come only for a better life and not for enrichment of their minds, except as a by-product of other pursuits. Their own ancient cultures have left them a cut above others who mill around them in their adopted land. Wearing the garb of preachers, the migrants, particularly from the Indian subcontinent, can purvey unsolicited advice to their fellow travellers not to allow themselves to be contaminated by the culture of the West, seduced by the libertine values, and to adhere to the straight and narrow path of the virtues imbibed by them in the country they left behind. Once they accomplish what they have arrived for—be it higher education or a nice nest egg or whatever the spiritual traditions enjoin them to acquire in the conduct of material pursuits—they should say adieu to this glittering world to return to their own tranquil and emotionally satisfying worlds. They should come into a new world but never forge ties that would bind them to it forever. From the ancient land they come, to the ancient land they must ultimately return.

The newcomers carry this heavy baggage until the settling down blues have been got over. Then they all get on a trajectory of new life—a trajectory which has originated from the mores they have left behind—which cuts the old values and beliefs at a new angle. The senses are numbed in the onrush of daily life and thought processes are muted. If they falter, the momentum of the trajectory will be lost. So they take the easy way out, pigeonholing their past, putting their memories in a black box. They must make their own what they see, do and experience. They become a part of the surrounding milieu if they have to survive in a new country and make a success of life there. They try to offload a piece of the baggage they have carried so long and so assiduously.

Yet they do not quite succeed in this endeavour. The trajectory of the new life is above the earlier surface but it cannot be joined with it. When children grow out of schooling, grow wings, new problems arise. The conflict between what was and is, submerged for long, wells up. A son or a daughter asks to go with a date and the parents are shocked. They then recite the holy scriptures to impress upon their children how virtuous were their Gods and forefathers. They even become autobiographical to let their offspring know how much they had struggled to come to where they are. The children, imbibing their knowledge not from books but from television and their peers in school, talk back, reminding them that the world their forefathers lived in is no longer extant. The parents then turn from moneymen to godmen, who too are obsessed with the thought of civilising the western world. They fly first class, move about in limousines, live in palatial houses, which is all called simple living and high thinking. Many associations of godmen have mushroomed where spiritual messages roll out in an incessant flow, but only in response to the reverse flow of money from the devotees.

Though thrown thousands of miles away, their nostalgia for their country's politics and culture grows in geometric progression. It is a status symbol to flaunt admiration for Indira Gandhi or Rajiv Gandhi or even the 1975 Emergency of Sanjay Gandhi. Gandhi is a magic name, after all. Many of them realised the Mahatma's greatness through Richard Attenborough's melodrama. Indira Gandhi was the empress because she brought about disintegration of the hated Pakistan. Emergency was good because it disciplined the unruly Indians. But the real reason is the suppressed guilt which disturbs their subconscious recesses. They have been luxuriating while millions of their fellow-beings are languishing back home. How else can one explain these Indians, in private palavers and at social functions, adulating Reagan and his administration? Perhaps, they have seen the unseen—the invisible bonds between the Republican regime and the 'garibi hatao' regimes of Indira Gandhi and her son. Journalists amongst them are not immune to these contradictory postures. In scores of community papers run by Indians in this country, the editorials read like press handouts of the Indian embassy or the Government of India. It is considered patriotic to defend everything that the authorities do back home, whether it is sending troops to Sri Lanka, denying the Sikhs their legitimate demands or making political capital from fake threats of Pakistani invasion which recur every now and then. For journalists, knowledge is information garnered from the Indian Embassy to which they make daily pilgrimage. They write about Indian events the way visiting politicians from India speak at press conferences in Washington. What these worthy ambassadors of the Fourth Estate despatch home is slanted summaries of what appears in American newspapers.

Cultural activity too reflects the ambivalence which becomes second nature. Plays are staged from themes which are evocative of days gone by, mawkish and melodramatic. There is no attempt to learn from the modern experimental techniques for which American theatre is known and which is making waves back home in Bombay, Delhi or Calcutta. Marriages are celebrated in gala fashion with a disco thrown in with *sari*- and *dhoti*-clad grandmas and granddads making their debut. The presiding priests use the function as a forum for lecture-discussions for the benefit of the few westerners amongst the audience. Temples are built and Gods are chosen depending on one's caste or regional loyalties, a legacy from the subcontinent.

This alternation of East and West in cultural and intellectual activity, this medley of values and beliefs, is a manifestation of the confusion of identity. They are neither fowl nor fish. This uncertainty as to their true identity leads to confusion in thought and action. There are some stirrings of late but these are faint. Unless they observe and analyse the surrounding scene, they cannot refurbish their image. American society has reached the acme of glory and it is now looking for new springs of resurgence which will come from the large waves of new immigrants who are being inducted into this society. After all, American society is an immigrant society—it is not German, Irish, British, French or Dutch; it belongs to all and therefore to none. Now the Hispanics, the Japanese, the Chinese, the Vietnamese and the Koreans are flooding in with their own distinctive brand of history, culture and tradition. The people of the Indian subcontinent are a part of this emerging new society. If only the Indians make an effort to discern what is best in the bewildering situation and adapt their own value system, retaining what is best and noble in India's ancient past, and fuse it with the best in the society they now live in, they would make the brave new world more livable, vibrant and human. It is no use harking back to the past, no use indulging in the nostalgia of John Denver's "Country road, take me home." But if you do all this to distil the best you see in the past to transpose it into the future, then you are on the right track.

Economic and Political Weekly, 13 August 1988.

2

A tale of two cities

IN topography, political profile and manipulative games, the cities of Washington DC and New Delhi could not have been more similar. Each nestles at the cross boundaries of two neighbouring states—New Delhi flanked by Haryana and Uttar Pradesh and Washington by Virginia and Maryland. Both are self-aggrandising capitals of the two federations, one priding itself as the richest democracy and the other the largest democracy though non-functioning only because of its teeming population. They have been growing by preying on adjoining territories, replacing farmland with the thriving conurbation, drawing sustenance from the expanding power of the federal government. Both inhere, as it were, the same architecture which a few may believe is traced to France—a country of old kings and queens and also the revolutions emitting messages of equality, liberty and fraternity. Both Washington and New Delhi boast a circular pattern in their traffic configurations, wide and long tree-lined boulevards and avenues. La Enfant designed Washington DC and Lutyen was the genius behind New Delhi's town planning and the vice-regal abode—two architects who had a shared legacy from the same French school of architecture.

But it is not only in architecture and topography that these two cities look alike. There are many other striking features that make them twins. The least important, and perhaps a coincidence, is that both are currently presided over by B-rated men—a B-rated actor and a B-rated pilot. Human as these statesmen are, they often run to Godmen or soothsayers to calm their frayed nerves. Don Regan, booted out for his involvement in the Iran/Contra affair, blew the whistle about Nancy Reagan's confabulations with an astrologer which, in his view, interfered with the business of state. For those of us in India and Delhi this should be news. Our ex-prime minister and the present one, the ministers, the president and all those who are in power or outside have some astrologer or godman not only to seek advice on how to run the state but also how to destroy the rival cliques. Poor Nancy, she rushed to the soothsayer only to protect her husband from another madman's firepower.

There is a constant stream of fixers, political operators and minions of industrial tycoons milling around Congress and the White House to manipulate some defence contract or the other or to get one's friend, dear one or even a mistress into some important position in the government. There are no licences to be issued here but certainly favours can be granted, inside information can be leaked, honourable women employees can be sexually harassed. Look at what the special prosecutor is unearthing to rope in Ed Meese, the guardian of law and order of this great democracy; the travails of a lady lawyer in the Security and Exchange Commission, who valiantly defied her employer for the last twelve years to vindicate her honour and in the process lost her money, mind and fair-weather friends; the underworld of buddy system in the defence organisation by which ex-officials have ensured their comfort and security after retirement by ripping off the federal government.

Why should we Indians be ashamed about our Bofors scandals? If such things could happen in the capital of the richest country, why not in the capital of the largest democracy struggling to survive? Maybe there is a logic beyond our comprehension. It is self-flagellation that Indians covet most, they say. If there are riffraff amongst the Indian Members of Parliament and Assemblymen, currying favour, peddling influence, wheeling-dealing in political power games and misusing their contacts in higher echelons of power for appropriating the spoils for their sons and daughters, Uncle Sam's favourite sons are no better. Senators and Congressmen are a favoured and feared tribe. Their moonshine occupation is to seek a 'quid' from businessmen for a quo of supporting some special legislation. Pork-barrelling is a picturesque American expression for it. They bend the traffic rules for their convenience—witness 'Stop' signs in front of their driveways, the same as the Indian legislators and ministers arrange to place 'No Parking' signs in front of their houses. At the airport in Washington almost one-third of the short-term parking area is pre-empted by these good-Samaritan legislators. Perhaps power-seekers and power wielders the world over are clones—they think, behave and act alike.

And yet these two cities stand apart in many ways. The Rashtrapati Bhavan, a red-stone palace in which the powerless First Citizen of India resides, is magnificence run amuck. Yes, it has been the legacy of the colonial masters but their liberated slaves have more than flattered them by imitation. They could, of course, rationalise it by saying that they got their back on the erstwhile masters by occupying those exclusive abodes. But what about the large bungalows—the former homes of the Commander-in-Chief and other military brass hats, which were converted for ministers' luxury living? Deep down, this was not a mere accident, amnesia or a sheer convenience amidst the availability of a large number of vacant houses after Independence. It was rather a manifestation of the imperial mould of our being deeply rooted in our history. If Americans prefer to live in hovels, it is their problem. In any case, their history spans only a couple of centuries; in fact, they have no history. But what about socialism, did you say, a vaunted banner that we have been flaunting for decades? For heaven's sake, by asking such questions you should not reveal your ignorance. Socialism is a dynamic concept, always evolving. In any case, who ever said that under socialism one should not live in comfort? Look at Stalin and other leaders of the communist world!

In Washington, the president, like our prime minister, often chooses the judges on the Supreme Court or other courts falling within the jurisdiction of the federal government. President Reagan used every opportunity to place men of his choice in the courts. He came out a cropper only once when the Derk Bork nomination was nipped in the bud. Almost all his nominees are of his persuasion, of a conservative mould, against abortion and also affirmative action. But see what has happened. The Chief Justice, Wilhelm Rehnquist, and other conservative judges of the Supreme Court stunned the Reagan administration and his fellow-travellers by upholding the Independent Counsel law, stoutly opposed by the government, and by expanding the federal anti-discrimination law for women and minorities. Even the worm can turn, the frustrated Reaganites are saying. Could it ever have happened in New Delhi? In the last few years the judiciary has been gravely politicised: the ruling party has saddled it with its subservient men. The same process was followed here but the results have been vastly different: they cut their ideological umbilical chord once they occupy the benches. This is not the first time that the judges of the US Supreme Court have denounced their benefactor. Justice Earl Warren did it earlier. Maybe the physical similarity between these two cities hides dissimilar inner chemistries.

In this city, ex-ministers and journalists too follow a path different from their counterparts in New Delhi. The ex-budget officer, David Stockman, chosen for his conservative philosophy despite his callowness, excoriated, once out of office, the Reagan philosophy of budget, which subsequent events have proved was disastrous. There was a lot of fiction in what he said but the facts he uncovered and the shenanigans of the budgeters he exposed, brought down the credibility of supply-side economics. Larry Speakes, the Reagan administration's press spokesman, lived up to his name by squealing. Michael Deaver, a close confidant of the President and the First Lady, through his memoirs published after his indictment for misuse of contacts in carrying out his consultancy business, spilled the beans about their private lives. And the last, Donald Regan, first the Treasury Secretary and then a Chief of Staff, after having been fired for his acts of commission and omission in the Iran/Contra affair, took revenge on Nancy Reagan, his bête noire, by revealing her astrological addiction. True, they made millions through these kiss-and-tell stories; but the way the American system of administration functions in the capital makes it easier for these ex-officials to stab their former friends or masters in the back. New Delhi had only one parallel to show, M.O. Mathai, Prime Minister Nehru's private secretary for many years. When his book came out, we all seemed to have been outraged. Maybe it was the difference in our inherited culture or perhaps Mathai was not sanctified by a number of dollars as were the American ex-officials.

Washington has its horde of journalists, eager to prey on the government. The press being totally independent of the government and journalists' freedom and remuneration being assured, they do not owe any debt to anyone in government, be it the powerful President of the United States or the Secretary of State or whoever. Richard Nixon, who was blatantly lying at a news conference, had to answer a question put to him saying he was not a crook. The Vice President, bushy-mushy George Bush, was hounded relentlessly by Dan Rather on CBS to get him to answer some unsettled issues on the Iran/Contra affair, and when he prevaricated, Rather moved the TV camera away from him. Maybe Dan Rather was insolent but it is better to be that than be servile like so many New Delhi newsmen, who ask the government dignitaries at news conferences either inane and superficial questions or paraphrase the government handouts because they reside in government-allotted apartments or serve the newspaper barons, who are eternally obligated to the government.

Washington has its best of times when men in power have a gladiatorial ride holding back from public gaze the secrets of statecraft—a My Lai is suppressed, the machinations of the President in illegally organising wiretap of happenings in the rival political party's office go undetected—but soon, the best of times are followed by the worst of times, when these men in power grovel in dust, when some 'deep throat' brings to light the misuse of power. New Delhi has its best of times, but its worst times are also its best of times. Justice often plays truant, as when the commission appointed to investigate the massacre of hundreds of Sikhs in the aftermath of the Prime Minister's assassination whitewashes the government's crimes, when the parliamentary committee supposed to seek the truth in the Bofors scandal sidesteps those who know the truth, when the skulduggery of partymen is covered up. But then how can you compare New Delhi with Washington? Is not New Delhi the capital of a nation with a long history and an ancient civilisation?

Economic and Political Weekly, 27 August 1988.

3

Children of a lesser God

EVERYTHING in life has its time and place—charity and cheating, affluence and dire poverty, swanky apartments side by side with shantytowns, mendicants and swaggering yuppies. All these contrasting situations abound in a poor country trying to break its traditional mores to enter the phase of industrialisation and modernisation. But pray, how can one see around him, in a country priding itself to be the richest in the world, a phenomenon of hordes of the homeless, denizens of a shantytown without there being one? These homeless swirl around American cities. They are black, white and brown, men and women, young and old, native Yankees and immigrants from the Andean countries, Africa and even Asia. A trickle a decade ago, their numbers are swelling. Dressed in drab and unwashed clothes, resting in sleeping-bags, these men with shaggy beards and women with dishevelled hair greet you at every metro station, bus stop, shopping mall and corporate office and the outskirts of international aid agencies. They invade chapels, shopping-centre floors and school corridors for night shelter and to answer the call of nature. They have thus become a major scourge for cities and government.

But who are these homeless and where have they come from? There is no mass unemployment nor migration from the declining rural hinterland to the urban centres that one comes across in developing countries. They are not even identified with the blacks, the perennial underdogs in American society, because there are whites and other non-blacks among them. Blacks may live in pigsties they call homes. They may be homeless with a home but not homeless without a home. Can economics of the marketplace, which is raised to the status of a high deity by the Reagan administration, throw light on it? Perhaps, but not fully. Market-determined demand creates over-development—you might get new models of cars every year, new designs of clothes every three months, new gadgets every few minutes at declining cost and price but not a roof over your head. The Republican regime has slashed spending on urban housing on governmental account on the specious ground that it is for the private sources to assume that role. Yet homelessness is not a consequence of over-development or mal-development, if one can use that expression for a change.

You know how these people are homeless, if you peruse their history. They are not necessarily poor, the kind we in India meet in our shantytowns. Many of them are well educated, once well stationed in life, some had enjoyed higher standards in the 1970s, but now have fallen on evil days. Pia McKay, one of them, holds a Masters degree of an Ivy League University, Columbia. She once taught in a Washington school system but has lived since 1980 in a shelter. She became homeless when she became psychotic as a result of the trauma of foster childhood. She lived this wretched life among other ladies of varying ages and nationalities. One in her late sixties defied her children willing to support her, regressing to childhood with its fading fantasies. Another chronic alcoholic kleptomaniac, who worked in a high position in the government for twenty years, shouted, "I don't want to be cured", when offered succour. She often got injured in accidents in her rounds of the city of Washington, was often raped, was disowned by her family, and was thrown out from various shelters; her abode is an awning of a restaurant. There is a handsome East European woman, once an apple of many an eye. She immigrated to the land of promise, being locked in love with an American. Deserted, she attempted suicide, after scampering around for a peaceful resting place. You also know a woman with college education, yelling for rights—heaven knows what they are—and occasionally resorting to prostitution. She became disorientated when she found her mother in bed with her niece! There is an exchange student from an Asian country, who came with great hopes of going to good schools; but some obstacle or the other, and she is left high and dry—no education, only joints and alcohol. She is constantly reading something or the other in preparation, she does not know for what.

Joining this phalanx are the grown-up men of between thirty and sixty. Many of them once enjoyed the luxury of high living. With their savings dissipated on unwanted wants and old-age infirmities, forsaken by their kith and kin and without the resources to enter the dorm for the old and sick, they have sought their destiny in the marketplace—a marketplace which the wiseacres of new economics believe would resolve all of America's problems. The marketplace may or may not clear the loads that flow to it but it brings in living bodies who become zombies, psychotics and prostitutes clogging markets without any demand for them even as a free commodity. If you have not seen the magic of a marketplace, do rush to American cities to be dazzled by it.

This frightening spectre of homelessness is not of a genre of the slum-dwellers of the impoverished population in our land. In some way it is sociological in its manifestation. Families are broken with divorce rates skyrocketing; 50 to 55 per cent of new marriages end up in smoke every year. The average life of a marriage has shrivelled dramatically from 25 years as of yore to anywhere between three and four years. Partners in marriage know each other as intimately and warmly as two strangers passing through a revolving door. Marriage is a procedure for fulfilling some immediate but transient needs. The two thus remain strangers as they grow and when a crunch comes at some point in the future, the whole edifice of beliefs, values and that invisible thread interlacing their souls is snapped. Things go even worse when the conjugal embrace brings forth a progeny without love, without care, embroiled in emotional tyranny. Riches may have banished the agony of hungry bellies in affluent societies but brought instead illness of the mind. How can one explain otherwise that beautiful, sophisticated, cultured and well-bred men, women and children can regress to childhood with total disorientation? Children may be there but they do not behave as children simply because they do not know who their parents are. Parents swap their marriage partners so often that they should be excused if they do not know whom to call their own children. Even those families which are not as much divorced as many others and whose children are relatively emotionally stable, refrain from placing much premium on the care and health of their wards. If the child is nineteen, he or she is a major and should be on their own. The parents figure out that once their children reach a certain age, they have fulfilled their obligations as parents. They are then free to enjoy their own life, what with a holiday trip to the world afar.

Economic factors operate but differently. There is an inner drive to earn more and spend more, even when incomes earned are sufficient to maintain a decent lifestyle. The psychological rule that motivates Marx's capitalist to accumulate and accumulate and accumulate also governs the consumer in this society—he has to spend more and more on newer goods all the time. This driven mentality in the conduct of daily life has ravaged the psychological apparatus of the people. This craze for satiation of unwanted wants has created a crisis. Is wantlessness a mere utopia?

So these homeless will continue to roam about in American society. Your moral sensibility may be outraged if you see a sunken-eyed middle-aged man, wrapped in dirty rags, with saliva dripping at the corners of his mouth, bundled out of a restaurant by the roughnecks. Your heart might bleed to see a semi-nude beautiful damsel of yesteryears begging for a dime or quarter for a peg of scotch. Under the present societal dispensation this show will go on. Men of conscience may agonise, a good Samaritan like Mitch Snyder may launch a Joshua-like crusade to wipe away the tears of this luckless humanity, but nothing basically will change, for a while at least. These high-minded people with goodwill, piety and compassion will face the dilemma of the minister of the Capitol Hill United Methodist Church. This factotum of God pushed away the worldly goods of a homeless one from the driveway of his church to the curb, from where they were tucked away by the garbage van. Losing everything he had, the hapless homeless looked back in anger: "You preachers are all alike. You live in nice homes with closets. You have places to put things." The next thing God's acolyte did was to raise the fence to shut out the homeless from entering the portals of the church. He was no doubt protecting the people of God such as him so that he could give in solitude a sermon from the holy scriptures to his audience. He could have instead recited the poem "Mending Wall" by America's national poet, Robert Frost. By raising the fence he was "walling in" the people of God; but whom was he "walling out?" Perhaps children of a lesser God?

Economic and Political Weekly, 23 April 1988.

4

Transformation of the blacks

WE Indians as a nation and a society are weighed down by the burden of over two thousand years of history. The history of the glorious past beckons us, brings to life our dormant ambitions and desires but only to depress us in the face of the unsavoury present. We then like to assert the unassertable, believe the unbelievable and act the unactable by spouting homilies to others, particularly the people of other continents and cultures. A favourite theme is the intrinsic superiority of the moral foundations of our polity and civilisation and the spiritual garb of our temporal existence. Egocentric and susceptible to flattery, we often mistake polite remarks on our society and culture as a seal of approval, without realising that we thereby give vent to our ingrained inferiority complex and intellectual barrenness.

These cynical thoughts crowd the mind on seeing the resurgence of the blacks in a white society where until the mid-1960s they were pariahs, scum of the earth, denied the right to live as ordinary human beings despite the ostentatious trimmings of a democracy. In the late 1940s the New York bus service personnel, predominantly white, struck work, not for improving service conditions or in political partisanship, but in protest against a black bus driver being allowed to become a conductor. As a bus driver he was screened off from the whites but as a conductor he was considered as contaminating the purity of the white skin. Until the beginning of the 1970s the blacks were condemned to the lowest of the low menial jobs of porters and janitors. In a span of over two decades the situation has been radically transformed. The proportion of blacks entering primary and secondary education has shot up by as much as twenty times; the number of trained blacks in all fields of higher disciplines is up by 10 to 12 times. This is very strongly reflected in the rapidly rising participation of the black workforce in white-collar occupations. In the ten top black cities of the United States, the percentage of the black workforce in white-collar occupations now varies from a low of 35 in Forth Worth to a high of 59 in Washington DC. The number of black businesses per 1000 blacks in metropolitan areas has increased substantially, with a high of 24.9 in Los Angeles to a low of 15.2 in Durham, NC; in Washington DC it is at 22. Yet another dimension to this black integration with American society is provided by the census on interracial marriages. The number of marriages in the US with black husbands and white wives has increased from 25,000 in 1960 to 121,000 in 1987 and those with white husbands and black wives from 26,000 to 56,000.

The real transformation of the blacks cannot be measured merely by these opaque statistics. Something has stirred up in their psyche and in fact their whole attitude towards their place in the sun. Yesterday's underdog does not want to remain an underdog any longer. There was a time when race and class were indistinguishable in America, with the black totally identified with the downtrodden. Now change with all its political and social connotations is in the air. In certain behaviour patterns, an affluent black and an affluent white are beginning to look alike. In stock exchange transactions, a black with high income apes his counterpart amongst whites, and a similar behavioural pattern is discerned in ownership of cars, use of credit cards, and so on. The emergence of the black elite has created different kinds of problems in American society. Though much of today's progress of the blacks is owed to affirmative action, the black elite are beginning to feel that government's welfare programmes tend to inhibit their self-confidence than to conduce to their welfare. A divorce of race from class is having its impact on political alignments. Blacks are no longer the unshakable anchor of political support to the Democratic Party; the Republicans are making forays into the black electorate.

The blacks' assertion of their presence in this society has sad echoes in the faint heart of an expatriate Indian whose land has been as starkly pockmarked by the problem of untouchables as America by blacks-related issues. Forty years of freedom from British rule have elapsed, but large masses of scheduled castes and other similar groups have continued to languish. History teaches by analogy but Indian society and the powers that be at its helm have not learnt any lessons. Scheduled castes and other backward classes command our attention only as vote banks. We rise to action only in lure of acquisition of power. Reservations for them in various fields are not taken as a means to elevate their status, to enable them to live their lives with honour and dignity, to ignite their self-respect, so that they can pull themselves up by their shoestrings. Everything done for them smacks of charity, a gimmick. Not that none amongst them has benefited by some of the largesse heaped on them. Some of them have but they have become vested interests through interaction with a peculiar chemistry of the Indian political process. They cling to the privileges arising from reservation; class is not detached from caste, even when a benefiting caste changes its class to the next in the social ladder, and therefore there is no attempt on their part to cut the umbilical cord of special privileges. The consequences of this perversion of a social policy are enormous. It has aborted the progress of scheduled castes by stabbing their self-confidence and pride, while giving a free rein to the parvenus amongst them to exploit the privileges reserved for the scheduled castes as a whole for the comfort of a few. This is why the continuation of affirmative action for backward classes has triggered a counteraction from the more advanced castes. Is it beyond the pale of human ingenuity to redefine the nature of affirmative action in such a way that it is a correlate more of class than of caste, of means rather than colour? The blacks in America are intermarrying more easily with the whites, can set up more businesses on their own, and the affluent among them have the self-assurance to drop the crutches than their equivalents in India. Why, one laments, is this not happening in India with its hoary history spanning over two thousand years?

Economic and Political Weekly, 21 May 1988.

5

Infinite majesty, infinite infamy

"The Heart of Darkness", Joseph Conrad said in his narrative,

> is experience but it is experience pushed a little (and only very little) beyond the actual facts of the case for the perfectly legitimately, I believe, purpose of bringing it home to the minds and bosoms of the readers.... The sombre theme had to be given a sinister resonance, a totality of its own, a continued vibration that, I hoped, would hang in the air and dwell on the ear after the last note had been struck.

NOW there is a dazzling light from that heart of darkness emblazoning the hopes and aspirations of the black people. The shame of ancestry has now become the hope of posterity; the letter of the law is now the reason of civil society. This metamorphosis has been achieved by a single black leader, Nelson Mandela, when he descended on America to turn the searchlight on apartheid. The seasons have seasoned him, incarceration for twenty-seven long years has toughened him, age has greyed his body, but unflinching faith in his mission has kept him evergreen. He has not shown even a trace of bitterness in his behaviour with his white hosts or black comrades. He was caustic on racism, not white racism but racism of all hues where the colour of the skin determines the destiny of human societies. He is not a 'nouveau statesman' with ambiguous messages. He did not spring on the screen out of nowhere. He was tested in the crucible of sacrifices for a long period, which kept his vision clear, ideology untarnished, his mission well contoured. Gaunt in frame, erect in posture, sharp in intellect, undiminished by any self-pity, unrelenting in his quest for justice for his people, and unbent even before the powerful president of the most powerful nation, he was gracious enough to see the civil and bright aspects of the country he was visiting.

He did not have to pose or be unduly modest. He realised that if he asked his host for understanding for his cause and his problems, he should not hold back on any issue where non-understanding could take place. He was frank but not rude, he was rational but did not indulge in word play, he came for support for his cause but was not ingratiating. He was personable without impersonating for a hero he is not, he was more than an icon but did not behave like an infallible God. At the first television show with Ted Koppel, he fired his first shot: "I am beholden to Yasser Arafat, Muammar Gaddafi and Fidel Castro". He did not want to be on the bandwagon of the dominant opinion in the rich western world. He did not want to let down friends who stood by his cause when he was down and out. "Your enemies are not our enemies", he told his interlocutors. There was a flutter, a commotion. What gumption for a man to come to this country and dare praise Gaddafi and Castro! Mandela was unflappable, held his head high and scaled greater heights when he met President Bush.

The President, welcoming him to his land, invoked Martin Luther King Jr, "a man who embodies the hopes of millions", to ask him and his movement "to renounce the use of violence and armed struggle to break free from the cycle of repression and violent reaction that breeds nothing but more fear and suffering." Pat came the reply from Mandela, unself-conscious, "the President had made his remarks about removing violence due to the fact that he has not as yet got a briefing from us." He reminded his host that "the ANC has considerably scaled down armed operations since 1986 and it will consider a complete cessation of hostilities once the South African government has removed all obstacles to negotiation." He added that President Bush and others of his kind should leave the issue of removing violence entirely in the ANC's hands.

Before Congress, Mandela was generous to American society. He paid it a tribute: "We are glad that you merged with our own people to make it possible for us to emerge from the darkness of the prison cell and join the contemporary process of the renewal of the world."

He recognised the vast changes that have come over the blacks in this white continent. The blacks, who until the 1960s were pariahs, are now proud citizens. Much has been done but much more will have to come. He warned American blacks to stand on their own power; they may have needed crutches in the past, now they have to learn to be on their own. Those who lack self-respect can never be great people. Borrowing the words of Thomas Jefferson, he spoke of the will of the future South African nation:

> In the exercise of that will, by this united nation of black and white people, it must surely be that there will be born a country on the southern tip of Africa which you will be proud to call a friend and an ally because of its contribution to the universal striving towards liberty, human rights, prosperity, and peace among the people.

In a subtle but clear fashion, Mandela revealed himself on the status of blacks in America, showing perspicacity, a sense of history, and knowledge of the social history of America. While he was for black resurgence, he suspected too that many American blacks fattened on the windfalls of affirmative action and used their colour to camouflage their political skulduggery. Almost as an off-the-cuff remark, he said black Americans do not have to deal with the colour bar that limits black opportunity and achievement in South Africa. American blacks can go to the courts and appeal to a legal system which allows them all basic rights that are available to other population groups. They can rely on the constitution and enforce their rights. Alluding to Supreme Court justice Thurgood Marshall, a black judge, he said that the blacks in America have risen to the top in the judiciary, which alone was a guarantee that justice would not be fugitive in America as far as the blacks are concerned, as it was in apartheid South Africa.

Such was Nelson Mandela's majesty—no bitterness but generosity, politeness but assertion of truth, not asking for special favours but insistence on what is the black people's due. By some quirk of history, there is another black leader to steal the thunder along with Nelson Mandela, but this thunder is in an area of darkness. Mayor Marion Barry's exploits in sex, drugs and money-making are in the public gaze. His trial on drug and crack charges is a simple trial for a simple crime, to which any ordinary citizen would have been subjected. But Barry, politician that he is, is blowing it up into a racial question. He is not saying so before the court but it reveals in his actions and pronouncements outside. He saw Mandela's visit as a godsend for his defence. In the beginning he was to banish himself from the Mandela hoopla, maybe in a rare moment of remorse and shame for the scandals he had shrouded himself with. But he soon saw his chance. He changed his mind and attended Mandela's rallies. When asked by a newsman about his change of mind, this brazen-faced mayor, a pale shadow of his lustrous past as a civil rights leader, snapped back,

> I think the media, unfortunately, has tried to link all of this together. My situation is going to go on regardless and Nelson Mandela's triumphant entry into Washington is so big as to overshadow anything that is going on. I can't hurt any thing—I have a long history here and the people here will tell you it would be unnatural for me not to be at this historic moment.

He wanted his black deeds to be whitened by Mandela's light.

Yes, Barry has a history—a history of making money on contracts, of asking his subordinates to satisfy his desire for drugs and sex, of preaching to innocent children of high schools in the District of Columbia to shun drugs and crack while himself indulging in them. He is now signalling that his trial is a trial of the whole black race. But he is not alone in this sinister game. Those other climbers, who occupied high political offices during the heady days of the civil rights movement, are his accomplices. Their privileged position is being threatened by wider awakening among the masses of black people, by their new-found self-confidence and by the emergence of an upright intellectual elite amongst them. Here they are playing their reverse racism and now Benjamin Hook, executive director of the NAAP, a black rights supporting group, has started a campaign against the trials of Barry, Bradley and many others, calling it "a hidden agenda to erode the power of the black elected officers." They are almost saying that indulgence in sex, drug crimes, and corruption in high office should be passports to black leadership. Roger Wilkens, Barry's one-time comrade in the cause of the blacks, said in sadness:

> Barry used the elders and lied to the young. He has manipulated thousands of others with his cynical use of charges of racism to defend his malodorous personal failures. This is a cesspool. Though we may wish his private person well and try to help him, the public man is history. He did it himself. And now he is doing it to our politics. Our blackness is all tangled up with his personal frailties.

> To build the black people and institutions, we need staying power and greater love for black people than for self-promotion. It does not mean sleazy networking by black politicians and their circling sharks.

Blackness meant discipline, courage, steadfastness, wisdom, strength and love. Mandela was the apotheosis of all these and so he symbolised that blackness to which the earlier generation of civil rights black leaders had aspired.

Economic and Political Weekly, 15 September 1990.

6

Football played with hands and mouth!

THOUGH America cascaded from the womb of Mother England, its genes differ in some ways. American English has its own sound, fury, cadence and phrases. You call staircases "elevators"; you give a "ride in a car", no lift; you give a "call", not a ring; and you always ask your friends while parting to "take care". This is no less evident in the area of sports. Americans get bored with cricket about which they know nothing except for its superficial similarity with their baseball. Cricket's American equivalent is football in mass appeal and hysteria, not the one we in the Anglophile world are accustomed to. Its name is a misnomer. It is a ball game, a cross between English rugby and soccer, played with hands most of the time except when the player kicks the football at the start; puts it away into the net in the end zone and punts it at the time of conversions.

American football is also played with the mouth off the field. Footballers are an unruly lot, with their own code of conduct. They freely shower epithets on all and sundry at newspaper interviews and this is fully reciprocated by a battery of correspondents and experts whose number is legion. At times mouths are widely opened with their big feet into them. When the playoff football games are on, it is a field day for all players, sports scribes, partisans, coaches and team owners to hold forth on all matters about football. The team owners would think aloud about firing this player or that, a quarterback or a full back or defensive coach or the head coach and expatiate on their sins of omission and commission. These compliments are returned with full vigour by those who are riled. This season a head coach, one

Mike Ditka of the Chicago Bears team, called a defensive tackle of the "Redskins" a man with "a grapefruit brain". The player, after his team trounced the Chicago Bears in a playoff game, sent him a basket of grapefruits with a message that he would need it for his new thinking next season.

But before the Super Bowl commenced, the plum prize for playing football with the mouth went to a sports scribe, Jim Snyder, called "Jimmy the Greek". Buttonholed at a Washington restaurant in a blaze of television cameras, he lapsed into the realm of American history, about which he knew nothing, saying that "blacks are now overtaking the whites in all spheres of football because they have been 'bred' that way." He traced it to the time of the American Civil War when a white slave master chose a "fat black woman to breed high-thighed, muscular blacks." He then concluded his grand thesis by predicting that only white owners and head coaches would remain in American football. Perhaps the times have changed; there was a furore all round and the CBS television network, for which Jimmy the Greek served as a football commentator for years, was forced to fire him.

In this American setting, the significance of the game of football goes beyond its appeal as a manly sport. Every football team has a quarterback, a sort of captain of the team on the field, and a head coach, its leader off the field. These between them principally plan, plot and play the game, which naturally requires brain. For the last fifty years, the blacks have played in all positions of the game but rarely as head coaches and quarterbacks. This has its own loud message: blacks have brawn but not brains—the overtone of racial superiority of the whites. So far there have been a few quarterbacks—maybe about two or three who were in the game but they were soon forgotten.

But the day of reckoning came in this year of grace when a black quarterback, Doug Williams, was brought in by the Redskins, a Washington team. A few years ago he was the quarterback of another team—the Packers—but he embellished the team more by sitting on the bench during the game than playing as a quarterback. Frustrated and disillusioned, Williams joined the Redskins not with a hope but a fear of being traded for another player in due course. But fate willed otherwise. The Redskins' starter quarterback, a white, suddenly lost his lustre, which ushered in Williams and up went the stars of the Redskins in playoffs. Williams made history by being the first black quarterback to play in the Super Bowl, which is a final game to decide the championship. On the eve of the Super Bowl, about two thousand sports scribes harried and harangued Williams, asking him whether he was bothered about being the first black quarterback to play in the Super Bowl. Looking calm and undisturbed he shyly said, "I do not know whether I am a black quarterback or not; I consider myself to be a quarterback of the Redskins." When the Super Bowl game started on 31 January, Williams was in the first quarter smothered, and smashed in his ankle. He left the field distraught and in pain but told his head coach that his injury was minor and that he would get back into the game after first aid. In the second quarter, he limped back on to the field with his opponents perched up in the game by ten points. In the next eleven magic minutes, standing on his one good leg, with a twinkle in his eyes and grim determination on his face, he passed the ball high and long in a hyperbolic curve into the hands of his receiver in the end-zone. Not once but four times in quick succession. It seemed for a while that he was not passing the ball, he was consigning to the dustbin of history the centuries-old discrimination, infirmities, injustices, and humiliation. With those four passes, Doug Williams exploded the myth of the blacks' intellectual inferiority; he tore down the walls of prejudice to smithereens. He proclaimed as it were, that "the black is my colour given me by nature; my manhood is my own." At the final Washington reception for the victorious Redskins for which the city mustered in large numbers, he was modest but proud. "What I achieved is not mine alone. It belongs to the whole world of the blacks; I am not a graduate of this university or that but I am a product of all the black universities in America. I may or may not play again, but many more blacks in future will play my game." These words will reverberate for all times to come in all continents wherever man has been inhuman to man, heralding the emancipation of the black from the shame and scandals of the past in the same way as a parting thud by Ibsen's Nora on the door of the house of her husband signified the unchaining of women.

---

30 January 1989, unpublished.

7

Million acres of darkness

A society—the most advanced, the most educated, the most democratic, the most affluent—is in dystopia. Ted Bundy from Florida state met his death in the electric chair. But who was Ted Bundy? A young man, with high school education, forlorn, deserted by family. And why did he die? The questions are easy but not the answers. Bundy murdered twenty-seven young persons. It took five years for the guardians of law to nail and hang him. A few minutes before he walked to the electric chair, he spoke out his mind, somewhat in a mood of remorse for the first time. He blamed his parents, rather his mother, a single parent, for not preventing him from falling prey to pornography. He was psyched up to commit the crimes by the free play given to his libido, seeing the pictures he saw and reading the literature he read. But was pornography the real reason for Bundy's depravity and ensuing criminalisation? Pornography may arouse your erotic emotions, foment your passionate urges, but no one knows why it should end up in a carnage and senseless bloodletting. Bundy is not alone. There are thousands of Bundys all over the land. The symptoms are detected, the deeper causes are slurred over. The new President made so much of the prison furlough granted by Governor Michael Dukakis in Massachusetts in the heat of the election campaign. Willie Horton may have won Bush his victory, but may haunt him for the rest of his presidency. Be it Ted Bundy or Willie Horton, they are thrown up by something that is rotten in the kingdom of America. Electrocuting the murderer may create an illusion of punishment but would not banish the causes of the crime.

One must hoe the soil around these crimes. Young kids grow up in the wilderness with none to guide, none to care, none to seek solace from in their formative years. Fifty per cent of the marriages are dissolved after two years and on an average a man and a woman change their spouses two to three times in their marriageable time-span. The babies born in and out of wedlock are dispersed. There is thus a new diaspora of the young. In a wide world, where they face the pressure to survive—in school from peers, in job from employers, in family from the ever-changing faceless parents—children gravitate to substances that opiate their waking lives.

The parents, educated and well placed professionals, too, join the joints. Look at Joel and Hedda Steinberg's trial which stole newspaper headlines for battering their adopted child Lisa to death. Here is a respectable highly educated lawyer who takes to crack, beats his equally educated wife, destroys her self-confidence and personality and hammers his adopted child in the same way he would have swatted a fly. Or open your eyes to what is happening around Washington schools. A boy watching his former girlfriend necking with another guy enters the school and shoots them both. The flowerbeds have become the killing fields of the young. They live in dread all the time, feeling that their lives have a short time span; they are resigned to the inevitable.

Asked by the teacher to rewrite a portion of Martin Luther King Jr's famous speech "I have a dream", delivered during the Civil Rights Movement of the 1960s, one schoolboy wrote, "I have a dream—that murder rates drop. The police need to get the drug dealers off the street, so children can go out and play." A girl, afraid of life inside and outside, explains her dream: "I have a dream that one day children can go outside and play without being hurt. I dream that all communities will be drug-free." But she is not sure if she will live long enough to dream of such a peace. "Well, if I live that long", she adds, "I will give speeches like Martin Luther King did to stop people from using drugs and killing each other. But I am not sure that I will live that long, if the thugs go as they have been going." Wisdom flows from the mouths of babes.

A psychologist, confronted with the shattering trauma, despaired: "The bottom line is that there are children who are living in a war zone, so what we are seeing are kids who are going to be combat casualties—psychologically if not physically." There is thus oneirolysis in the lives of the young. Martin Luther King dreamt, as only a visionary like him could do, but he at least had the time to see a part of his dream come true, before he met with a violent death. For these young lives, the dream is just a pause on their way to the cemetery.

Rock music evokes emotional turmoil amongst youths, aspirations, hopes, successes and failures in a life yet to unfold, and its words are their poetry. Tracy Chapman, a young black singer, this year's Grammy Award winner, has articulated the fears and foreboding of the children in her song, aptly titled "Behind the Wall", sung without instruments, with gravity, sadness and fatalism:

> Last night I heard the screaming loud voices behind the wall
> Another night without sleep for me won't do no good to call
> The police always come late, if they come at all
> Last night I heard the screaming
> There is silence that chilled my soul
> I prayed that I was dreaming
> When I saw the ambulance on the road.

The album has sold in millions. The children for whom there is no tomorrow might have figured out that they should celebrate in song, if not life, at least its demise.

From schools where the future is moulded, you go to the courts, where the neglect of children and their abuse are tragically written in the dockets. The judge throws up her hands: "It has become more and more difficult. I look back to the good old days of heroin. It did not destroy the ability of its users to be human the way crack does." Drug abuse has destroyed families. But most family court judges believe that crack use has been a sinister influence on families, producing an epidemic of children being beaten, raped and murdered. There are cases galore of children becoming disoriented and being victimised by family surroundings and becoming mental wrecks. A homeless woman approaches the court to claim possession of a baby born with AIDS whose parents are in jail. A girlfriend of the father's brother, she pleads that the ailing infant will recover in a few months. The court denies her plea. Another drug-abuser smuggled her seven-year-old grandson out of the hospital. He was left there by his mother because the grandmother's boyfriend had abused him, driving him to suicidal behaviour. The judge decides that the child will neither be with the mother nor the grandmother. Such neglect cases are mounting. Many parents do not even show up. Children vanish in the wilderness. The grandmother, mother and child chase each other's tail in a sordid drama of family disintegration and a spreading metastasis of the societal edifice.

President Bush wants the "thousand points of light" to be even more luminous. But those thousands points of light are not the guiding stars; they merely puncture the millions of acres of darkness so that those who lament the horrendous tragedies and vanishing old family values should be shaken out of their cosy existence. The thousands of lights let men of compassion and idealism see the decadence of human institutions and values which are enveloped in pitch darkness. You may succeed in sending to the gallows those who commit murders in a frenzy, you may deny furlough to others incarcerated for lesser crimes, but that will not banish the crimes or the drugs. Police action is no surrogate for social engineering.

Economic and Political Weekly, 13 May 1989.

8

Romance with two words

WHEN words become non-words, the world becomes a bedlam. George Orwell, master of English prose, discovered the joy of words, their sound and association, and used that facility with words to "face the unpleasant." Politicians in all climes and places may not have Orwell's command of words but they are skilled enough to twist words out of shape and substance when faced with unpleasant facts. Look at what has happened to that unhappy word 'liberal' in today's America. It has become an abuse, a dirty word, as if it stood for some child molester or criminal or traitor. A grammarian will tell you that 'liberal' is an adjective describing representational form of government rather than an aristocracy or monarchy, assuring maximum individual freedom possible in civil society in matters of personal beliefs and expression. Adam Smith, Hobbes, Hume, J.S. Mill and all those hedonistic philosophers would turn in their graves if they knew that that king of malapropism, mauler of grammar and mangler of sentences, George Bush, who has just won the race for the presidency of the United States of America, uses liberal as a synonym for one who resorts to government action to help the individual to satisfy his needs.

But such political shenanigans have worked because the one at whom the word was flung did not take up the gauntlet. Michael Dukakis, in his anxiety to enter the Oval Office, shied from being a liberal and instead used a political oxymoron to defensively plead that it was not ideology but competence that mattered. This was sheer chicanery. It did not bother him getting mileage from the parallelism with Kennedy's quest for the presidency; perhaps superstition overwhelmed him. Who knows the similarity between the circumstances in which Kennedy entered the arena of politics and his own might catapult him into that hallowed place by some divine dispensation. Dukakis went into a closet, whining that "labelling is bad and if he had put aside a dollar every time Bush threw at him that label, he might get a tax break." But being clever is not being honest.

He should have defined what liberalism really meant and exposed Bush's ignorance not only of language but also of politics and American history. Liberalism of the Kennedy era helped bring the blacks into mainstream American society. The human and humane visage of America owes it to those very liberal values which have made Jefferson and Lincoln such hallowed deities in the American pantheon. To discard those values is to make American society crueller and not kinder, contortive and not caring, myopic and not regenerative. These values would be denigrated once you renege on ideology as the main fulcrum of your political platform; you then become irrelevant. Why Dukakis followed this evasive course is easy to understand. He was chasing that chimerical group—the so-called Reagan Democrats. In the process, he lost the support of his natural and traditional constituency. He should have been proud to be a liberal, those who gave America its glory in the 1930s and 1950s, and should have given an exposé of what liberal meant in word, substance and ideology. The tragedy is that government action, which the word 'liberal' is twisted to connote, would be required in abundance in future. The Republicans may delude themselves that everything is hunky-dory. Real issues today relate to childcare, parental leave, housing for the middle-income and the poor and education system overhaul—all would entail persuasive government direction. And these are issues both candidates have been dodging during their campaigns. For losing the election Dukakis should blame his pusillanimity in not confronting Bush with issues and not convincing the electorate that if issues mean liberalism which they want to denounce, then there are no issues to fight for.

If Americans have forgotten their English language, Indians have not. If liberal means more government action for individual benefit, contrary to its true meaning, its derivative liberalisation means in India exactly what it should. But it has come to be an obscenity, for the very reason that the term 'liberal' has become an expletive in America. When the young prime minister came to the throne four years ago, he was in a hurry to skip to the twenty-first century and liberalisation was placed on the agenda with great fanfare. For a while the policy of liberalisation resonated in the country, but soon it was realised that the arrangements to which all of us have been inured over the last forty years are at stake. The brave new leader developed cold feet when the Congress Party *apparatchiks* sensed the threat liberalisation posed to their interests. If controls are removed, licensing is buried, who would pay them money under the counter? With the Congress ideology—if there was one—in a shambles, with the depletion of the pre-independence capital of popularity and sacrifice, and with the gushing of scandals, shame and corruption, the only way to survive is to keep the show of socialism going, so that the sources of illicit money do not dry up. The industrialists who until recently denounced controls and licensing also foresaw their empires crumbling in the wake of liberalisation. How else could they prosper with their inefficiency? They can batten only on protected markets. The writing on the wall was seen by the prime minister, and he and his cohorts changed their tune. There was a sudden emergence of touching concern and compassion for the poor and the downtrodden. Liberalisation was slowed down and a search was on for a proxy word.

Indian communists alone knew what liberalisation stood for and they opposed it. Though consistent with their past, they were at variance with their comrades in the communist world and in uncertain tryst with their destiny as descendants of the dynasty of Marx, Engels and Lenin. With the bankruptcy of sick industrial units, if liberalisation is allowed unimpeded, organised labour which is their constituency would suffer. But their knowledge of communism has stopped at Marx, Engels and Lenin. They forget Rosa Luxemberg's comment that "the organised labour is as tyrannical as the organised capitalists." Who dare say they do not think for themselves? The ragbag of other opposition parties is also the ragbag of opposites. That great champion of liberalisation, V.P. Singh, suddenly rediscovered that his brand of liberalisation is a part of his socialism. Liberalisation for him has become the instrument to bastinado the tax evaders.

Orwell was wrong that words have power. It is power and the lust for it that change the innards of words. Politicians of all hues fall in love with words and fondle them until they age. And when they fail to rejuvenate them, their romance with them is over, though their company is kept. The epiphany will have to wait for another time.

Economic and Political Weekly, 26 November 1988.

9

Law's aim is crime

LAW is a binding covenant of a civil society because the condition of man is a condition of war of everyone against everyone. The predators have to be reined in by law, this was the ancient gospel. Reason is and should be the life of law. If freedom is traduced, honour is besmirched, violence runs amok and if human life is to be more than an interregnum between birth and death, some codification of behavioural rules is necessary. But we are not currently living in a Lockean world where the beginning of law marks the end of tyranny. In these civilised times, laws become a burden, weighing us down at every stage of the conduct of our business. Democracy, they say, is rule by law, which gives you security, certainty and a certain predetermined course for your actions. Yes, democracy is the antithesis of dictatorship with its law of the jungle. And yet living in the world's most enlightened democracy, to which not only ordinary people like us but also the Gorbachevs and Zhaos of the declining communist empires are paying homage, we are constantly lost in the jungle of laws and their diabolical practitioners.

If you are born, the lawyer is there, like a doctor at the birth of an heir to the throne of the British empire, lurking in the distance to verify whether you are a test-tube baby, a baby of a surrogate mother or a baby by your legal father. In a society where 50 per cent of new marriages are dissolved in two years, and 40 per cent in the next five years, it is the lawyer who becomes your guardian angel and also godfather. If you fall ill, lawyers hone their wits to save you, not necessarily from death, not even from the doctor's bills, but from his maltreatment, if only he can prove it so. You may be touched by his kindness when he tells you that you should not worry about his fees. He is a do-gooder with the interests of all at his heart. You just give your consent and he will get you the compensation by proving in court that the treatment by your doctor or his coadjutors was wrong. He will be modest enough to keep for safe custody one-third of what he would collect from the doctor. If you survive, you will be a millionaire; if not, your progeny will inherit the windfall, if your lawyer does not get into the act further to settle your inheritance.

But you should not be a sloppy moron to shed tears for your doctor. The doctor is safe with his malpractice insurance policy and an ever-growing phalanx of lawyers has seen to it that they and those insured are well protected. The laws devised are complex, periphrastic; institutional memory is non-existent; case law is law which changes with every case. Lawyers are touchingly humanitarian; they have large hearts and have an abiding interest in those who are indicted for crime or fraud. Isn't presumption of innocence a basic tenet of their praxis? A Chinese was indicted a few days ago for the old-fashioned crime of murdering his wife for the old-fashioned reason that she had a paramour. A clever lawyer and a cleverer judge saw this tragedy through a prism of sociology and a bit of anthropology. They put the blame for the murder on the cultural background of the husband and he was set free. The Chinese in China, perhaps because of their preoccupation with the struggle against Deng and Li Peng, may not have heard of this verdict. Otherwise they would have rediscovered their lethal weapons of punishing others.

Lawyers in America have spawned such a strange culture that one benign soul despaired for the future of this society: "There is no tragedy without liability, no vice without villains." See what havoc this litigious frame of mind of Americans has caused them. A woman in California, who guzzled half a bottle of bourbon every day during her pregnancy, delivered a retarded child. On her lawyer's advice that it could be a product liability suit, she sued the makers of Jim Beam bourbon for failure to "warn her that drinking bourbon during pregnancy would cripple her child." There is another who smoked incessantly and was hospitalised with cancerous lungs. Since the cigarettes she smoked caused the cancer, she sued the tobacco company and was awarded $400,000 in compensation. A young couple rented an apartment in a condominium owned by an orthodox

Catholic lady. When she knew that they were not married, she gave them notice to quit on the ground that an unmarried couple could not indulge in sexual activity, at any rate in her condominium. The couple was awarded handsome compensation.

Bizarre as these cases may be, such suits have been elevated to a fine art by lawyers and political interest groups to mulct rich clients. For the lawyer who won the case of the cancerous woman against the tobacco company, it was his investment in future tobacco litigation. The Bhopal disaster might have killed thousands of people in that unfortunate city, but lawyers here were roused not by moral outrage, not by the gigantic human tragedy; they saw in it a golden opening for plunder and booty.

Even a teenager's simple prank is exploited to the hilt by lawyers for self-aggrandisement, without any concern for its social and moral consequences. A little black girl, intrepid, callow and footloose, absconded from home for fear of being smacked by her stepfather for absence from home late at night. She allowed her imagination to run wild and told the police, who found her on a heap of garbage, that she had been raped by some white boys, beaten up and left unconscious. The lawyers saw their chance for both money and publicity. Knowing fully that the story was a fib, they created brouhaha about race relations and made unsubstantiated charges against the defence attorney. They almost succeeded but the truth was eventually out. The girl made up the story to save herself from a battering. But the lawyers, knowing the truth, did not relent and almost ignited racial conflict.

It is a great conundrum of American society why lawyers and their cohorts are dominating not only the government but all other echelons of the social structure. Look around and you will see lawyers in the ranks of politicians, economists, academics, sportsmen and even scientists. The overpowering position of lawyers points to the way social and political relations have evolved over the last two hundred years. The President of the United States seems all-powerful and yet he is not; Congress is supreme and yet it is not; the Supreme Court is the apogee of justice and yet it is not. Every organ of the government is hostage to every other hand; each one can be strong if it is allowed to be. It is bargaining all the way which ultimately climaxes into policy for the nation for good or evil. The government is only a mirror image of the society which is a potpourri of the diverse national and cultural groups which emigrated to America and they all survive by striking deals. And deals have to be negotiated. Social intercourse is conducted as a business. If guns are sought to be restricted, there is a lobby to fight the move; if restrictive practices in the medical profession are to be torn down, there is the Medical Association to wage a battle to prevent it. If some foreign country wants a change in US policy to favour it, there are consulting firms galore, staffed with people with a talent for casuistry. Even law and order is negotiable with those who break it with impunity. Judges interpret the law but also encourage plea bargaining. You commit a heinous crime, then plead for a lesser punishment by squealing on someone else. This is a game-theoretic model of democracy; for every move of yours there is a countermove. Who can do it better than a lawyer who, like Scarlet Pimpernel, is everywhere?

The American educational system may not throw up scientists, mathematicians, biologists; but lawyers are cheaper by the dozen, though the price they command defies the laws of demand and supply. They have made a bargain out of everything—your life, your death, children, patriotism, justice, wife and marriage. If you don't play that game, you will be thrown by the wayside. In this kind of democracy, the lawyer is a necessity.

Oliver Cromwell said of law and lawyers: "Necessity has no law. Feigned necessity, imaginary necessities are the greatest cozenage that men can put upon the Providence of God and make pretence to break known rules by." But then who called Cromwell a democrat? Law and lawyers are part of democracy's kit. Those innocent Chinese students, slaking their thirst for democracy, were shouting hoarse at Tiananmen Square in Beijing for "law and not party." If only they knew what lawyers have made of the world's greatest democracy with its laws and all, they might perhaps have asked instead for "not party, not law, not rarefied democracy but reification of democracy."

Economic and Political Weekly, 22 July 1989.

10

Parting with heroes

NOW in this year of grace, we are at the cutting age of re-evaluation of the era that is bygone and the men who dazzled us both when they lived and after their death.

The 1960s were exciting, alluring and erotic. The millions of dead in the Second World War had faded from memory for the baby boom generation. The Beatles set new tunes, new images and new sartorial and tonsorial styles. In their wake came the lilting pop tunes that spellbound the youth. All that mattered were pleasures of the body, the affluence of the present, and the dream of life without pain. The old mores broke down, the language changed, and restraint gave way to a release of both the baser and the nobler instincts. It was in such fertile times that John F. Kennedy, with his handsome face, beautiful wife, dashing youth, bewitching smile, ghost-written speeches and books and synthetic cosmopolitanism appeared on the American political stage. His career from being an unknown Congressman to being elected President of the United States of America was only of a few seasons, but books written on him and his presidency would have equalled those on a dozen presidents. The myth surrounding his life pulsates even today. Like perennials, it blooms all the time. But the truth is different. Like annuals, it surfaces now and then but perishes soon after.

That he was a popinjay is only now being realised. The best and the brightest he gathered around him—whom a cynic called "honorary Kennedys"—kept his myth alive. So-called historians like Arthur Schlesinger were merely hagiographers, intellectual harlots, forming an institutionalised forum for blarney, who used rhetoric to cover up the machinations of the Kennedy presidency. Kennedy was a lucky man. He got credit for every discreditable act, while the hapless President Johnson was discredited for every honourable act. Kennedy's famous "Let the word go from here" speech was the harbinger of his most aggressive foreign policy which brought eventually on the nation the disgrace of the Vietnam defeat. It is scarcely remembered that by the time Kennedy died, there were sixteen thousand American soldiers in Vietnam. The seeds of the Vietnam debacle were sown then and there. The Bay of Pigs was known for being a fiasco; but his culpability for Vietnam has gone unrecorded. Unsurprisingly, some of his hagiographer coxcombs like Kenneth O'Donnell and Arthur Schlesinger still insist that Kennedy, if he had lived, would have resolved the Vietnam imbroglio.

There have now and then been a few dissenting voices. The new Left had been shouting itself hoarse for years that Kennedy was a prime progenitor of the Cold War and that his loyalty to expansive capitalist interests delineated his approach to American misadventures abroad. But their cry was in the wilderness. If the Leftists do not turn leftward, who would? asked the court historians. But the Left were not the only dissenters.

There were occasional ripples amongst feminist groups. Nancy Gager Clinch, a leader of the feminist movement, wrote way back in 1974, defying the conventional view of Kennedy, that his and his father's hyperactive sexuality shaped his macho view of leadership. Till then, many had known that Joseph Kennedy rose to fame, prosperity and political eminence through bootlegging during the prohibition period of American history, but none was aware of his enduring contribution to a new psycho-historical theory of political leadership. There were titillating stories about John Kennedy's sexual liaisons involving Marilyn Monroe and Mafia moll Judith Exner, but far from diminishing Kennedy's image, they lent credence to his manliness which those who could not rival him in this game could only envy. And the Kennedy myth went on to become a legend, to make him a demigod in the American political pantheon.

But the moment of truth seems to have arrived with the publication of a new book by Taylor Branch, *Parting the Waters: America in the King's Years*. The book is on the life and work of Martin Luther King, the visionary leader of the American blacks, but it has become famous more for revealing the black side of John Kennedy, in the same way as Michael Holroyd's book on Lytton Strachey is remembered more for unearthing the closet exploits of John Maynard Keynes. Until Branch's book was out, it was widely believed that John Kennedy was a champion of civil rights and one of King's benefactors. The truth has now been laid bare. Branch describes how in the 1960 campaign Kennedy opportunistically exploited a phone call he made to Coretta Scott King while her husband was languishing in jail, and exaggerated his friendship with her to draw on the vote bank of the blacks. Branch has also revealed how Kennedy allowed the then FBI director, J. Edgar Hoover, to tap Martin Luther King's phone. Emperor Kennedy had no clothes but he stole King's clothes when it came to taking credit for asserting the American blacks' civil rights. He paraded as the president who tried to bring the blacks into the mainstream of American society.

Poor President Johnson, for all he did for the liberal creed and the blacks, is remembered only for the uncouth manner in which he displayed before newsmen in his Rose Garden a scar on his stomach. Kennedy, master publicist that he was, knew how to exploit the chances that came his way to build up his own myth. He seduced newsmen through blandishments of various sorts to shower panegyrics on his presidency and his supposed intellectual exploits. It is now known that his Pulitzer Prize-winning book *Profiles in Courage* had been ghost-written and the prize it won was manipulated by Arthur Krock, who was the Washington Bureau chief of the *New York Times*. One need not be in the employ of the Marwari press to be bought for a nickel; it can happen in a country with the freest of the free presses. A puzzling dilemma about Kennedy could be explained in terms of the anatomy of power. "As witnesses not of our intentions but of our conduct", wrote Hannah Arendt, "we can be true or false and the hypocrite's crime is that he bears false witnesses against himself." Perhaps, if Kennedy had not died the way he did, his life would have been worse than his death.

Once you begin to part with one hero, it becomes a habit. Nearer home the hero is Jawaharlal Nehru who was born in November, the month in which Kennedy died. The year 1989 was the centenary year of Nehru, which was celebrated with fanfare, publicity and extravaganza. One is not sure whether it was done in perpetuation of his memory or in celebration of his death, which paved the way for the Nehru dynasty. Hagiographers are busy churning out folklore about the great leader, unifier of the country, great socialist, mighty planner and, above all, great democrat. Here was a democrat who helped establish a dynasty with first his daughter and then a grandson following him on the throne. He loathed dissent from any quarter. Whenever he saw someone of substance even at a distance, he banished them into the wilderness. When he saw Morarji Desai emerging as a leader after Govind Ballabh Pant's death he was quick to split the Congress Party's leadership in Parliament, allocating it to two leaders. He was a democrat who pretended to agree reluctantly to his daughter being appointed president of the party and turned a blind eye to her managing the ouster of the democratically elected Kerala government on trumped-up charges. He had no remorse in defending two state chief ministers, his buddies, against all constitutional proprieties. For him his edicts and judgements were more sacrosanct than the letter and spirit of the Indian constitution. He was a democrat who set a shining example of what an ideal democrat should be, by sacrificing his trusted defence minister after the China debacle. If his ministers followed wrong policies it was their fault and not his, though he was prime minister. He defined democracy in the mould of dictatorship, in substance if not in form. He was a democrat who refused to step down even after suffering a stroke at the Bhubaneswar Congress meeting and foisted his disoriented and feeble leadership on a country that was in a crisis. Whenever the government was attacked for inefficiency and corruption, he sent his ministers and chief ministers into the woods. He was a democrat accountable to none.

Yes, he was a nationalist but he wanted Foreign Service officers, at the inception of the Foreign Service, to be trained at Cambridge, Oxford and Harvard. A clipped English accent and table manners were far more important to him than an understanding of the society and people they were supposed to serve. Toadies and nincompoop princelings were the first recruits to this hallowed service. He thus Indianised the Foreign Service, but denationalised it in spirit.

He was a federalist but had no qualms about concentrating all power at the centre, on the specious ground that the nation otherwise would disintegrate. He was a socialist who nationalised many industries to promote statism, which was the instrument used by special interest groups for accentuating income inequalities. As the first prime minister of independent India, he presided over the creation of stratified housing colonies for government servants in New Delhi, segregated according to status. The great socialist that he was, he and his ministers occupied the luxurious mansions left behind by the viceroys and commanders-in-chief. He superimposed new classes on the old classes.

Yes, he was a leader of the nation. He led India for seventeen long years, believing firmly in his own indispensability and revelling in it during tranquil times. But when China licked the Indian army in Bomdila, this leader of leaders went on the radio and cried, when the honourable course would have been to resign. He acquired his mastery of the English language and his English etiquette from England, but he forgot what English prime ministers do when they fail to deliver.

This was Nehru, hero of our youth, leader of our nation, social engineer of our society, democrat. But the dream dried up like raisins in the sun. Maybe we are cruel in our judgement on our hero that was. Not that Nehru was an ordinary man. His contributions to the independence struggle were monumental, his secularism was above board. When in 1947, Hindu madmen were burning Muslims in the Delhi riots, it was Nehru who jumped into the fray to save Muslim lives. Whatever has remained of India's secularism owes not a little to him. But even here, the chill of history overlays his achievements. Could he not have gone in for a common civil code for all Indians, making them all equal before the common law? But electoral calculus was stronger than concern for the minorities. The result is there for all to see. After forty years of freedom, Muslims and other minorities are still outside the mainstream of Indian society. One can then ask, more in sorrow than in anger, why was Nehru's leadership flawed? The answer is easier than the question. It is the ancient truth—the spell of the lust for power, once you get inebriated on it, never goes away. If only Nehru had been aware of the limitations of power, he would have shown his other face to his countrymen and the world. "No one is fit to be trusted with power—no one", said C.P. Snow.

"Any man who has lived at all knows the follies and wickedness he is capable of. If he does not know it, he is not fit to govern others. And if he does know it, he knows also that neither he nor any man ought to be allowed to decide a single human fate."

When heroes lose their lustre, whether John F. Kennedy or Pandit Jawaharlal Nehru, they leave behind debris for their erstwhile followers. It is a painful process to put 'fake' against their names. But to leave them untouched by critical evaluation for fear of hurting fake historians and courtiers is to betray one's conscience. Our trust in any particular hero cannot have a safer basis than an attempt, even a failed one, to challenge it. It is better to live in a world without heroes than one where heroes turn into anti-heroes.

Economic and Political Weekly, 6 January 1990.

11

Jealousy of possessions

A few centuries ago, Columbus came to the shores of what is known as modern America and called its natives 'Indians.' It was sacrilege then, as it is now. How could anyone call the cultureless, 'tribal' people, steeped in ritualistic cannibalism, Indians? The people of Aryavarta, who created one of the greatest civilisations of the world and enriched a philosophical domain, deserved better than to be identified with the barbaric natives of America of a mere four hundred years ago. The Indian (from Bharat, that is India) now comes to the America of Columbus, besottedly trying to establish his identity. When he meets an American he harks back to his Indian prototype and then curses himself that the American does not behave like an Indian. He is distant, callous, artificial, synthetic, outwardly pleasant but inwardly rude. He visits a department store but what troubles him is the 'deafening discord' he hears from the metronomic beep and stutter of the cash register. That evokes in his mind the picture of a "wisened old man back home who gingerly put the weights onto his scale, weighed the potatoes, counted the change, and talked about his son." He goes to a bank to open an account and feels put out that the bank identifies him not by his name but by an alphanumeric symbol. He is disquieted by his alienation, but he wants to remain in a society where he sees neither his past, nor his present, nor his future; he consoles himself that "maybe constant alienation is a healthy anecdote to the threat to individualism in a foreign culture."

If the young man who arrives in America thinks in old ways, the old man who comes here to settle thinks in ways befitting his ancient traditions, scriptures, and culture. He will see divorces around him, and mope over the decadence of American families; he will see young girls and boys dating and curse their sexual promiscuity while reminiscing over the virtuousness of his youth. He will look at the morning papers for news about India and set them aside as useless. If India does not figure in the news or is given only a little space to describe some railway accident or communal riot, he will condemn the self-centredness of American journalism. Yet when newspapers flash on their front pages the riots following the Rath Yatra or the Kashmir insurgency or the Punjab shootings, his blood boils. These cussed Americans revel only in showing the worst that is happening in India. Why are American art critics raving over Peter Brooks' *Mahabharat*? Bhisma is black, Karna is black, Gandhari is black. How can Aryans as fair as the Greeks be black? Even our greatest epic is vulgarised by the West. They then conclude that the society which they are blessing not only by their visits but also by hankering after permanent resident visas is rotten to the core.

But time is a healer. The ardour for identity evaporates with the efflux of time. The Indians' loathing for Americans undergoes a radical change. After all, if we live in America, what can we do except tolerate them. And if you tolerate them, why not choose the best among them—the whites. The blacks, they come from the bush; they live in slums; they are drug addicts; they are violent; they are not people we should break bread with. And relationships with them by marriage? Never! With white Americans, yes, of course.

As they feel increasingly American, they give up their obsession with an Indian identity and strive constantly to disidentify themselves with Indians. You see many Indians who, running into other Indians for the first time, will try to use every device to identify their caste, their language, and their possessions. Somebody's last name sounds unfamiliar, somewhat unusual. Who could he be? A Tamilian, an Andhrite, a Brahmin? Is he well placed? Otherwise he will be a pest; he will ask for some favour which I cannot, do not want to, bestow. Why should I, when he does not belong to my caste, does not speak my language? Better preserve my powers to do good only to the privileged few. If Indians are holding important positions in international organisations, they have to guard themselves from contamination by other Indians. What if they were to ask for favours? How would I look in the eyes of the Europeans or the Americans, if I am seen helping the brownies? I have to maintain my image as an international civil servant, above board in every respect! After all, it is wrong to expect a highly placed Indian in an international organisation to be a Salvation Army man offering succour to all and sundry Indians. Not doing good does not mean doing bad is expunged. You can be a hatchet man for someone above you, and damn if the victim is an Indian. This too proves your non-parochialism. So the excluded Indians almost say to themselves what President Vaclav Havel said when he assumed the presidency:

> I would only add that, in my opinion, the hidden motivation driving all my dogged efforts is precisely this innermost feeling of being excluded, of belonging nowhere, a state of disinheritance as it were, of fundamental non-belonging. The real reason I am always creating something, organising something, is to vindicate my permanently questionable right to exist.

However, the malign neglect of the unlucky fellow Indians suddenly becomes benign if perchance he falls on evil days. There will be gallons of crocodile tears shed. Some help may be offered knowing full well that things have gone beyond redemption. In social relationships Indians reveal their arithmetical and mathematical skills. If one is prospering, they divide his virtues; if one is down and out, they multiply his vices.

The Indian society in the US thrives on jealousy—caste jealousy, religious jealousy, language jealousy, the jealousy of one's own possessions and the possessions of others. As in the case of the Pacific Islanders jealousy of possessions is the key to the Indians' culture. Thus, their identity is with their old habits, old mores, old modes, while they are busy disidentifying themselves from their compatriots. They are like philosopher Kant's timber, "so crooked as that from which man is made, nothing entirely straight can be carved."

Economic and Political Weekly, 25 May 1991.

12

India's prince charming

HERE comes a prince charming as the new Indian ambassador to America with a basketful of memories of past glories not only of his ancient country but also of his royal ancestors. Before his arrival a series of planted news items appeared in the US press, highlighting that the new ambassador was of blue blood and a scholar extraordinary, who could hold forth on religion, philosophy, civilisation and culture. The advance squad of public relations men portrayed him as a prince, a Kashmiri, a close confidant of the Nehru family and, above all, an aficionado of all that is beautiful, intellectual and noble. They did not forget to slip in casually a reference to his presidency of the Vishwa Hindu Parishad. Some journalist was innocent enough to ask him how he could square his espousal of Hindu militancy with the secular order in India. To which his answer was that Hinduism was a universal religion, it was a philosophy of all philosophies. The Khalistani Sikhs felt offended that a self-confessed Hindu chauvinist should be sent to represent India. But the prince charming was undeterred. He had a ready reply to disarm his Sikh critics. Was not the great Ranjit Singh helped by the great-grandfather of the ambassador? Anecdotes, real or imaginary, were thus thought to be answers to serious questions of politics. Yes, Ranjit Singh had been a pal of his great-grandfather, but how had a Sikh problem surfaced, endangering the political stability of the Indian nation? He did not explain the origin of the Sikh issue, why it is allowed to fester, why the Longowal-Gandhi agreement was disowned, why the issues of Chandigarh, river water allocation and realignment of borders between Haryana and Punjab were still hanging fire. But the ambassador is a prince and a scholar. He cannot be expected to answer general questions not having to do with his family or his own experiences.

His first priority on arrival in Washington was to flaunt his parentage and his wealth. A style section of the *Washington Post* went to town over his antique collections valued reportedly at some three million dollars. The prince and his wealth were in the forefront; India, poor India, was in the background. Yes, what is the point of displaying and advertising Indian poverty before the rich Americans? That is a task for fellows like Satyajit Ray and Louis Malle, not for the honourable Indian ambassador. In his interview he swaggered about his artistic sensibilities while berating, not very subtly either, his predecessor for lack of taste. No one asked how he had managed to bring treasures out of India.

Karan Singh does not want to be only an ambassador, he is a master of serendipity. He has discovered four 'notable truths.' On his arrival, he found that America and the American people did not love India and Indians despite India's ancient civilisation. He almost suggested that all Indian ambassadors before him had failed in their job and he had to make up for their failure. The first 'notable truth' then is that India "is peripheral to the consciousness of the United States." How could the Americans be so mean? Is not Indian civilisation one of the world's two most ancient civilisations? And what about our great poets and philosophers, not forgetting the Taj Mahal? And what about India being the greatest democracy in the world? Americans are silly. They do not realise that "the future of democracy itself depends on the state of relations between India and America." The diplomat excelled in *non sequitur*. America can love our great poets and yet dislike our policies in the same way Indians can admire Lincoln and Jefferson and yet denounce America's national and international policies, as India has been doing for years. He was particularly proud that he and his generation were mesmerised by John Kennedy. But perhaps he does not know what Kennedy thought of his great leader Nehru when they met. Yes, Karan Singh is a scholar but history is not his strong suit.

The prince is also unhappy about the second 'notable truth'—that India does not receive enough media attention in America and the younger generation of Americans are not sufficiently exposed to political events in India, despite Attenborough's *Gandhi*. The other two 'notable truths' are that though America ignores us we adore it and are eternally grateful to it for its generosity; and that India will no longer accept 'the lopsided perception' in America about India.

All the four 'truths' that His Excellency harped upon are well known. Indian civilisation and culture need not be lectured on by ambassadors. Nor is it necessary to tell Americans how much we love them. Asking Americans to love us and assuring them that we reciprocate their love is not going to refurbish India's image in American eyes. Karan Singh could have turned the light inward to figure out why his country's democracy does not command respect. Yes, it is the largest democracy but the largeness is made up of millions of the miserable. It is a democracy by accident and those who have been entrusted the responsibility to sustain it have dismally failed. Holding elections on the basis of universal franchise is not democracy. When ministers are charged with corruption, there are no commissions to go into the charges and if at all there are any, they are managed ones; criminal cases involving high-placed ministers are soft-pedalled; norms of decorum and decency, which are a hallmark of democratic government, are given the go-by; the public media are exploited to build the image of the ruling party and its leader and to disseminate misinformation; when the auditor general, a watchdog of public probity appointed under the constitution, exposes skulduggery in the Bofors affair he is called names and threatened with impeachment. Contrast all this with what happened to Speaker Jim Wright of the House of Representatives, whose slight indiscretion cost him his position. Democracy does not reside in numbers but in the integrity of those who run the political system. A shipping agent of yesteryears becomes a tycoon by bribing politicians and officials and subverting the government machinery. Economic policy is made hostage to the greed of this or that moneybag. Invoking the name of Mahatma Gandhi is not going to fool Americans when they know that the old Gandhi has been dethroned long ago and a new one has misappropriated his name and his deeds.

With the emerging alignments in international relations, India is beginning to lose whatever importance it had in the Cold War years. Stalin's and Brezhnev's Russia has become Gorbachev's Russia, which is drawing closer to the western powers, politically, economically and strategically. India cannot beat the drum of its non-alignment much longer. There are few buyers now for that useless symbol of independence and equidistance from the superpowers. Gone are the days when for every trouble in India you could blame the CIA. India, from now on, will have to be on its own. With the western powers' attention riveted on the disintegrating Eastern bloc, their money will flow there, leaving India and others like it high and dry.

Economic and Political Weekly, 9 December 1989.

13

Indian royalty: An equal exchange

THESE nosy, lotus-eating Americans have a strange fascination for Indians and India, which may not be their staple food, engaging their interest and time constantly and continuously, but could occasionally be their exotic smorgasbord, often dreamt of but untouched by their palates. Indians congenitally have a low attention span, always bubbling with so much wisdom, pickled and marinated by the well-congealed philosophical scriptures. They can rattle off a flood of words in answer to the most trivial of questions. Yet Americans are riveted by both Indians and their country. The old prototype of India being a land of *maharajas,* snakes, astrologers and the rope trick is now fading, but not because the Yankees have ceased to believe in that image of India. The reason is simple: Americans have now been co-opted in some ways. Rattlesnakes have come to be the gourmet's delight in French restaurants, the rope trick has been put in the shade by wheeler-dealers like Michael Milken of Drexel, Burnham, Lambert—the tenth wonder on Wall Street, and astrology and astrologers are making inroads into the inner chambers of the White House. Even *Swamis* are all over America, the latest being the itinerant Chandraswami who is making waves in India currently. The American grapevine is buzzing with stories that some leading lights of the Administration are occasionally found closeted with the fabled *swami,* and at Watergate of all places.

With all this, one thing in which America and Americans have not been able to match India and Indians is the legacy of the *Maharajas*—their pomp, pageantry and dynastic halo. They feel so lacking in this particular area of one-upmanship that whenever something happens in India, particularly of a political nature, their imagination flowers, and somehow they seek to find some analogue for events and persons in the regal heritage of India. Besides, American journalists are fond of etymologising. Whenever they refer to Indira Gandhi or her prince in succession, Rajiv Gandhi, they would not forget to add that this Gandhi is no relation of Mahatma Gandhi, no matter that in the process they often mislocate the letter 'h' in 'Gandhi'. You should not ask why this etymological research wanes when it comes to their own people. If Ronald Reagan appoints Donald Regan as his chief of staff or treasury secretary, it is just a question of a missing vowel. If a Don Kennedy emerges as treasury secretary, there is no question of tracing his genealogical tree to find out if he could be any relation of John F. Kennedy. How can any kin of John F. Kennedy be a minister in a Republican administration, they could well rationalise. But then India is different from America—it has a history of over two thousand years.

The media here really had a problem when Indians elected a new prime minister. All they could say, at the first shock news of V.P. Singh's election, was as usual an etymological dissection of his name. They let their readers' minds at rest that "Singh means a 'lion' in Indian language, but he is not a Sikh." And at that moment, they got out of their amnesia. If India's new prime minister, who ousted a scion of the Nehru dynasty is not a lion, could he not be a king of some unknown kingdom of yore? Rajiv Gandhi's exit came as a bit of a shock to them. They fondly remembered his princely deportment, his lineage from the great Nehru, his blue blood, his economic liberalisation, his giant leap, aborted in mid-air, towards the twenty-first century. He also was in a western university, imbibing the essential western values to be a modern man. If he was sent down there, so what? Did they not say, not failure but a low aim is crime? But then who is this V.P. Singh if not a lion? Ah, the puzzle is solved; traditions are not broken, history is not disowned.

Yes, the Indian people did not let them down. What a delight when they discovered that V.P. Singh was a prince—if not born as one, at least through adoption. Royalty, after all, is the name of the game. If the poor, illiterate and ignorant electorate could show this discernment, three cheers to them. This is a democracy with a difference, it ensconces royalty at the centre of power. This is eastern mysticism at its apogee. If the kingdom from which he hailed is only a small principality, it does not matter. A kingdom is a kingdom and a prince is a prince, and it speaks for the acumen of the Indian common man that a new prince is made to succeed the old one. All is well so long as the royalty is in place with all its appurtenances. India's prime minister, mercifully, is not some yokel drawn from just any social class in that decadent society, who cannot speak English or shake hands with foreign dignitaries in the royal fashion. On this discovery, their research mills started churning out stories of how V.P. Singh was adopted by a childless *Raja*, the family feuds and the machinations of other pretenders to the throne, how the palace intrigues led to his seclusion—ideal material for a glossy Indian film.

Fortunately for V.P. Singh and unfortunately for the American news media, they could not locate his harem, though they did not overlook the two wives of his adopted father, who between them could not conceive an heir. But there is always a compensation for every loss: V.P. may not have a harem, but his wife is a princess, too.

In their quest to trace V.P. Singh's royal provenance, the media has been at a loss to know what made him what he is. For a prince, he is rather well educated. He did not have to do rope tricks to clamber on to the prime ministership. He came from nowhere to somewhere, though he was not a jail-going Congressman. He is from a new brand of politicians of post-Independence India. Catapulted as chief Minister of Uttar Pradesh with the blessings of Indira Gandhi, he had the courage to renounce it, when he saw his writ had been whittled away, with dacoits running amok in the state he ruled. By this one act he did what his then mentor Indira Gandhi could not do when the Allahabad High Court annulled her election. But all these things are to the American media a second order of smalls. Perhaps they wanted a like for a like, not an upstart, not a bumbler who did not know what the West is or the East is not.

But royalty was not the only virtue; the economic liberalisation era is also the handmaiden of V.P. Singh, which warmed the cockles of their hearts. Was he not the finance minister in 1985 when India threw open its doors to foreign investment, diluted industrial controls, unshackled the restrictive regime and allowed the hounds to run? In his zeal he might have consigned some fat cats to jail, put the fear of God into them and brought to book some tax-evaders. But all this could pass muster in the game of politics so long as you are a liberal at heart and do not talk the language of socialism. So this is the time for rejoicing. One royalty is exchanged for another and it is an equal exchange. There is no fear that India's economic policies will change gear and America has no reason to beat its breast for the end of an era, the end of a dynasty which meant so much for so many for so long. So why worry? Turn the page and proceed. Everything is hunky-dory in India.

Why this anxiety among the westerners to seek a surrogate for anything that belies their expectations from the political history of the colonies of the yesteryears? With illiteracy abounding, how can they read? With unread masses how can they understand? With opaque thinking, how can they vote and call themselves democrats? Something is amiss somewhere and it has to be sorted out by and by. The undulating ocean of humanity that is India, throwing up leaders and institutions, does not fit the westerner's model of rational expectations. And if they are not rational, there must be something terribly wrong. Hence this eternal search for empty royalty, empty gestures and meaningless symbols to explain happenings in India. We know that there can at times be rational fools though a curiosity, but the world and India in particular should not deviate from conformity to the general law of irrational fools.

Economic and Political Weekly, 18 April 1990.

14

Differently similar

IF you want to make your mark in this Capital City, you should be able to impress others with your frequent appearances at social events. However, mere presence is not enough, you have to meet two tests. First, you have to be seen at social functions which are graced by relatives of the President of the United States, by high officials who have the ear of the President, and by other dignitaries. Second, your conversational gambit should aim at convincing those around you that your tiny tots attend high-achievement, high-tuition-charging, early-childhood schools. If you succeed in doing this, then you truly belong to the 'U' class and are not 'a barrel of laughter' like others who do not make the grade.

There was, a few years ago, a Canadian diplomat's wife, Sandra Gottlieb, sprightly, smart, something of a litterateur who could write delightful stuff in *The Washington Post* on the goings on in political and social circles in this city. Her favourite conversational starter "You are the wife of" used to open a window on the person being talked to—who she was, what her husband did, how important the personages around her were. What she wrote amused many because her column with its smirky levity revealed the foibles and vanities of diplomats and journalists, social mountebanks and cringy acolytes of the high and mighty, bureaucrats from the affluent countries and those from 'how to beg from my neighbour kind' countries of Africa, Asia and Latin America. But Gottlieb also disturbed many with her slings and arrows. And one day the party-giving pressures got her into hot waters. At one of her evening dinners an important Reagan official, Counsellor Richard Darman, did not turn up and Gottlieb was so upset that she slapped her social secretary on the face in the presence of her guests.

But such quirks of hostesses have not taken away the glamour and glitz of socialising. To be or not to be at parties is what makes you a success or a failure. Mere presence is not enough, you should have the *savoir faire* to show your closeness to important personages at parties. A story goes, and not an apocryphal one, that an Indian lady, mature in years, in her late fifties, at an embassy party wanted to show her intimacy with a European ambassador. While the people around were discussing something else, she tried to steer the conversation to how she knew the ambassador in school and then college and how close their families were. Such is the addiction to partying in this political city.

There is also the experience of a young journalist in wartime Washington, who could not get enough to eat because of wartime shortages. Being a minor journalist, yet to make a name for himself, he found a sure way to attend these parties without being invited. He assiduously read in the daily newspaper the list of guests invited to various embassy parties, picked up one name at random for himself and started attending the parties. He did that quite successfully until, one day, the person at the party to whom he announced himself happened to be the person whom he had been impersonating.

Partying in this town is a status symbol. But there are parties and parties. You may attend several of them and yet you may be left out of that charmed circle. If it is a party where the President and his acolytes who are the parvenu power centres are present, then you make it to the 'A' list. If not, then you slide fast down the social ladder. Only second stringers passing through the sieve figure on the 'B' list. Yes, like the grading of students in schools and universities, parties in Washington are graded. 'A', of course, is the top. You may have millions, you may be an intellectual of Nobel rank, but if you do not make the 'A' list, you fail the test of being a socialite. You come anywhere near Georgette Mosbachev, the glamorous red-haired wife of millionaire commerce minister Robert Mosbachev, and you have done it. Unlike the grading in academia, this social grading is flexible. You are in 'A' category if you are today's secretary of state, treasury secretary or at least a special assistant to the President. But grades change when the administration changes. Yesterday's men are good only for 'B' category social parties. But the process can be reversed, you can fall to 'B' from 'A'. White House chief of staff John Sununu, until he assumed that office was on the 'B' circuit; his new office promoted him to 'A'. Those who had met him on the lower rungs earlier, first thought he had missed his way when they spotted him at a party attended by President Bush after assuming office two years ago. They did not know even how to pronounce his name. Some thought he was an 'Eskimo or a tanning salon' or what the Pacific islanders call 'susu.' The hostesses, always 'strategising' to attract 'A' list guests to their parties, suddenly woke up to Sununu's importance in his new incarnation. The 'A' list was chipped and chopped. A simple test for weeding out is to figure out who is in power and who is not. Don Regan and Michael Deaver could be slipped into a stepney list, euphemistically called an 'invitations list', to be drawn on only in emergencies when VIPs and VVIPs drop out at the eleventh hour.

Whether a guest is in power or out of power is, of course, the first criterion. The other is the state from which the President or a high dignitary like James Baker comes from. California is now passé; Texas is the place to be from. And what about the newspaper man who had played dirty by the President during the campaign? No, he should not be on even the 'B' list. And what about those who were forging documents about the alleged psychiatric ailment of Michael Dukakis? Yes, of course, they should get onto the 'A' list.

If to be on the 'A' or 'B' list is one life-and-death question for the socialites, placement of tiny tots in good private schools is the other. Attendance at the right kind of parties and enrolment of children in high-charging schools determine your importance on a scale of one to ten. There is a good theory why this is the case. A tale was floated by some school entrepreneurs anxious to have their pre-kindergarten classes filled, that if a child does not start in the high-cost highly touted kindergarten, it would not get into first grade private schools later. This raises the blood pressure of high-achieving Washington parents who are swept by the competitive culture of the city. The higher the fee (which often reaches up to twenty thousand dollars) the better, of course, the kindergarten—money in the cradle enriches the civilisation. To get admitted into the school is an elaborate affair. The parents of a three-year-old child are the first to be interviewed. "What is your philosophy of education?" is the first pre-tested question. Whatever your answer to it, quick comes the second question, "What work do you and your husband do, and what is your level of education? Is it from any Ivy League school?" If you survive this, then the final lead question, "Can you name a good family friend?" This is not straight but guerrilla warfare. If you just mention a good scholar as a reference, it won't do. But mention Barbara Bush, James Baker, or even Ed Meese, and then the answers to all your earlier questions are washed away. Your child is in the best school and its future is made. You can then proceed with your name-dropping game at social parties.

Doesn't all this evoke images of what goes on in our Delhi and Bombay? Of course, but with minor variations; some differences are unavoidable. Is not our culture different? Are we not a different people, and are not our values different? We are more spiritual and not addicted to material comforts. So if you find that what happens in Delhi and Bombay does not replicate exactly what you see here, then you carry out a factor analysis to attribute the deviations to the uniqueness of our culture. Categorisation of social events in Delhi begins with categorisation of your residential location. You are on Pandara Road? Okay, just fine. You are in the midst of the high and mighty, the rich and the beautiful. If not, you are untouchable riffraff, but not always. You can have a right surname which reveals that you are some relation of a high-ranking civil servant or of a politician who has not yet lost his ministerial position. But the 'A plus' social events are those organised by the embassies. The best heady stuff is flowing there, of course, but more important is some influential personage from an international organisation or aid agency or a highly endowed university. You can strike deals for visits abroad, for scholarships for your—needless to say—brilliant children and, by the way, for tax-free jobs in international agencies. Maybe they treat our country badly when it asks for some loan, they offer unsolicited advice and impose those silly conditions. But this should not deter you. Advice can be ignored, conditionality is ephemeral, but the jobs for you and your children are permanent. It is, after all, a small price to pay.

Your importance is determined by the rank you hold, the caste you come from, the wealth you possess, the company you keep, and by how you speak the English language. However, these are necessary but not sufficient conditions. Your standing also depends on where your children are educated and their deportment. So you get into the parvenu network, people with high connections, and send your children to the right schools by appropriating a seat from the quota reserved for hardworking civil servants or donors to the schools or politicians. Once in a good school, always in a good university, and in due course a foreign one.

India may be poor, but its people are not a whit less talented, enterprising, gracious and generous than the Americans. We can match wits with them, we can throw social parties as glittery and extravagant as they do; we also educate our children by booking seats for them in the best schools while they are still in the wombs of their mothers. But we are not demeaned by the lust for material goods. We have maintained our spiritual heritage and have been enriching it even in distant America, not least by building temples for all possible Gods and Goddesses.

Economic and Political Weekly, 2 March 1991.

15

This picture and that

AMERICA has its riches of research institutes in all spheres of social sciences, liberally supported by private endowments. They take up issues of public policy of the day of relevance to the country and of importance to its relationship with the outside world. They have their biases, their ideological colouring, but issues on hand are dealt with in a cohesive fashion and policy options are set out. Whether it is immigration or trade policy or protectionism or education, each is subjected to a thorough analysis despite its political complexities and the conclusions are released for public debate, even when they seemingly contradict the prevailing stance of the political party whose cause they espouse at any point in time. The papers that roll out from these institutions are scrutinised rigorously through internal and external reference processes before they are published. Few of these institutions boast permanent staff members, many of whom gravitate to them from the universities or the political parties or even the corporate world. Their work is time-bound and subject-specific. Once the job is done, many of them go back. Their salaries and perks are equivalent to what professors and lecturers get at universities. They occupy modest cubicles and work in a cloistered environment. There are no permanent positions; there are only permanent interests—that is, to articulate reasoned views on the questions of the day according to one's lights. Those who finance these institutions are not allowed to attach any strings and, if they insist, the institutions go without the endowments. Come elections, their work provides inputs into the political platforms of both the political parties in the country. They do not encourage basic research, which is better left to the universities, which too draw financial wherewithal from corporations and affluent individuals to pursue knowledge in the areas of their concern.

There is Brookings Institute, privately funded, focusing on the leading economic, political and social problems that agitate the minds of the leaders of the American polity. It has its bias towards the political philosophy of the Democratic Party but it does not slavishly toe the line of the party. The premise is the party's but the conclusions are what follow logically from the premise, regardless of whether or not they receive the approbation of the party. There is another Democratic party forum, the Overseas Development Council. It is a major 'think tank' with resources not amounting to more than six million dollars a year. But its policy influence goes far beyond what its resources would indicate. The Republican counterparts are the Hudson's Institute in California and the Heritage Foundation and Enterprise Institute in Washington. The Republican eggheads and the Republican moneybags are their main pillars. But the quality of research, whatever its ideological hue, is professional. If the conclusions are unsavoury to the government, so much the worse for it but they do not modify their analysis because the conclusions are inconvenient. The importance attached to the work of these institutions may be gauged by how it has changed the course of government policies. The Carter administration embarked on a major overhaul of the immigration policy because institutional research convincingly revealed the adverse impact of restricted immigration on the future economic growth of the American economy. Primary and higher education reform was similarly triggered by the solid and well-founded reports of the Carnegie Endowment for International Peace.

When you turn away from this picture and see what has been happening in India, you get on to a different planet. Most of the research institutes in India, if not all, are creations of the government in one way or another. Their fields of operation are not clearly demarcated, and it is not uncommon that more than one institution engages in the same area of research and often with the same data set and sources. Each such institution is lavishly funded by government—central as well as state; when the funding cannot be done through budgetary provisions, public sector financial institutions are asked to chip in. If some inventive person decides to add up these sums, they might find that the total is large enough to finance the five-year plan of one of the bigger states. As if this were not sufficiently generous, these institutions receive contracts from government for special projects. This has twin advantages: the permanently employed government economist, who should have been working on these problems, instead spends his time in attending meetings or goes on foreign tours and drafts inane speeches for his ministers; secondly, he gets enough time to indulge in politicking. Much of the work now contracted out used in the good old days to be done in government departments or ministries, but with the emergence of the research institutes an easy way out has been found. Thus, much of what comes out from these research factories is of ephemeral value, conveniently vague, often text-bookish, and devoid of any significance for the problems facing the country.

This is not surprising. Like the proliferating government bureaucracy, the tribe of researchers has also grown. But quantity has not generated quality. The number of research institutions is so large that a number of positions go begging for want of qualified personnel, so that lesser talents crowd in. There is no peer review, internal or external. Whatever is produced and approved by the directors of the institutes is lapped up. There is no dearth of publishers to accept even low-quality work of the institutes. There is a compact between them and the publishers that a certain number of copies are bought back by the sponsoring institutes to be distributed amongst visiting dignitaries, particularly from foreign countries or international institutions. All concerned are happy with this arrangement. The institute can flaunt the number of publications to its credit; the publishers can make a neat profit without risk and members of the institute's staff might be blessed with a foreign invitation.

True, all is not bleak. There have been some shining examples of high-quality research but they are so few. Not long ago, dedicated men of ability, conscience and commitment used to pursue research in their small institutes without government crutches and defined themselves and their organisations as trustees of society. Compromises of convenience, sycophancy and conviviality were not for them. Their concern was to see things clearly and dispassionately, so that the larger interests of the polity were served. One hopes, maybe in vain, for some Sachin Chaudhuri, who founded the

Economic Weekly without money and manpower, and who had the spunk to turn his back on a tempting offer of aid for fear of losing his freedom, to show that good research is powered by brain and intrinsic interests and not by money and patronage.

Economic and Political Weekly, 24 September 1988.

16

Trashing the Trumps

AFTER he untethered the blacks from the shame and scandal of slavery, that great president of the United States of America, Abraham Lincoln, had a masterly vision of creating "a family of man", in which the distinction between large and small, former slaves and former masters, the rich and the poor, the pompous and the meek, would all wither away. More than a hundred years have gone by and in this land of Lincoln, 'the family of man' has remained a pipe-dream. It has become a cruel joke. The progeny of the descendants of Lincoln have debased that family. In this time and clime, when history is unfolding in black Africa, with the release of Nelson Mandela, with diehard apartheid champions beginning to atone for their sins, when Mandela by grand statesmanship and generosity of heart is prepared to forgive and forget all the tortures and humiliations he went through in prison where he spent his youth, this America of Lincoln and Jefferson is exhibiting the morbid curiosity of its educated elite, the greed and glitz of the captains of its financial world, the infinite lying capacity of its ex-president, Ronald Reagan.

New York and, close on its heels, Washington are agog with juicy stories of one billionaire, Donald Trump, casino king and owner of airlines, his sexual escapades and gambling extravaganzas. Who is this Trump who has been stealing the headlines of all newspapers and the television media? Is he a war hero? Or has he made a grand discovery which has shaken the world? Nothing of the sort. All he did was to cheat his wife, Ivana Trump, a former Czechoslovakian night club moll. The story leaked out that he proposed to divorce her. It seems that in a pre-nuptial agreement, Ivana had committed Don

Trump to $100 million alimony and a palace worth a few million dollars more. Not satisfied with this pittance, she sent a notice to her husband laying claim to a larger share in his billions. This was enough for the newspaper hounds. They first filled their pages with an interview with Ivana and then searched for Don Juan. It took a few days for them to locate his hideout. Perhaps all this was make-believe news media hype, to rouse public interest. At last they found him. He flatly denied that he had ever threatened a divorce. Prompt came the reply from Ivana that "her hubby is either lying or laying someone or the other."

This bestirred the two cities—the commercial capital New York and the political capital Washington—no end. As if nothing else was happening in the world, except Don telling someone something and Ivana crying. The news hounds' efforts were at last rewarded. They traced the cause of the marital discord of the Trumps—one Marla Maples, a heartthrob of Don Trump and another night club entertainer. But Trump finally played his trump. He announced grandly that Marla would appear at a bash at the Taj Mahal, a hotel with a casino in Atlantic City, in April. Marla Maples has now acquired the grandeur of Shah Jehan's Mumtaz. One may have perhaps commiserated with Miss Maples' parents whose only daughter is being so publicly paraded as a strumpet. But no. Her father too soon joined the jiggery-pokery of public shame and private greed. Not to be outdone by Donald Trump's money-making shenanigans by using his daughter, her father announced, "I said everybody but the family is making money off her situation and it was time for her to gain some monetary benefits." No one has remained a saint: everyone is a recidivist, sanctified by lucre, lust and levity.

Leave for a while poor Trump and his hapless lady and imprudent lass. After all, Don Trump is a mere individual though anointed with greenbacks. Now turn to the sanctum sanctorum of high finance, the symbol of much-sought-after capitalism and all that you cherish in this material world. In the midst of the titillating Trump saga came the startling news of the demise of the giant of an investment firm, Drexel, Burnham, Lambert, Inc., which had almost convinced the world that "if it had not found the fountain of youth, it had indeed discovered a fountain of money in the junk bond." This firm and its wonder boy, Michael Milken, invented those high-risk, high-yield, appropriately named bonds for corporate takeovers. The market for junk bonds ballooned to $200 billion in the early 1980s. The world was held in thraldom that here was a man, his firm and his country, all making money by just shuffling papers, while others were struggling to make ends meet by the mundane activity of producing goods. It was all a world of magic which drove everyone insane and made all immune to what this freedom to cheat would ultimately portend for the American financial system and myriad small investors. Henry Kaufman, that sage of Wall Street, known for his probity and sagacity, had warned right at the inception of the junk bond market that "we are drifting toward a financial system in which credit has no guardian." Felix Rohatyn, himself an investment banker and a man who stands for public interest, lamented that "the junk bonds fathered by Milken and Drexel would turn the financial markets into a huge casino, leveraged buy outs, financed by junk bonds, bet the company on a combination of continued growth and lower interest rates, with no margin for error." But everyone was staid as the Buddha; no one would get into conniption. The editors and the public media are more concerned with Trump-like stories of sex and wealth and gambling or the politics of drugs and crime. Congress did not feel any urgency to stem this rot because none in that august body thought that the danger of fraud was imminent.

And now the rot has set in with Drexel filing for bankruptcy. But bankruptcy for what? Junk bonds were a fraud, of course, and with their collapse they also brought down many savings and loans associations. But even when the impending bankruptcy was staring the Drexel managers in the face they went ahead with impunity, giving each other bonuses—not one or two million but a good 350 million dollars, with some individual bonuses amounting to 10 million dollars apiece. Now it has come out that the excess of liabilities over assets of Drexel was not far above the creditors' dues. The managers of Drexel thus bonused the firm into bankruptcy.

A playboy, an investment firm, and now the turn of the actor-cum-ex-president of the United States, Ronald Reagan, who was ordered by the court to depose before the court, enquiring into the involvement of John M. Poindexter, a former national security advisor to the then president Reagan in the Iran-Contra affair. Reagan testified without batting an eyelid that

> we don't break the law and I am confident that my former national security advisors, Robert McFarlane and Poindexter, replied truthfully to Congressional Committee seeking information about secret White House efforts to help Contra rebels through the US arms sale to Iran.

But McFarlane has been found guilty of perjury and Poindexter is before the bar for his involvement. Reagan, of course, is a master of malapropism and known for his feeble memory, but he did not hesitate in telling a lie either, that

> because Khomeini may not live out a week, a group of individuals, citizens of Iran journeyed to a third country; contact was made with them that they wanted to discuss with us how better relations between Iran and the United States could be secured. We were not doing business with Khomeini.

But the testimony before the Tower Review Board unfolded a totally different story. There was no group of individuals from Iran involved at any of the secret arms sales, and no delegation of Americans. The idea of sending American-made arms to Iran was broached by Israeli officials working with an Iranian middleman. Such is the ex-president of the great nation and an heir to the great Abraham Lincoln who wanted to convert the world into a 'family of man' and to Thomas Jefferson who wrote, "Ignorance is preferable to error and he is less remote from the truth who believes nothing, than he who believes what is wrong." How then is Reagan different from Donald Trump who tramps his way to wealth and fame, lying and laying; or from those financial wizards of Drexel, Burnham, Lambert, Inc. who not only lied to the innocent investors who entrusted to them all they had and to the employees who were sacked without compensation? At a time when President Vaclav Havel was telling them that the salvation of the human world lies nowhere else than in the human heart, in the human power to reflect, in human meekness and in human responsibility, these personages have abdicated all the elementary values. Greed, unvarnished greed, overpowered them all—to the shame of this great nation.

Economic and Political Weekly, 19 May 1990.

17

Whose life is it, anyway?

AMERICA, this land of the Bill of Rights, whose one great leader decreed three freedoms—freedom from fear, freedom from hunger and freedom of speech—is a strange land. When opulence is gushing, the body is in good shape, and the spirit is undying these freedoms spruce up the pleasures of living. Society is designed for physical fitness. But when you are past the prime of youth, the purse shrivels with healthcare, the infirmity of age is asseverating in all directions, the body takes a beating, the joy of death takes precedence over the pain of living.

The oracle of the Supreme Court of the United States of America has spoken. If you are sick and infirm and in a vegetative state, endure, rot in your bed with sores, heap anguish on your dear and near ones but take care not to die. Heavens will not fall if your parents go broke and go to a nunnery but do not stop bleeding them white financially and physically. This is the profound message of the nine learned Supreme Court judges. They in their wisdom asked her parents to desist from removing the life-support system for Nancy Cruzen, a 32-year-old Missouri woman, so that she continued her useless comatose existence. Don't be foolish to ask why, because the answer will be even more foolish than the question. The court argued that the patient enjoyed the constitutional right to refuse life-sustaining medical treatment, but since the patient was not in a state of consciousness to say whether she wanted the life-supporting system or not, others, be they parents, husbands, wives or doctors, have to remain helpless witnesses to the lifeless body. So proceed with your mummified existence. The message of the learned judges is clear: if you are healthy, do not fall ill; if you are ill, do not fall into a vegetative state; if you are physically alive but clinically dead, do not try to die by removing the artificial aids. If you do, you will be committing a sin against God and society.

The Supreme Court verdict, however, applies only to the sick who cannot decide for themselves. But those old and young, who cannot rely on others to decide whether they should live or die, have already taken their lives in their hands. The old live to die. There was the 80-year-old couple who quietly tiptoed to their death. They deliberated long and deep. Justine De Witt Bowersock and his wife of sixty years, Betty Bruce, planned their death for a year. They took an inventory of their goods, evaluated their assets, made their inheritance will distributing their legacy between their two surviving daughters, tidied up the closets and, after forewarning their understanding daughters, quietly swallowed sleeping pills with alcohol. "We are old and we are happy", they wrote in their last testament,

> but we do not want to be a burden to our daughters nor to society. Through honest means we made our nest egg but we would not like it to be wasted in preserving our relics, which have neither use for the old as we are, nor for our busy daughters nor the community. With the inhuman medical system that we have, we will unhappily live to die.

Thus they went into one long slumber.

The Bowersock couple is like any other in American society—middle class, good income, no great pretensions. So their voluntary death caused a mere ripple. But not so with a psychologist and a well-known one at that, Bruno Bettelheim, who came to Washington to die as others come here to live. He was not an ordinary man. His lifework was on the psychology of the young and he was a beacon of light to the despondent. Tortured in a Nazi concentration camp, he was always full of life and hope. "This is the man", said Jacqelyn Sanders, his colleague at the University of Chicago's Sonia Shanhmen orthogenic school, "who told us that you struggle for life, that even though it is very difficult, life is worth living. How is it that he committed suicide?" He sought meaning in everything the child did or said. For him children's lives were laden with meaning. Bettelheim, despite having gone through the crucible of torture in his youth, remained optimistic. In the introduction to one of his books he wrote,

> If we hope to live not just from moment to moment, but in true consciousness of our existence, then our greatest need and most difficult achievement is to find meaning in our lives. It is well known how many have lost the will to live, and have stopped trying because such meaning has evaded them.

It is an enigma to his admirers and friends why such a man put an end to his life.

For strange reasons, in this society there is more in death than to life. If the old live to die, if the forsaken and the forlorn in this affluent society feel that life is a burden, it is understandable. But in this society, the loveliest, the youngest and the best have smiled, said 'good night', and gone to rest. A young girl, hardly thirteen, wrote to her mother, "I can't see how I can cope with this high pressure society. I have no one to call father. I have no one to call a friend." It was for her the age to dream of glorious youth and the beauty of life, but she preferred the wings of death to ageing in youth. A boy, just out of high school, had to part with his father when his family split. He could not take it. "Can I leave my father and call your husband my dad?" he wrote in sadness in his last letter to his mother. Two boys, eighteen years old, entered a suicide pact. A school counsellor prepared the report on their death. Both had dropped out of school in the tenth grade, had drifted through menial jobs, had had brushes with the law and had dreamt of becoming mercenaries. Music too resonates with odes to death. In one album, "Beyond the Realm of Death", the band sings, "Yeah, I have left the world behind. I am safe now in my mind, I am free to speak with my own mind. This is my life, and I will decide, not you."

It is easy to understand why the old want to exit. But why the young and the innocent who don't know what life is? Do the sociologists and the psychologists have any answers? But even they despair and end their lives, as Bruno Bettelheim did. Can Karl Marx help? There is, to be sure, alienation from family, alienation from society, alienation from life. One can go back to jejune and hackneyed theories for explaining this strange fascination for death. Can one invoke Sutton's law of medicine—if you do not know what the trouble is, grab the biopsy and study it because that is where the problem is—to explain the death wish of the youth? But what part of social organisation do we dissect to search for the ailment of the youth? Maybe the family as a unit is disintegrating. Maybe the pressures of living in the midst of plenty are mounting. Arthur Koestler might have said that the youth in America "have regarded the universe as an open book printed in the language of physical equations, but as their consciousness grew they found it as a text written in invisible ink." In their struggle to find meaning in life, they may not have succeeded in deciphering even a small fragment of it.

It is a different story with the old and the infirm. If they have lived full lives, the best way they could, and now have reached the end of their tether, why should they be prevented from exiting? The right to freedom from unwanted life is as precious as other kinds of freedoms. Arthur Koestler, who practised what he preached, described euthanasia as a means of reconciling man with his destiny. "It is a process of being unborn", he inscribed in the manifesto for his last mission in life. "Entry and exit are the gates of human existence. Just as man needs a midwife to aid him to be born, he should also need similar means to be unborn—to die peacefully without fuss from old age."

Economic and Political Weekly, 25 August 1990.

18

No need for defenders

WASHINGTON DC is a beautiful city. It is a capital city, ever expanding, ever improving. It is a nation's capital becoming international, housing those hated gnomes of finance capital known as the World Bank and, worse still, the IMF, which are out—as any Indian would tell you on the streets of New Delhi and Bombay—to subvert poor countries in Asia, Latin America and Africa. The city is beautiful, but ugly within—the inner visage revealing itself more often to the world's leftists. But these leftists can now be ignored; their laws of historical evolution have been falsified by current happenings around us. But the leftists are not alone in the hate parlour. Now a man with his own law of gravity has joined their company to hate this city. These are happy tidings for Indian communists. The *yogi*—and an Indian *yogi* at that—has pronounced that Washington stinks like capitalism.

The *yogi* is none other than Mahesh Yogi, who claims to be a former professor of physics and explains the conundrums of modern living in the idiom of physics. He and his cohorts had made this capital city the seat of the Mahesh Yogi Institute of Transcendental Meditation. The institute thrived, it spread its gospel, it proselytised. Many groups mushroomed all over Washington, propagating the cult of transcendental meditation. Wives divorcing their husbands were helped by this spiritual nostrum. Not that they retained their husbands, but they got hefty alimonies for comfortable living. Congressmen were saved, not from the glare of publicity for their sexual escapades, but from electoral defeats. Functionaries in the presidential office may not have been saved from losing their jobs, but they were rewarded with plum lobbying contracts. Transcendental meditation became a craze. Then something went amiss. Familiarity breeds contempt, some would say. There are some naughty detractors of the swami who say the reverse may have also been true in his case. Mahesh Yogi is now disenchanted, disgusted with this city. He is running away, his followers are on the run, his university is levitating to Fairfield, Iowa state, where a sprawling Maharshi international university has been spreading the Yogi's gospel.

"Plague on all of you, this government, this city", the incarnation of the Hindu god is using the biblical metaphor. You should ignore the lapse; it happens even to a yogi and the anointed Hindu prophet who travels to the West so often that the inevitable jet-lag momentarily enfeebles his spiritual and mental powers. "I would not advise anyone to stay in Washington, this pool of mud; save yourselves from the criminal atmosphere—if your business justifies your presence, then limit your stay to those few hours", sermonised the yogi. One of Mahesh Yogi's western alter egos, Robert Oates, went even further: "Living in and near Washington is like living near Chernobyl. All the stress of the world's collective consciousness impinges on DC plus the incredible rate of violence."

All is not, however, lost. The yogi has laid out the escape routes. There can be some green between Washington residents and the city. They can go some distance away. A score or two of Yogi's followers have already sold their homes in the city at throwaway prices to move away—though that is not the reason for the free fall in housing prices in the area. Who says Indian sovereignty is being undermined by the western countries? No, it is the other way round. The subverters are Indians—Mahesh Yogi and his converts and, before him, Ravindra Batra who concocted an alchemy out of modern economics and Anand Margi philosophy to predict a crash in 1990. It should not matter that the date has proved to be somewhat off mark. There are good prospects that the recession, which takes on, like the Buddha's life, different forms—shallow to deep to flat to shallow again—may as well end in a crash. So the Indian messiahs, Mahesh and Batra, may save western civilisation, after all.

Why then has the once-galloping TM movement of Mahesh Yogi, which drew to itself politicians, criminals, intellectuals, psychotics, actors and actresses, lost its steam midway? There may have been material causes for the spiritual dissipation. Rumours are rife that many observers, eager to see the levitating TM-sters, found that they never did fly. Mahesh Yogi failed to enlist US government support for a collective meditation programme. Unlike our mythological Valmiki, criminals did not change their souls and crime is in full bloom in the city. The last straw was the rebuff the yogi got from the federal government which turned down his request for $20 million to ward off the risk of a Gulf war. The war came and went, the commissar levitated, and the yogi was sunk.

The woes of Washington have not, however, ended with deflation of the all-knowing Maharshi. There has come a professor of history, Paul Fussel, a bored American who has become an Anglophile and whose credo is 'great crappiness is all American.' His disenchantment with America and Washington is based on materialism; there is nothing spiritual about it. On seeing a woman eat french fries in a restaurant, he explodes, "Look how bad is America. Look at her! She is eating french fries. I want to rush over to her and say, madam, stop! I know chips are good but she could ruin herself, her figure." A woman's figure for the professor is his figure of speech for America. All that America symbolises is bad. But "bad things are merely 'bad', which is to say merely 'not good'. Bad is something phoney, clumsy, witless, hairy, untalented or just boring." In his mould of badness are "airports, colleges, food, ideas, magazines, movies, poetry, television and ... the President of the United States" and the city he lives in.

Maharshi calls Washington a "pool of mud." Professor Fussel has a more eloquent phrase: "cesspool" of, of course, intrigues.

> Washington is a middle-class bad. Terrible people from Kansas trying to come on as aristocrats, you know. Did you read the nasty things I wrote about embassy personnel? They are like field-grade officers just obeying orders. Gentlemen never obey orders. Washington is filled with that kind of thing—people like Olie North pretending to be a gentleman, pretending to be independent, and Ronald Reagan, pretending to be the President. But one is only an employee and the other just an actor and not a good one.

Fussel would not stop. There is so much to say in so little time. Did he find anything that might redeem this hapless city under assault? No, nothing. The lifelike sculpture added to the Vietnam Veteran Memorial ruined its throat-catching understatement and simplicity. Unfortunately, there is no audience for such architecture in Washington. Fussel misses an audience with subversive wits.

Does Washington need the defenders? By no means. The greater the crime rate, the greater the outmigration of the blacks, the cheaper the land, the more beautiful the buildings that come up on the ruins of the old. The trooping in of international diplomats for conferences on the Israel-Palestine question or on the on-and-off crumbling Russia and its splintered states, the arrivals and departures of international finance men and bankers to strike deals, keep its skies roaring with aeroplanes. No matter if the city stinks, as the maharshi and the professor would like us to believe; it will be a magnet for the powerful and the weak, the rich and the poor, the holy and the profane, the promoter and the subverter from all parts of the world. Do we not know that for all the well-advertised bankruptcy of the American economy, its deepening recession, collapsing savings and loans associations and the unethical behaviour of the security exchange dealers, the world's wings keep flowing to Wall Street, which is having the biggest bonanza in its history? Wall Street is the role model for this much-maligned city.

Economic and Political Weekly, 22 August 1992.

19

From there to eternity

THE greatness of American society shrivelled with that cruel verdict of the biased white jury in Los Angeles. Here was a simple incident of police brutality—the beating of one Rodney King, an unemployed black, for no fault of his except his accidental presence. The inhuman treatment meted out was viewed on television by the people of this civilised nation. All were revolted by what they witnessed; the media poured scorn on the police; the civil rights groups were up in arms; the blacks, subjected to indignity, racial slurs and brutality, took it in their stride, hoping against hope that the judicial system would punish the guilty police through the normal processes of law. They waited for nine long months; they endured, remaining patient even when the site of the trial was shifted from Los Angeles to Sim Valley, following the plea of the defence lawyers. Why? Because the Los Angeles area is dotted with blacks and the jury's deliberations, it was thought, could not be free in such an emotionally surcharged atmosphere. But what is good for the goose is not good for the gander. In Sim Valley the population is predominantly white—out of 10,000 people, only 2 per cent are black. What is even more startling is that some 2000 of them are active police officers. There was not a single member of the black community on the jury. Oh, this is not fair criticism, they would say. How can a fair-minded black be found where blacks are only drug addicts and former jailbirds? A change of venue for the trial and an all-white jury, and still the blacks did not demur, did not agitate, did not set fire to buildings. They kept their counsel and their cool, preached patience and calm. The judicial system would prevail, the black leaders assured. The fateful day came in April; the whole thing exploded in the face of ugly America. The blood of hundreds was spilled; tattered bodies of the dead were sprawled on the streets, reminding one of Anselm Kaifer's painting: "They are much more ambiguous and much more charged in the way that they mix irony with deadly seriousness, and in the way that they force fixed conventional images to take on fluid meanings." What would history say about this tragedy—a tragedy of perverted justice, of inhumanity to the downtrodden ignorant mass of the black people? Historians like Otto Namier are wrong. The crowning attainment of historical study is not to achieve an intuitive sense of how things do not happen; it is the other way around; it should acquire an intuitive sense of how things happen and why.

Far from the leaders of this nation being shaken out of their torpor, they have been fiddling around. The greatest leader of the greatest democracy has been crowing that "no system of development has nurtured virtue as completely and rigorously as ours, and we have become the most egalitarian system in history and one of the most harmonious." This was said in that hallowed seat of learning, University of Michigan, by President Bush. But when the Los Angeles tragedy erupted, that same president, without any shame or anguish, reacted: "... the court system has worked; what is needed now is calm, respect for the law." But where was the rule of law when the site of the trial was shifted to a white locality? Where was the justice when the entire jury was made up of white men and women? Maybe even with all this, the verdict could have been justified, if the evidence was merely circumstantial. But the lurid drama of the beating of an innocent black had been seen, like a violent sitcom, on television by the whole world. And yet this president of the United States of America, a lawyer by profession, a descendant of Jefferson and Abraham Lincoln, a world preacher, sermonising to the fading communist world on the importance of a civilised society surviving on fairness and equity, has the spunk to say that the court system has worked. Blacks—even Rodney King who was trampled under the booted feet of the police—have asked for calm and restoration of order, and also for the rule of law—which the President believes has prevailed in this case.

And now evidence is piling up to show that the entire judicial system in America is biased against the blacks. If a rapist is black, the court is prompt enough to hand down a guilty verdict and the most severe punishment. But if he is white, his sins are whitewashed. Rape perhaps is not rape if the perpetrator is white; it may be harmless sport amongst two youth and understandable. The conviction of blacks on drug charges, larceny or other petty crimes is more common, certainly, while whites more often than not go unpunished. Any crime charged against a black is believable, whether or not it is committed by him or her. A stereotype of a black is that he is more criminal than civil, a hangover from America's ugly and tyrannical past. There was a story a few months ago of a man in Boston having murdered a white woman. The very fact that the victim was white was enough evidence to indict a black—any black who was around the place of the crime. All the newspapers came out with stories of a black murderer until it was accidentally found out that it was the husband of the murdered woman who had bumped her off. The stereotyping of blacks as criminals or rapists, not only in the public mind but also in the judicial courts, is enough to damn the US judicial system.

The origin of the Los Angeles riots and similar riots in Watts 26 years ago and the almost daily occurrence of drug trafficking and mayhem in cities like Washington have to be attributed to the pathology of deprivation of the blacks. The Orwellian obverse rules supreme in America—all are unequal, but some, the blacks, are more unequal. The National Research Council reported in *A Common Destiny* that between 1959 and 1986 the share of black male wage-earners actually dropped from 8 per cent to 5 per cent. A recent article in the *Harvard Law Review*, "Invisible Man: Black and Male under Title VII", highlighted the misery and metastasis of the black community." In urban areas, black male unemployment rose from 5.4 per cent in 1969 to 23.4 per cent in 1982." A sociologist from Los Angeles recently calculated that about 70,000 industrial jobs had been lost in the south-central Los Angeles area over the last three decades. It is the devastating impact of unemployment and social neglect that has driven the black male beyond human endurance to crime and punishment. In this state of destitution, the blacks cannot even maintain their families intact let alone imbibe those family values which President Bush and his Republican cohorts harp on.

And yet the leaders are unfazed, even in the face of the unfolding of a great social tragedy. The President's coterie has been attributing the tragedy to the consequences of the Great Society programmes of

President Johnson: "Those poverty programmes", Bush's press advisers brazenly declared, "ignored the relationship between people's pride in their community and having a job–having the hope of income and improving their lives, and being able to own their own property or homes to give them a stake in the community." How can blacks have pride when they have no access to jobs? Nobody answers that. Entitlement programmes may have degenerated but they had a rationale when they were introduced. You can own property, a home of your own, love your family, only if you have security. But this is denied. It is true that joblessness is not confined to the blacks but they bear the burden more than the whites. When the initial conditions are unequal, the distance between the two races widens through time. But for Johnson's great social programmes, the blacks would not have progressed as much as they have; a new middle class has emerged in the community, with confidence in their own ability. If Johnson's social programmes had not been there, there would have been riots and social unrest in America perpetually, tearing its social, economic and political fabric. But the Bush administration is awash with apologia for its incompetence. Maybe Johnson was wrong, but what have the five Republican administrations done since the end of Johnson's presidency?

The present and the past have been cruel to President Johnson, but the future will certainly beckon to him. He may not have had the social graces of a Kennedy; he may not have had oratorical flashes; he may have had no great wealth before he became President; he may have been crude in his personal relationships; but he had a great vision and sincerity of purpose. He declared 27 years ago before Howard University, a black university:

> In far too many ways American negroes have been another nation: deprived of freedom, crippled by hatred, the doors of opportunity closed to hope. Men are shaped by their world. When it is a world of decay, ringed by an invisible wall, when escape is arduous and uncertain; and saving pressures of a more hopeful society are unknown, it can cripple the youth and it can desolate the men. We, therefore, must seek not just freedom but opportunity. We must seek not just legal equity but human ability, not just equality as a right and a theory, but equality as a fact and equality as a result. No single answer is available to your problem. Jobs are a part of the problem; decent homes are another part. Social programmes to help

> the happy family is another part. And yet there are other answers which we must strive to find as we go along.

Johnson's was a grand adventure. It is the betrayal of his ideas and idealism by the inhuman Republican presidencies which followed him that has brought American society to its present sorry pass. To fasten the blame for today's social ills on Johnson reveals only the bankruptcy of Bush's leadership and his opportunism, which will begin to haunt him in the coming months. What one old Republican said of President Wilson could be aptly said of President Bush:

> He is a man of ability, but he bas no intellectual integrity at all. A man can change one or two of his opinions for his advantage and change them perfectly honestly, but when a man changes all the well-considered opinions of a lifetime and changes them all at once for his own popular advantage, it seems to me that he must lack in loyalty of conviction.

These are sombre times in America. The glue of anti-communism was binding them, not Americans only but all people in the western world. Now, as the glue has lost its property, the ethnic diversity is dissolving into racial division and conflicts. So these are times to speak up and speak up loudly, even if one is lynched in the realm beyond the Mason-Dixon Line.

Economic and Political Weekly, 25 July 1992.

20

Heartbeats of America

EVERYTHING that is best, attractive, appealing and seductive becomes a heartbeat of Americans. Turn to the sound bites on television, and you are taken in by a lilting line from a crooning soprano, that Nissan's aquiline Infinity is a heartbeat of America. You turn, another time, to your set, and you will end humming a tune of Coco Chanel being your another heartbeat. You then see a stunning beauty, sensuous and smashing, and you fall head over heels calling her your heartbeat. Everything that is beautiful, makes your life pleasurable, is your heartbeat. And yet you do not know the agony and anger of the hearts that miss their beats. Now a startling story is out in the media about two drugs that are supposed to save the lives of people with a heart problem, but instead of relieving their heart ailment, these drugs and their life-saving qualities may well induce lethal heart attacks. Even those with sound and healthy hearts may be in jeopardy, knowing the fate that may await them, should they have to take these drugs any time.

A paladin of the new heart-treating drug TPA is the prestigious Genetech, now majority-owned by the Swiss drug company Hoffmann-La Roche. One dose of it costs $2200 and if you survive at all with this drug, you may pop off when you receive the bill. Medical practitioners have a Panglossian faith in this drug that it would dissolve easily clots in the arteries. If what has now come out about it is known to heart patients, a clot in their arteries may be dissolved but another in their brain may develop. There is another drug, Streptokinase, equally potent and with more or less the same properties, which has been selling for the last few years and is priced around $100 per dose. The question is why on earth Streptokinase is not prescribed in this land where 30 million people are without any medicare.

To ask such questions is to make a fool of yourself, is a smidgen on your intelligence. This country is a country of not-so-hidden persuaders, who force you to buy a costlier drug when a cheaper one is available. It is a case of forced freedom. And hear this hair-raising story of how this freedom is forced down the throats of heart patients in America, both literally and figuratively.

The battle of the two drugs is on; it started with a marketing blitzkrieg by Genetech by spending millions of dollars. There is no difference between TPA and Streptokinase, Genetech's phoney research to prove otherwise notwithstanding. A well-known cardiologist in California, Harold Karpman, excoriated Genetech: "They continue to always find a reason, cleverly so; those studies proving TPA better than Streptokinase are not valid." Stanley D. Bleich of Tulane University was more forthright. "I cannot in my mind morally, ethically, say, I really think this drug is better, but I am not going to use it because it is more expensive. If it was your heart, what would you want?"

Even so, TPA grossed $210 million in sales against $5 million for Streptokinase. Did the patients foot this bill on their own? Certainly not. The medical profession is mortgaged to Genetech. Some cardiologists who bought Genetech shares conducted clinical trials sponsored by the National Institute of Health to compare TPA and Streptokinase. Two cardiologists who acted as counsellors to the firm were offered a stock option. The House Committee on Government Operations found "repeated examples of more positive evaluation of TPA by scientists with relationship with Genetech compared to scientists without such relationships." Some doctors quickly published information from the Health Institute's trial that was favourable to TPA; but data showing some drawbacks they published two years later. An Alex Bosky, a Michael Milikan could go to jail for inside trading but not these doctors who recommend drugs on false grounds and buy the stock of the firm producing them. The medical practitioners are untouchable like the Chicago gangster Al Capone. They are beyond not only the law of the Securities and Exchange Commission but any law of the land.

Two heart drugs have disproved two laws in economics, Gresham's law and the demand and supply law of pricing. Unlike Gresham's law, under which bad coins drive good coins out of circulation, one good drug drives another good drug out of the market. Again, who says that a high-priced commodity is competed out by a low-priced commodity with identical attributes? The pharmaceutical companies producing these heart drugs and the medical profession have discovered a new law of demand and supply. The low price of Streptokinase made it impossible for its producers, Astra Pharmaceutical Products and Kabi Pharmacies, to hold their own in the market against Genetech. So they raised the price of their drug to $300, so that they could spend more on marketing. So you brush up your economics: if a product is priced higher than its substitute, the substitute's price should rise further.

The phalanx of Genetech salesmen, some 300, is on the march with egregious sales techniques. They cook up arguments, falsify trial test results and even use threats subtly. One Dr Perry betrayed his character when he said that he chose TPA not on the basis of scientific literature and his experience but because Genetech marketing influenced him. "I cannot deny that more arguments you hear from one side, there is no question there will be influence." Another doctor from Mount Zion Medical Center in San Francisco was anguished that the Genetech salesmen "made our lives miserable. There was a time that drug representatives were a help to me. Now it is not unlike insurance salesmen and car salesmen. All they care about is a bottom line." One common gimmick has been to play upon doctor's fear of malpractice suit. They would go into physicians' offices and say, "If you don't use TPA, you are setting yourself up for a liability", said one doctor James Selevan. They also ask devastatingly, "Which drug would you prefer, doctor, if you were to have a heart attack?" The issue is clinched.

Guerrilla tactics have also been adopted. Genetech gets hold of nurses in the emergency ward and pays them richly to train others in the use of drugs. It has also tried to interfere with clinical trials that could challenge the superiority of TPA. The coordinators of the American parties of a recent trial known as Isis-3 complained that Genetech salesmen told doctors that they would be endangering their patients by enrolling them in the trial instead of administering them TPA.

This is not merely a tale of two heart drugs; it is a tragic saga of the whole medical care system in the country of Abraham Lincoln. Today there is one drug, tomorrow it is another given to patients with mental depression. Doctors have prescribed it, the Drug Administration has approved it, the mentally ill people have taken it. Whether depression has abated is a moot point but the patients have damaged their brain cells and this was discovered after fifteen years. With sunken eyes and ashen face a tottering body of an AIDS-afflicted girl in her teens, Bergalis, narrated a story of man's sins against women, of lawmakers' insensitivity to the tribulations and trials of the helpless in society and of the criminal apathy of the medical profession. Visiting a dentist to cure her ailment, she met a worse fate. When she heard that he died of AIDS, she got her blood tested. It was HIV positive. She knows she will soon be no more but she wants to spare other innocent people her tragedy. She and her hapless parents carried their battle all the way to the US Congress to convince the government that they should do something to improve disclosure requirements for doctors. Sure enough, the medical lobby was up in arms with convoluted arguments against a dying girl. Thwarted in her mission but undefeated in spirit, she screamed in her feeble voice: "You bastards are the murderers of the young and the innocent. You commit sins but they are visited on poor us." Mothers cried, fathers were enraged, but the lawmakers passed to the next item on the agenda. It was another day in their busy lives.

One never knows how long a band of doctors would go on as a death squad. For a large majority of people, medical care is beyond reach. The cost is prohibitive not because the cost of medicine is high; not because techniques have become expensive. It is just the making of an unholy alliance of lawyers, doctors and politicians, and is made so by the greed of this acquisitive society. If the government is sensible, the medical system can be changed on the lines in Great Britain or Canada. But this country is a lawyer's paradise and a haven for doctors. They restrict entry into the profession without raising anybody's eyebrows, artificially rig up the cost of drugs in tandem with the pharmaceutical companies, and resist all rational reform of the medical care system. They all dance a tango to the market economy and its virtues but conveniently ignore what a market economy in their neighbouring country Canada has achieved in setting up a humane medical care system or what West Germany has done. This is not the 'kinder' capitalist system which President Bush boasts about; this is predatory capitalism.

Not for this society are living bodies. It sheds tears only for babies unborn; they beat their breasts for the useless foetus flushed out through abortion. For them it is a real thing, not the young girl dying of AIDS because of her doctor's crime, nor the young boy fighting his mental disease with a wrong drug.

An American visiting India will write in righteous wrath about the *dais* in India's villages trampling on the bellies of pregnant women to pump out their babies. It is cruelty in all its hideousness. They would term it annihilation of the female if they see in Indian cities doctors applying the amniocentesis test to women and aborting them on determination of the sex of the foetus. It is all an unpardonable crime against humanity, but at least it has the extenuating circumstance of ignorance and superstition bred by cultural and economic backwardness. What would you say about the most advanced society and the richest at that, where millions of people cannot afford medical care because of low income or artificially jacked up medical costs? They live in one abominable hell. Perhaps the number sanctifies the deaths that occur here, as it did in the world of Charlie Chaplin's Monsieur Verdoo.

Economic and Political Weekly, 22 February 1992.

21

A season of mothers

IN this world of quick television sound bites one can see the ancient war in ancient India and the modern war in the modern world with different messages. Lord Krishna of Peter Brooks' *Mahabharat* is sombrely chastising Americans and others in the western world that 'victory is defeat', but the vibrations from the modern Gulf War are different—for Saddam Hussein defeat is victory. Saddam may have been defeated in the mundane vocabulary of ordinary people, but he has conquered the English language. If you see on television the shambles to which Iraq's hapless people have been reduced, the ashen faces of babes and the wizened faces of the old, screaming mothers clutching morsels of food, slaking their thirst with foul drain water, holding their babies to their milkless breasts, and the hordes of defecting Saddam's army men with craven faces hanging on to American soldiers' epaulets, begging for shelter, just ignore all this as the Americans' dissimulating pranks. Saddam Hussein has won a great victory through his defeat. He called his war with the allied forces "the mother of all battles." As a result so many mothers have mushroomed all over, in the lingo of statesmen, journalists, scientists and factotums of the President of America.

The first to come in the aftermath of the Gulf War was the mother of all world orders. President Bush declared that the old order had ended and a new world order was being born through the midwifery of America. What is this new world order? Israelis and Arabs would be friends not foes, they would relive the Old Testament; West Asia would be a zone of peace. But wait a minute lest you get it all wrong. 'World order' is what you heard. No, in this society of political pluralism you talk only in plurals. It is not a new world order but new world orders. Kuwait's reconstruction is on the agenda and the losses borne by Turkey and Egypt are heavy and need to be compensated. Orders for new goods and services will be there. But if the new world order is to be firmly and permanently in place, there should be new world orders for armaments and ammunition. Saddam Hussein's mother of battles may have perished, but the mother of all world orders for armaments has taken her place.

But what about a mother of all defeats? The leaderless, fatherless Democrats cannot escape such a mother. Many Democrats had stood up with courage against the despatching of GIs to the Gulf. They lost and hopelessly and helplessly watched President Bush's electoral stock soaring sky-high during the war. The feedback from their constituencies was frightening. They tried to backtrack and put some gloss on their opposition. But the Republicans hammered away ruthlessly at the 'unpatriotism' of the Democrats. The Democratic party is not getting anyone to be a presidential candidate for the 1992 race. Everyone is chickening out. By not voting for the Gulf War, the Democrats fear losing votes in the 1992 elections—the mother of all defeats.

From Desert Storm has emerged a new storm of political wheeling and dealing by ex-president Reagan and ex-vice president Bush in cahoots with their acolytes, CIA, Casey and Co., Gary Sick, professor at the University of Columbia and former Carter aide, has come out with the stinging charge that officials in the Reagan-Bush campaign had made a secret deal with Iran to delay the release of 52 US hostages until after the election. This has triggered an enquiry by Congress. So the Democrats, poor souls, should not drown themselves in sorrow. Their mother of hopes, presidential hopes, is waking up from deep slumber; she is smiling.

Mother of all hopes, did you say? Yes, it is not only the mother of all hopes but a most fecund mother at that. Alan Friedman and Lionel Barber, of the *Financial Times,* have come up with a sensation. The Bush administration pushed through a $1 billion loan guarantee to Iraq for exports before the invasion of Kuwait. And this despite the solid evidence available to the Administration that Iraq had abused US funds with impunity, manipulated the US banking system illegally to fund its arms purchase programmes and collected generous kickbacks, including armoured trucks, as a part of the loan deal. All this was in defiance of the advice given by highly placed US government officials at the time. The Democrats have been blessed with a heaven-sent opportunity to transform their mother of defeats into a mother of presidential hopes. Adding to the glory of the Democrats' mother of hopes is what Robert Woodward of Watergate fame has revealed. Bush's war against Saddam Hussein was his own, not General Colin Powell's, not Jim Baker's, not even Dick Cheney's. The Gulf War was, oh, a mother of Bush.

The mother of all Bushes is perhaps the right description. The other day Bush was celebrating his great victory at a gathering. A wag asked him, "What role did Barbara Bush play in the conduct of the war?" With a coast-to-coast smile and his usual distorted syntax, the President said, "She is a mother of all Bushes." For Indians who are used to Indira Gandhi being the mother of all Gandhis this may sound rather jejune, but not in this society. The mother of all Bushes must have brought into this world the best of all children. But newspapers are naughty; they flashed the news the next day that Neil Bush, one of the sons of the mother of all Bushes, was reprimanded by the superior court for his conflict-of-interest entanglement in a fraudulent savings and loans association.

And here comes the mother of all deceptions. There is a sordid story making the rounds in cocktail circles for the last five years, though nothing emerged until recently. There is a small computer software firm, Inslaw, which signed a contract with the federal government in 1982 to supply all 94 US attorneys' offices with software it had developed. In early 1984 the government terminated the agreement and Inslaw as a result slid into bankruptcy. The company went to court, charging the government with stealing its property and software "by trickery, fraud and deceit." In subsequent appeals, the Attorney General's office brought pressure on court judges and, by various machinations, thwarted Inslaw from getting justice. But the firm did not let up and has now convinced the House Judiciary Committee that it should see through every document connected with its plea. Many heads may roll as a result.

But if this is one mother of deception, there are two others. Bush's Chief of Staff John Sununu had made 90 trips in the public interest, using government transport and money, to visit his dentist in Boston and play golf in New Hampshire. When asked, the President justified all this by saying that he needed to have "voice contact" with Sununu when he was away. But Sununu could not get away with this. His minions, to whom he had denied these goodies, have blown the whistle.

Shenanigans amongst Bush's coterie are now seeing the light of day. The disease has spread fast. Robert Clarke, Controller of the Currency, is found to have indulged in conflict-of-interest transactions. Asked about this impropriety, his answer, like that of all honest men till they are found to be dishonest, is that "according to his interpretation of the rules, his act was permitted."

Even the hallowed educational institutions have not escaped the mother of all deceptions. A congressional investigation committee has identified several educational institutions, including Stanford, Harvard and Yale, as having fudged the aid given to them to cover expenses extraneous to the purpose for which it was given. Most of the culprits are Ivy League colleges; only two are state universities. Money has been spent on interesting projects: Cornell had billed thousands of dollars for executive jet services for its president, Frank Rhodes. If you want an explanation, here it is: the president, being a tall man, is uncomfortable in commercial airplanes.

In the midst of all these too many mothers—mother of all battles, mother of all world orders, mother of all deceptions—one is confused about which one to love. But the predicament is not new. There are different kinds of mothers—biological mothers, stepmothers, live-in mothers, surrogate mothers, and casual mothers. Yet a riddle remains. A mother of battles? A mother of deceptions? Why not a father of battles? One is not only naïve but also a backward walker in the terrain of knowledge. Invoking mother and not father was a stroke of genius in this epoch of fatherless children who can be manufactured through in vitro fertilisation.

Economic and Political Weekly, 20 July 1991.

22

Metastasis of parenthood

THE elementary question of why parents desire children becomes elemental in American society. Parents have their broken marriages, fathers their sexual perversities, administrators of educational institutions give vent to their sexual fantasies and custodians of day-care centres sexually abuse and physically torture their wards. A man fights not for his own present so much as for the future of his children; he seeks riches for their welfare. But see what is happening in America—children are shamelessly used for sexual molestation, not by lumpen child-lifters but by the parents who brought them into this world.

There is a saga that has just ended—poignant, tragic and inhuman. Dr Elizabeth Morgan Foretich, mother of a seven-year-old daughter, hid her from her husband, a doctor, whom she accused of molesting the child when she was two years old. She was jailed for two years following a court order to bring her daughter back from hiding so that her father could exercise his visiting rights. Only when Congress amended the law was the mother released. When she came out of jail under the special dispensation of Congress, the first thing she did was to remarry. Soon after her release the father of the child, who had employed professional detectives spending thousands of dollars to locate his daughter's hideout, eventually succeeded in tracing her to her maternal grandparents in New Zealand. The judicial fight moved from the American court to a New Zealand court. The judge in New Zealand has now given his verdict that the daughter should remain in New Zealand with her grandparents without being visited by her father. The judge ruled that visits by the father would place the daughter "in the midst of parental conflict with the inevitable disruption of her emotional security." Did the judge find any evidence of incestuous behaviour by the father? Not at all, and yet he did conclude that Elizabeth Foretich and her parents had often told the child, Hilary, about having been abused by her father and for Hilary this became the reality, whether or not the belief had any basis in fact. Who is guilty? Father? Mother? Mother's new husband? Grandparents? Or all of them who used the child as a weapon in the parents' marital warfare?

From medical doctors you turn to a respected, tenured professor of nuclear engineering at a Maryland University who was accused by his grown-up daughter, now married, of subjecting her to incestuous sexual abuse since she was eight years old. She waited eighteen years to take her father to court. The court released the father but not without challenging the character of the daughter. There seemed some shred of evidence—flimsy and speculative—that the daughter wanted to extract money from her father with which to help her husband to meet his alimony payments to his first wife. A daughter could have conceived of a thousand other accusations against her father, but she chose the one which was symbolic of the modern era. Right or not, credible or not, parental sanctity is being assaulted day in and day out. And it tends to acquire credence because everyday families are being destroyed, despite the Republicans' sales talk about the nobility and sanctity of families in American society. There is something mysteriously amiss in all this. Accusations of incestuous crimes do not come out of thin air. The social mores of this sociologically disturbed society are changing. If the wife does not care for the husband and the husband does not care for the wife, why should sons and daughters care for their parents? If Ann Landers' daily column mirrors changing American society, it offers plenty of evidence of these perversities surfacing at different layers of society. One recent letter from a daughter asks Ann Landers why she should not marry her father when he needs the care and attention which her late mother gave him.

And a startling indictment of the surrogate parents in the day-care centre has recently come from California. The whole family—father, mother, son and daughter—who have been running a centre for young children were indicted for child abuse, ranging from sexual perversities to inhuman beating of the hapless innocents.

One would like to believe that these stories are not typical of this society and that, as in any other society, they represent some stray aberrations in behaviour or some psychic disorder. But now comes a new phenomenon, which is superficially different from the libidinous misadventures of parents or day-care centre guardians.

A couple, Abe and Mary Ayal, have decided to have a baby. It is not a surprise that they should have a baby, but it is certainly more than a surprise to be told that they want to conceive the baby to use a part of that baby to save their other dying baby. The grown child, 17 years old, is dying of leukaemia and she can be saved only by a bone-marrow transplant from a donor having compatible genetic characteristics. It is as if they want to have a child to provide 'spare parts' for another. The parents know that removing bone marrow from an infant child is risky; the child may well die of shock. They know, too, that there is no more than a 25 per cent chance of the older child surviving even with the bone-marrow transplant. Perhaps the child they have raised for 17 years has a greater right to life than the one that is just born. Why beat your breast? Do you not champion abortion to slow down population growth? Newly born children are little more than a developed foetus; the aborted one is a little less. Both have life and if one's life is to be destroyed to save another's, is it not better than the elimination of life, which is what abortion means? This is a democracy, and freedom is precious. What if the right to choose supersedes the right to live?

This is not Huxley's brave new world; this is a selfish technocratic world where biotechnology, genetic engineering and Freud's libido are spiralling in a devilish dance. You yearn for children and you generate them, if necessary through in vitro fertilisation or by creating surrogate motherhood or by the bastardisation process. But then why destroy them by use of the same technology? Is it another kind of manifestation of the law of haves and have-nots?

Daniel Moynihan, a Democratic senator of the US Congress, is moving heaven and earth to improve the lot of the nation's children through new welfare legislation, because he found that 22 per cent of children born in the late 1960s were dependent on welfare. But his perception that "the problems of children in the United States are overwhelmingly associated with the strength and stability of their families and that our problems do not reside in the nation but in our behaviour" is not totally off the mark. Children suffer not from malnutrition or hunger as in much of the world, they are tyrannised by the decay of moral values, the ruination of families, the dehumanisation of society brought on by the onslaught of the mindless advance of the new biological sciences. The malaise is deep; the children, those beautiful flowers in life's garden, will wither away even if they are kept alive through the transplant of spare parts.

Economic and Political Weekly, 29 July 1991.

23

Peacocks of war

WE are not Benjamin Franklin with his virtues and statesmanship to pronounce that "there never was a good war and a bad peace." His times were different from ours. This is an age where there is both a bad war and a bad peace. Even if a war is started by a bad man and a good man joins it, it does not become a good war. This war, which exploded on 16 January, is certainly not one of that genre, and the peace that may break out after the carnage and cruel exhibition of modern destructive weaponry is not likely to be good either. In the meantime, business will be as usual, with a few kings, some sheikhs and maniacs shuffled around. Saddam Hussein, foolish and vain, menacing and Mephistophelian, is counting his days but those who would come in his trail would be more of those ruthless demonic personalities who will preside over the 'generation of meaningless deaths' in the Middle East. Why this horde of carnivores? Why this death dance? Why this dying when you are already dead—not only physically but culturally and historically? Today it is the defence of Islam, tomorrow it is the espousal of Shiism, and it is the honour of the Palestinians the day after. But the enemies are not neatly defined. The other day the Shias were at the throats of the Sunnis; then they together ranged against the Jews; and now those who lacerated the sky with 'Islam in danger' are fighting each other.

The enemy of Arabia is within itself. Iraqi poet Abdul Bayati, famed for his prophetic vision, lamented that "he dreamt of democracy and peace in his land and that sounded right". After three score and ten years, he gave up—going through disillusionment, prison tortures and a perpetuating mendicancy. Not being a fatalist, he fastened the blame for this tragedy on to his leaders. The defeat in the Middle East wars, he ruefully says, is the defeat of "these peacocks" who were left behind.

> A generation of meaningless deaths.
> In the coffee houses of the East we are defeated by
> the war of words.
> The peacocks who strut in the halls where pride is dead.
> And the essays of the obedient hacks.

But the peacocks are not only in the Arab world. They are here, too, in good measure. The peacocks with their colourful plumage do not see the ravages of war. President Bush, a war leader now with an approval rating of 80 per cent, is riding high on popular acclaim. "Cost in lives during war is beyond the administration to measure in the same way as the cost of not resisting aggression is beyond mankind to imagine", he thunders. Yes, how can you measure the cost of war? On television there is an awful display of modern electronic weaponry with night vision contraptions, Patriot missiles, and precision instruments, which wipe out miles and miles of long rows of houses and factories. How can one add up the unimaginable amount of dollars sunk into the manufacture of this weaponry? No, no one can measure the cost of war, whether it relates to weaponry or human lives. Men, women, and children just melt into a thickening liquid. In Saddam's Iraq, children are dragged out of their homes without knowledge of their parents. In Bush's America, they are just called in, if they at any time had used military service as an interim arrangement to support their education or families. And then how can you treasure the cost of tears, the emotional devastation that is wrought on the families of men and women on the warfront? There is a picture on television of a young girl, newly married, bidding goodbye to her young husband going to the front. Tears roll down but more tearing are her words, "But whose war are you fighting?" The distraught father, seeing off his son, about to be a doctor and an only breadwinner, saying to his departing son, "I don't believe in this war, but you can't avoid it." There is a dairy farmer, whose husband is a reservist called for duty in the Gulf. Being a reservist, he had to forgo his income. When asked how she copes with the loss of income following her husband's departure, the wife, pale and wan, pointed to her ailing father who is helping her in milking the cow and broke down sobbing. Yes, this is the cost which is beyond the administration to measure but certainly not beyond humanity to imagine. As Bayati mused, "We are the generation of meaningless deaths", which is costless for the peacocks who rule the destinies of modern nation-states.

But it is not all doom and gloom. There are some oases of bloom—of daredevil soldiers, upright journalists and public men of conscience. Death in Desert Storm is staring at them, the uncertainties of the morrow are unnerving them, darkness of the night is enveloping them, the sand dunes of the sprawling desert are taking them into the bowels of the earth, but the soldiers, the foot soldiers on the battlefront, singing and dancing, regale themselves with a vision of their fiancées, dream of their future happiness:

> Come eh, come eh,
> You, the beautiful one
> But if you don't find me here
> Then let us meet in heaven.

One scene fades out and another fades in, with a young black soldier struggling to call his mother on the emergency phone. He shouts, "Hi mom, I am Robert, what are you cooking now? Please remember me when you eat my favourite dish. Let me tell you how grateful to you I am for bringing me into this world. If I die now, it is because I lived well under your care. And mom, I made my peace with Dad." Then he laughs and laughs till be breaks down. No, these are not the costs which can be calculated by humanity or even by the Gods.

It is not war if there is not disinformation or misinformation. Dreading a free media, the Pentagon did not allow non-pool arrangements for journalists to report the war news. But one Peter Arnett, an intrepid CNN television correspondent, braved all these adversities and stuck to his mission in Baghdad to relay pictures of war devastation in Iraq and the killing of civilians. He was scrupulous enough to add that his news coverage had been cleared by the Iraqi authorities. But he did not shirk, even within those bonds, from announcing to the world what Allied bombing was doing in that country. But Republican Senator Alan Simpson has flung a verbal Scud at him, saying that he is doing a dirty propaganda job for Saddam Hussein. However, this Scud attack at Arnett has been repelled by most leading journalists with 'unpatriotic' missiles. In the process they have exposed the skeletons in Simpson's and other senators' cupboards. Simpson, when he met Saddam Hussein a few months ago, had told him that "the frightful things being said about you and your police state must be the work of a maligned press. I believe your problems are with Western media and not with the US government." Another, Howard Metzenbaum, had assured Saddam, "after listening to you for about an hour, I realised that you are a strong and intelligent man and that you want peace." It is these men—peacocks, as poet Bayati described them—who flaunt their colourful plumage rather than those fearless journalists who disseminate the truth, who betray their people and egg them on to the abattoirs of war. During such traumatic times, the best in men and women surfaces and it is before this that one bows one's head and pays homage to a free and democratic society. Is such an act by a journalist conceivable in India which boasts of truth, non-violence, and high moral values? It is high time some Indians jog their memories hard to recall a forgotten Bengali journalist who exposed the hollowness and falsity of the reams of paper prepared by the Historical Division of the Government of India to prove India's claim on the McMahon line.

A war without destruction of life and property would not remain war and yet, when you see the bodies of women and children dumped in broken bunkers, your soul cries for those innocent people who escaped from the living tyranny of one misanthrope into the silent cemetery of another. Only those who survive them mourn them; for them, it is like another day. With such annihilation of life, one's mind harks back to another place and time—Dresden in Germany in February 1945, where 35,000 people perished under British bombing. The tragedy lives on in a painting by Wilhelm Lachnit, called 'The Death of Dresden.' There is a figure of death and a mother sitting side by side, their heads collapsed into their hands, the ruins of the city stacked behind them in the spoiled light and a powerless sun. The mother's son stares out from the picture, his small hands draped over the mother's lap, palm facing out towards what remains. The peacocks of the world with their plumage of glorious and gory colours have always left behind such paintings for eternity.

Economic and Political Weekly, 11 May 1991.

24

Prometheus unbound

IN these days of newspaper hoopla in America, anyone who can lay claim to some oddities, stock exchange fraud, sexual peccadilloes or predatory aggression can steal the headlines. But it is a wonder when this honour goes to one not so much for doing something unusual or eccentric as for doing his job honestly, conscientiously, and earning his keep. Justice William Brennan of the US Supreme Court stepped down from his high office in July last year rather reluctantly after 34 years of service as a justice. And what he did in this period changed the whole complexion of American society. He made it more humane, egalitarian and civil by the sheer force of his intellect, personality and idealism. "The nation and the Supreme Court changed", they say, "but not Justice Brennan." The nation changed with the civil rights revolution, modern notions of equality and equal opportunity, environmental and consumer protection, individual privacy, freedom of the press, the rights of criminal suspects and defendants. The Supreme Court changed from being strictly 'constructionist' to a body which legislated to capture the spirit of a civilised society. Brennan wrote more major opinions from 1956 to 1978 than Chief Justices Earl Warren and Warren Berger combined. He authored dozens of the landmark rulings for which the Warren Court then and the Supreme Court under other justices now have become famous or notorious, depending upon which side in this conservative society you are on.

Brennan started his career as a scholar and a Republican at that. His upbringing, his orthodox family background and his Catholic beliefs made him the ideal choice for a seat on the Supreme Court, from the Republican Party's point of view. President Eisenhower thought him convenient for his purpose of revamping the dynamic legacy of the Supreme Court that Roosevelt had left during the New Deal era. His mentor and professor at Harvard, Justice Felix Frankfurter, promoted him for the high office. But from the very beginning Brennan repaid his debts to both of his benefactors by being himself. He cut the umbilical cord both to the men who promoted him and the views he previously held. He grew in his job to become a mighty intellectual giant, imbued with the spirit of a universal man, to the chagrin of both his mentors. When asked whether he had made any mistakes as President of the United States, Eisenhower replied, "Yes, two, and they are both sitting on the Supreme Court." He was referring to Brennan and Earl Warren, his nominees. Felix Frankfurter stewed in his own juice. He always espoused the right of every man to think for himself and assert his independence. But when he had to swallow one judgement after another of Justice Brennan on the burning issues of the day, he was constrained to remark ruefully, "Always encouraged my young students to think for themselves, but Brennan goes too far."

It is intriguing why Justice Brennan was transformed so radically after joining the Supreme Court. For him the Bill of Rights was a living document replete with spacious, flexible phrases intended to protect individuals, especially the powerless poor and minorities from the increasingly sophisticated and centralised powers of the government. This conviction guided him in his entire career at the Supreme Court. When President Reagan's Attorney General, Edwin Meese, and his conservative coterie theorised that the "Constitution must be read narrowly according to the original intent of its authors", Brennan went public to challenge that theory in excoriating language: "This theory is nothing more than arrogance cloaked as humility. History is only a starting point. It is arrogance to pretend that from our vantage we can gauge accurately the intent of the framers on applications of principle to specific contemporary questions."

In this law-addicted society, where the convoluted legal system and the hungry wolf packs of lawyers play ducks and drakes with the lives of men and women, Brennan's voice brought in a whiff of fresh air. He scolded fellow-lawyers who were quick to abandon public-interest law to make money or those who tolerated racial discrimination.

> The idea that the public sector should be serviced by young lawyers while older, more experienced lawyers concern themselves with more lucrative private practice is a pernicious one. The talents and experience of the older practitioners are sorely needed in the public sector. Lawyers must bring real morality into the legal consciousness.

That Brennan was loathe to leave office even at the ripe old age of 84 might warm the hearts of many Indians who are chronically habituated to office, come what may. But Brennan's reluctance was not because he loved the perks of office or his paycheque or the halo of the social prestige. All that and more were already his without asking. His anxiety was that his exit would pave the way for a conservative Republican government to change the balance in the court. He, along with Justices Marshall and Hugo Black, were the only liberal judges left. And among them he was the only one who could turn a minority view into a majority by his rare ability to forge alliances, orchestrate liberal rulings, and write powerful damage-control dissents. With his departure all that would change and the conservatives who were bent on "only interpreting the law and not legislating it" would have a field day. What the Supreme Court had achieved over the last fifty years in the fields of social justice and minority and women's rights would go down the drain.

Brennan had thought of retiring since 1970, first because of the illness with cancer of his wife of fifty years and then his own affliction of cancer of the throat. But he survived it all to continue his career as a justice. Only towards the end did illness and old age hasten his departure. People are greatly agitated over his successor, David Souter. If he turns out to be a conservative, the Supreme Court will be a totally different body from what it has been and the ethos of egalitarianism and liberty will take a beating. And yet one never knows how the new incumbent might shape up. The chemistry of the Supreme Court has been strange. People who join it are transmuted, as happened in the case of Earl Warren, Hugo Black, and William Brennan.

The Brennan episode both exhilarates and depresses us Indians. It exhilarates us because one's faith in the intrinsic fairness of a democratic polity is strengthened. It depresses because of the contrast it presents to what is happening in India. A Supreme Court judge fudges his travel bills to claim compensation; two High Court judges indulge in mutual recrimination, accusing each other of corruption; some court luminaries encourage their kith and kin to plead cases in their own courts; the government, throwing to the winds all canons of fairness, ethics and decency, transfers judges from one court to another or promotes them on grounds other than their work; judges of the Supreme Court and High Courts relish being courtiers of the government in power. This sickening subversion of judicial sanctity has come to pose the greatest threat to the survival of Indian democracy.

Economic and Political Weekly, 16 February 1990.

25

Scatological chaos

A few years ago, a British sociologist was holding forth on the BBC Third Programme about the receding twentieth century and oncoming twenty-first century, delineating the characteristics of each. The erudite speaker, to the surprise of his audience, called the twenty-first century a century of food and that, too, Indian culinary extravaganza. For many disillusioned with the twenty-first-century prime minister of India, who promised more than he could understand, it was a cheering thought that Indian food, if not the Indian prime minister, would make its mark during the twenty-first century. But in this America, which has had sex to its brim, there is no sign of any of the best Indian cuisine making its debut in elite restaurants, as the twenty-first century is beckoning to us all, and sex is getting sexier, with every passing day, whether in the domain of art, academia, music or theatre. A titillating era began with the release of the Swedish film *I am Curious-Yellow* and the staging of the British play *Oh, Calcutta!* in the 1970s. We all turned blue from yellow and yet the libido of men and women here remained unsatiated. The way sex is still rousing the passions of this passionless society is simply amazing.

Here is a highly respected president of an American university in Washington, a physicist of repute, who was found one day by the investigating police to have been calling women in charge of day-care centres for children and indulging in obscene telephone talk about children. His paedophilic adventures had been going on for a few years. After exposure he, of course, left the university and went into a psychiatric hospital for treatment. It was pleaded on his behalf that he himself was molested in childhood by a woman relative and his behavioural misdemeanour was the hangover. Perhaps, enough would have been enough if he were asked to leave. But nothing of the sort. Recently, the trustees of the university offered him a hefty compensation of a million dollars. When opposed by the students, faculty and the general citizenry, the deal was changed. Now he will come back to teach with the same salary and status plus about four hundred thousand dollars for relinquishing his presidency of the university. What an example for the young to follow!

The president and the executive board of another university—University of the District of Columbia—have gone one step further. It is perpetually short of cash, its faculty programmes have gone sour. The accreditation of some of the faculties is withdrawn either because of low-calibre teachers or a lack of equipment. It has always had a stormy and troubled existence. And yet the DC local government has been squandering money on projects very remotely related to academic studies or improvement of the students' skills. A few days ago, the university authorities accepted a gift of sculpture from a sculptress, Judy Chicago, called 'Dinner Party', which dishes out not a palatal tingling cuisine so much as an exhibition of the worst kind of offensive nudity. It is a free gift, but the cost of housing it in the university campus would be about $2 million. The students, the trustees believed, would be enthralled by the display of nudity. But they disappointed them by staging a strike and asked that the money to be spent on 'Dinner Party' be used for buying computer equipment instead.

The distance from academia to a sports stadium is short. In Foxboro, Massachusetts, a group of naked football mastodons emerged from the shower to girdle a female reporter interviewing another player. While seated in the locker room, they positioned themselves in front of her face, exposing themselves and orally abusing the reporter with taunts and sexual overtures. The National Football authorities, after a thorough enquiry into the incident, instead of giving them the boot, fined them trifling amounts. It is just a misdemeanour, not a crime, they pronounced.

Then comes the crowning trial of Dennis Barrie, a director of the Contemporary Arts Centre at Cincinnati, for exhibiting the photographs of Robert Mapplethorpe, a self-confessed homosexual but a most talented artist who is no more. Barrie was charged with encouraging obscenity, even when the same exhibits were shown earlier at the Washington Project for the Arts. It was first to be shown in the famous Corcoran Gallery of Art in Washington, but it created a furore as the gallery was federally funded. The Republican members of Congress, who often show touching concern for freedom of speech, pressurised the organisers of the Corcoran and succeeded in cancelling that exhibition. Those who had the best interests of art and are not unduly concerned about the bogus notions of obscenity agitated against this ban and eventually succeeded in ousting the management of Corcoran. Notwithstanding, the local administration in Cincinnati prosecuted Barrie and his collaborators. The proceedings were hilarious; and had they not been without tragic overtones, could have been good theatre at Broadway. The witnesses were two law-and-order policemen and an 'expert' who knew nothing of art, sculpture or photography. Witness was asked to apply 'content analysis', which did not make any sense to the art gallery director, other artists, or even to the witness. She looked at one of the five photo exhibits of Mapplethorpe shown to her and said, "There is no face, there are no eyes, there is no aspect of human body that would tell us anything about human emotion or feeling. This is an anonymous picture. There is no anger, fear or horror or sadness." Then she used the lightning techniques she acquired in her speech communication studies and argued with self-assurance that "the focus on private part of the subject shows the part but conveys no human emotion."

With such witnesses for the prosecution, Barrie did not need any further defence. He was exonerated from all obscenity charges, restored to his job and the prestige of the art centre was unimpaired. But what is gnawing is not the existence of pedlars of virtue in this land. Why this intense obsession with obscenity? You go to a theatre or a film, it is not without bedroom indulgences; you can witness the entire Kama Sutra being unfolded. If you study at the universities, you see the homosexual clubs functioning unabashedly. You go to the beaches, and you wonder how a man or woman would look if dressed properly. But why does a good piece of art or literature stir occasionally the guardians of morality in this society? Is it boredom that follows affluence, as night follows day? Or is it a neurotic psyche of this well-meaning, highly aggressive, self-assertive, perpetually-hungry-for-success society? Or else, is it a mere regurgitation of conscience which otherwise slumbers most of the time? A perceptive American wrote:

We are so enamoured of ourselves that we are dissatisfied if our exploration brings us face to face with any image but our own. We are a generation marked by a desire for stimulation and narcotics—fear of responsibility, of open places, or closed places, fear of society, fear of being alone, fear of fears, fear of contamination, fear of everything, lack of decision in trifling matters, hopelessness...

This anguished cry was written in the 1880s. So there is light after darkness, after all. When you are depressed, hopeless, disoriented, fear yourself, then use sex as your enemy, make a devil out of it. It will make you look morally right and civilised. You can then safely wait for the twentieth century to kick the bucket.

Economic and Political Weekly, 29 December 1990.

26

Wreckers united

AN Indian, in his teens, out of the intruding social environment of his country, shelter of his doting parents, and the company of his nosy compatriots, waded his way to America, not as 'a dreamer of dreams' but a 'seeker of abstractions.' He did not want to be a 'living cliché of immigrant fictions that Vidya Naipaul and Salman Rushdie conjured up. He would rather call himself "the modern Steppen Wolves blown around by his undergraduate idealism." But he was discombobulated by the language of this America, which could describe two scenes in two countries—India and America—so differently. Yes, it is all right to say that the streets in America are crowded, but why are they 'teeming' in India; fans only 'briskly whirr' in America but why should they 'listlessly drone' in India; those without homes are 'homeless' in America, but why on earth should they be 'destitutes' in India?

But the young man would soon learn the difference between the two cultures; it is a function of time and cogitation. He will learn what Tocqueville, that Frenchman, on landing in America, learnt. He left his cultural baggage back home in France, and became an adulator of America. He perceived the deeper forces at work which made America what it is in the twentieth century. He wrote:

> I know of no country indeed, where the love of money has taken stronger hold on the affection of men and where a profounder contempt is expressed for the theory of the permanent equality of property—it is the vehemence of their desires that makes Americans so methodical that it perturbs their minds but disciplines their lives.

Yes, methodical they are both in making money, using it for religious passions and also for wrecking what they build. Building and wrecking has become their very favoured game over the years.

This nation, they say, is built by the founding fathers who evoke awe by their vision, sacrifices and selflessness. Building has its antonym in wrecking—that is what many Americans have now been indulging in. A whole lot of finance men have gone berserk. The debacle of savings and loans associations, it was thought, would be avoided with massive injection of government money to bail them out. The dollar amount is ballooning. Now it may go beyond three hundred billion dollars and the income of generations to be born would be mortgaged. Many heads are rolling, including that of the son of the President of the United States. And yet the savings and loans associations scandal is the tip of the iceberg: the heat generated may melt that massive iceberg into a ravaging flood.

Those who were at the helm of the savings and loans associations are not the only wreckers. Now it has come out how airline companies, who carry the lives of millions of people on their daily flights, are flouting the regulatory authorities with impunity. A federal jury has indicted the Eastern Airlines' two high officials with criminal conspiracy to fake records to conceal unperformed aircraft maintenance work—an act the nation's top law enforcement officer said "strikes a raw nerve in anyone who has ever boarded an airplane." This was not a crime committed by some stray individuals or in isolation. It had an imprimatur of the high management. The conspiracy to defraud was directed from Eastern's Miami headquarters, under former vice president of maintenance—one Edward Upton, still occupying a position in another airline. Eastern used its centralised computer system to falsify maintenance records and keep FAA from grounding improperly maintained aircraft. Though these crimes have now surfaced, a warning had been sounded by the airlines pilot unions and the workers a few months earlier when Eastern filed for bankruptcy. But their cry was in the wilderness and now the chickens have come home to roost.

The wrecking saga takes on a different coloration when charismatic tele-evangelists go to town. Jim Bakker, a sect leader, made a business of his religion by setting up television centres for dishing out sermons to his faithful. He raised 158 million dollars by promising to his viewers lifetime, three days-a-year lodging packages for $1000, among them elderly devotees on fixed incomes, then diverted a large part of it in salary and bonuses to support his lavish lifestyle. He used a widow's mite for his obscure gratification and pleasure. He was corrupted by money and power, and in turn corrupted those around him, until he became "a ruthless man who loved things and used people." Bakker, for once admitted in atonement, when convicted and handcuffed, that "he made mistakes" but added brazenly that "never in my life did I intend to defraud anyone." Perhaps in the lexicon of this Godman the words go through a metamorphosis.

From finance to airlines to religion to scientific research, everything is a business here. The prestigious National Institute of Health is bedevilled by one scandal or another. Robert Gallo's AIDS research is being challenged as plagiarism and awaiting verdict by the investigating panel but a well-known researcher, C. David Bridges, at the Purdue University is now found to have stolen information and ideas for experiments from a Harvard University manuscript, which was given to him for refereeing. The paper, published two years ago, was on the biochemistry of the pigment in the eye's retina. A few years ago, an assistant professor, an Indian, at Yale University passed on as his own the research results from the papers he was asked to evaluate for a journal. This maltrading in somebody's intellectual property has assumed serious proportions and several congressional committees have gone into this with a view to preventing such scientific fraud. In American academia, the 'publish or perish' philosophy has gone overboard. Some academics are perishing without publishing; many others are perishing by publishing somebody else's work through fraud or deceit.

The greatest indictment of the present administration for wrecking America has come not from Democrats, the congenital opponents of the Republicans, but from one of the gurus of the Republican Party, Kevin Phillips, who was a close adviser of President Nixon and his successors. In his book *The Politics of Rich and Poor: Wealth and American Electorate in the Reagan Aftermath,* he has revealed some startling facts. Between 1977 and 1987 the income of the richest one per cent of American families increased by an average of 74.2 per cent. In 1986, America's richest 420,000 households alone possessed 27 per cent of the nation's wealth; between 1981 and 1988, millions of Americans got left behind, especially the poorly educated and single mothers. The medium income of male high school graduates fell nine per cent, the medium income of single mothers rose a meagre 26 per cent.

Those who asked for it got it and now they cry foul. But why should this great affluent and democratic society be heading toward wrecking what was built before? Is it because "the love of money and wealth", which Tocqueville identified as "the principal and accessory motive of all that the Americans do", induced them to run their government as a business corporation? Corporation is a metaphor for American society, making profits the sole *leitmotif*. Build a corporation if it makes profit, wreck it if it does not. Poor Founding Fathers—they did not know that wrecking is the antonym of founding.

Economic and Political Weekly, 13 October 1990.

27

A tragic odyssey

LIFE is an absurd theatre. Mitch Snyder, that self-proclaimed messiah championing the cause of the homeless, was no more on one humid evening of this tormenting July. The manner of his death was like the manner of his life—nothing predictable, nothing respectable, but full of surprises and contradictions. Berated by his father, he swore to himself that he would not do to his kids what his father did to him—not leave them forsaken and forlorn. And he did precisely that—abandoned his young wife Ellen and his two sons, without any succour. He was attracted to the religious life and had a deep and abiding belief in God. "Now the vast majority of people who live here are not religious", he often screamed to his followers, tearing his long and unruly hair locks. And he went on to cash bad cheques, stole a car, snorted crack. He fought against the injustice that was the Vietnam War, against the use of 'Tiger cages' by the US government. But he was impervious to the injustice he inflicted on his colleagues in the community of 'creative non-violence.' He went on a fast in 1984 lasting over fifty days, and brought that actor president of the United States to his knees before election day. But he battled against his weight problem and could not resist secretly hoarding candy in his rooms when he was not fasting. He had a problem with women and treated them as encounter groups. When challenged by women colleagues about taking more food than his collaborators, he often went nuts; his tragic end was because of his unrequited love for Carrol Fennelly. And yet he was as equally at home with the strung-out residents who were hallucinating as with the wives of cabinet officials such as Susan Baker, who took up his cause and visited him during his long and arduous hunger strike.

He came to social causes *via* his protest against the Vietnam War. The war was lost, and that put him in search of a new cause. He came to a mission without knowing what that mission could be. Once invited by the University of Maryland, he told his admiring students to leave their classrooms.

> Why do you think kids would run our of class if they could? Because classes are not what the kids want or need. We don't listen. We create, and have created a society of people who will accept any injustice, any absurdity, any insanity and will step over the broken bodies of bag ladies, who are mentally disabled, raped repeatedly, freezing to death and eating out of garbage pails.

Fired by this idealism, he set out to form 'the community of creative non-violence.' He raised money, not always by fair means; he cajoled the news media, even tried to blackmail them at times; but he at last put the homeless in some shelters.

This stormy petrel ran into sand somewhere. Was it because Mitch identified a woman with a cause or cause with a woman? He was infatuated with Carrol Fennelly, he made no secret of it. They decided only a few days earlier to get married, announced their wedding plans, and then came the news that the plans went askew; marriage, after all, was not on the cards. Or did Mitch lose his steam because 'Initiative 17', obliging Washington, DC Council to provide shelter for every homeless, was voted out? Or was his charisma wearing thin and the finances were unstable? There was gossip that if Mitch were to starve himself again for the homeless, they might as well allow him to do so.

If a man can end his life for a woman, could he be the leader of men? No one knows. He loved a woman with a cause and a cause with a woman. Life need not necessarily be intransitive. If a man can love and die for her, he can always die for a cause. Mitch's quest for social justice, concern for the homeless, empathy for the Vietnamese people, was not a mask. He was not an epigone of the saint of Assisi who gave his clothes to the naked. He was an extrovert, but he espoused the cause of the homeless and carried it to a point that the conscience of entire America was roused. See this Mitch Snyder and see the other Snyder—a sports scribe who about three years ago said at a restaurant: "The blacks are overtaking the whites in all games because they are bred that way. Slave masters chose a fat black woman to breed high thighed muscular blacks"—and you will see that an idealistic white, fighting the unpopular causes is something to be applauded in today's America. Mitch did it, according to his light, for the poor, the blacks, the raped, the Hispanics—for all the scum of the earth. And when the time came, he may have ruminated,

> sleep after toill;
> port after stormy seas;
> ease after ware, death after life,
> does greatly please.

Mitch's suicide raises inconvenient questions for all in this prosperous society. Today it is Mitch Snyder. Yesterday it was Abbie Hoffman, who ended his life with an overdose of sleeping pills. Can this be called the American phenomenon? For Mitch Snyder, maybe it was the discontinuity between his persona and his idealism. A man had abandoned his wife and hapless kids, which may have haunted him. One who leaves home—can he be champion of the homeless? In the last months of his life he was thinking of going on a sabbatical to a Trappist monastery. He was despondent about his failed love. He told his friends that if he and Fennelly could not get together one of them would have to go. Was it an admission of a failed love or failed cause? It was different with Abbie Hoffman. Rebel that he was, he saw no new revolution on the horizon. For him, all revolutions were arrested revolutions. Without revolution, life for him was ennui. Not for him the lotus-eating ways of American society. He wrote in a leave-taking note for his followers that his death was a celebration of life.

That is why the suicide of Mitch Snyder was a tragedy, a tragedy for the cause left undone and the man. He chose a cause which contradicted his emotional inner self. What he could not do for his family he could not hope to do to his society. He loved the woman to end his life; he did not love his cause to live. In dying, Mitch had locked the outside door to his bedroom at the homeless shelter, then unlocked the inside door to Carrol's adjoining bedroom so that she should find him dangling at the end of an electric chord. Perhaps a Sod's law governed his life and his mission: every wrong he avoided doing was done. Mitch, for that reason, was disregarded as a friar, despite his strong religiosity. He was resented even by those following him in his endeavours as a golliwog, with strange quirks of character and eccentricities. Reverend John Steinbrack, pastor of Lather Place church and an advocate for the homeless joining Mitch's caboodle of followers, said in anguish, "It means to be immersed in a sea of despair and not to have concrete victories. I will cry in my own way. I also feel like I want to curse him." Homeless Danny Hitan did not sound different: "Mitch could not have done it for me or the other homeless people. Things will still happen for the homeless but may not be as fast."

An odyssey Mitch Snyder may have ended by his death but not the tragedy of his life.

Economic and Political Weekly, 1 December 1990.

28

Family in distress

A nation with families in ruins is at last waking up to define family and family values. Familiarity with family has not bred contempt for its meaning. Vice President Dan Quayle is quailing about Murphy Brown, a television sitcom character, mocking the importance of a mother bearing a child alone and calling it just another life-style choice. Quayle, who does not quite know how to spell 'potato', is indulging in an etymological search for the meaning of family. For the family to exist there should be a father, a dutiful wife, and a cluster of happy children around. A single-parent family—fatherless children and husbandless wives—does not fit into his definition of family. He, therefore, wants America and Americans to hark back to families and family values to make America great. But has Quayle got the meaning right? Wordsmiths like William Safire are on the track. Who first thought of family? The great Samuel Johnson was invoked. Yes, he was master of the English language and culture, and if he did not know something then it simply did not exist. Somewhere, Johnson had said that "his lexicon might become a concomitant to the Family Bible." Some other wiseacre came up with the origin of family in 'famulus', meaning 'servant', which includes Christ's wife, children, and domestic help. Did they get it all wrong? If family is a group of servants, what about a happy family and family values? Something has gone wrong somewhere.

Dan Quayle, whose ascent into the professional stratosphere has not exactly been an example of reward for hard work, should have been careful about hitting the bootstrap circuit. Fatherless children have become a symbol of modern America, not because there is a sexual revolution, not because the youth have gone berserk, not because there is rampant use of drugs. Fatherless families have come out of the womb of a society sociologically and technologically transformed; they are also a tragic legacy of the Vietnam War. The phenomenon is complex and baffling and has nothing to do with Murphy Brown's television sitcom or with the vulgarisation of values in Hollywood films. For most men, a wife and a child are a sort of a package deal. Once the marriage breaks up—or if there was never a marriage, once the relationship breaks up—most men find it difficult to stay actively involved in their children's lives. In the span of a single generation of Americans absent fatherhood has become pandemic. Some 35 per cent of children now live away from their biological fathers, double the percentage who did so as recently as in the 1970s. Family disintegration in the black community—a common phenomenon—is not the legacy of slavery or Jim Crow. The disintegration is progressing with time. The out-of-wedlock birth rate for blacks was roughly 20 per cent in 1900; by 1989 it had shot up to 60 per cent. The out-of-wedlock birth rate for whites, while starting from a far lower base, has exploded in the past generation from 5 per cent in 1965 to 19 per cent now.

There is no dearth of explanations for the emergence of a fatherless society. A political scientist's poetic fancy attributes it to the socialisation of the male. For biological and evolutionary reasons, this socialisation is not easily achieved and some substantial part of what is called the under-class problem arises from the incomplete and increasingly more intractable task of socialising some males. These are all, however, intellectual gymnastics, pastime of ivory tower scholars. Nobody tells you what socialisation of the male means. In American academic portals empty words conceal empty thoughts. The villains of non-family in the ghettos are welfare mothers who prefer the regularity of a monthly cheque to the uncertainty of a marriage and a wayward father whose notion of child rearing begins with sexual conquest and ends with birth. No doubt there are real cads who measure up to this stereotype, but the explanation that the young girl opts to produce children because she receives monthly cheques is far from convincing.

Could it be that values were debased by the Vietnam tragedy, which not only disgraced America and demoralised its youth but also bred fatherless progeny when American soldiers made Vietnam a whorehouse? Twenty years after that heartrending tragedy, the wages of the lust of American soldiers are being visited upon American society. Thousands of fatherless children from Vietnam have flooded into America in the last few years, searching for their fathers and seeking a brave new world. The Red Cross Society is offering a free search service to these fatherless children to help identify their fathers. Shunned in Vietnam as American bastards, they try to regain their honour through father-identification, but in vain. The Red Cross found that most of the fathers identified have asked not to have their addresses given to their offspring. There was a letter written by a man who lives in Connecticut, sent to Catholic Charities, after officials there called to inform him that two American children had arrived in the United States. The letter says:

> Let me tell you one thing right now, never and I mean never, will you call any member of my family concerning any item involving or in reference to events in my past. You will not ask questions or pressure anyone to accept responsibility for my past life.

These fatherless children, forsaken by their legitimate fathers, are eking out an existence in depravity. And yet US leaders are waxing eloquent about family values.

The lack of socialisation of the male, the welfare cheques and the illegitimate children of American soldiers are not the only causes of the 'fatherless-ism' of the American family. American society has been rocked by the misdemeanours of doctors who are supposed to be the trustees of society. Cecil B. Jacobson, a well-known fertility specialist, inventor of the amniocentesis test, has been indicted for fathering more than 70 Washington-area children by using his own sperm without the knowledge of his patients who approached him for fertility treatment. This is no ordinary doctor: he is eminent in the profession. He gave his women patients hormone shots that triggered false pregnancy tests, used phoney sonograms to perpetrate fraud and then told them their foetuses were dead and would get reabsorbed in their bodies. Desperate for children, they agreed to artificial insemination. But the doctor, on the sly, used his own sperm without disclosing its source to create fatherless children amongst respectable childless women. The victims were devastated by the facts that came out during the doctor's trial. Now those reluctant mothers will spend the rest of their lives holding on to their offspring, without love and perhaps with hatred. Many of them may well become psychological wrecks, prone to depression and suicide. Who created these fatherless families—the unscrupulous doctor? the new biotechnology? or the whole tribe of conspiring fellow medical practitioners? As someone said, there were no whistleblowers amongst doctors: they stuck together. One doctor with conscience, who saw a patient of Jacobson's in the late 1970s, concerned about Jacobson's fertility fraud, mentioned it to a couple of his fellow members on the State Board of Medicine. Now he confesses that he was advised to back off on the specious plea that all he would have achieved was to wind up in court. Defamation laws are so lax and sweeping that Jacobson would have tied him up in legal knots.

So if Bush, Quayle and the Republicans are so concerned about family values and survival of the American family, they should turn the light on their own philosophy of life. Social and political leaders have abdicated their responsibilities towards the disadvantaged, the meek and the lowly in the economic and social backwaters. If children can be produced without fathers, why should families not be fatherless or single-parent? If American soldiers in Vietnam and elsewhere left behind the children they bred, can you blame their mothers for caring for their fatherless children? You debase human nature, the noble instincts of man, debauch science and technology and treat civil society as military barracks—and you get the family you deserve: drug-addicted, promiscuous, AIDS-afflicted, alcoholic, and trigger-happy with the predatory urge for mayhem.

Yet eggheads in America indulge in logic chopping and legal casuistry in their search for solutions to American society's descent into social anarchy. Now comes a jurist-cum-sociologist-cum-economist, Richard Posner. Inspired by Nobel laureate R.H. Coase, who brought legal ratiocination to the centre of economic arguments, he is seeking guidance from free market economics to explain family, children, and libidinous indulgences. "Emotion and morality are irrelevant in understanding human relationships", he says. His bizarre pronouncements are causing a stir as much for their novelty as absurdity and shocking implications. For him "prostitutes should compete with wives and girlfriends and that is why they differentiate their services." Posner cannot understand why there should be opposition to baby selling in the open market, which he terms as a 'parents' right.' Stretch his profound economic analysis and you will know why family has declined in America. In his book *Sex and Reason,* Posner has argued that

> The maintenance of conventional Victorian type sexual morality is impossible when women are economically emancipated from men. When women are extremely dependent on men, then they will exchange their chastity for the male's financial protection. But once they are out in the market, they work with men, they have their own income and they cannot be repressed as effectively.

The Republicans are being hoisted with their own petard. The family has been subverted by the rising self-assertion of women. And this deserves the support of the economic analysis of Posner and Milton Friedman. Those of us, who for years have been waiting for some new idea in this dismal science and are about to write its obituary, should bestir ourselves. Economists may have failed to explain the present turbulence in the international economy. But it is no small success that they are so willing to enlighten us on why the family and family values have perished.

Economic and Political Weekly, 28 November 1992.

29

A society on the rampage

A dense scatological air is polluting American social life these days. The sexual bravados and escapades associated with the American presidency may be indecorous and unbecoming but not unusual and predatory if they were to occur in the life of an ordinary person anywhere. But the demonic dance of the libido in this land is now surpassing even the wildest imagination of humanity in a civilised society. It has now moved to the arena of school and family, which are nuclei for fostering noble instincts of compassion, civility and creativity to assure living in a better and happy world. No child is safe from perverse sexual aggression in school, at home or in a day-care centre. Social thinkers are at their wits' end to figure out the nature of the virus that is threatening to destroy the foundation of this society.

A year ago, a girl of 5 in Denver, paraded by her rich parents as a beauty queen, went missing after an all-night bacchanalia on Xmas eve. The mother reported the news tearfully on television the next day and begged the suspected kidnapper to return to her the child. On investigation, the police found the child dead in the basement of her parents' house, sexually assaulted before being strangled to death. The stepson of the girl's mother appeared to be the culprit. But the whole investigation and judicial process are stalled because the parents, invoking the Fifth Amendment, refused to testify before the public prosecutor. For the mother her daughter was just a beauty queen but her love is showered on her adult stepson. For the father his reputation as a millionaire and his affection for his second wife superseded his feelings for his own dead daughter.

If this tragic incident is not traumatic enough to give you goose bumps, here is another. Well-known author Michael Dorris, whom his admirers described as "someone who, when he walked the earth left some footprints," committed suicide when his latest novel was making big waves with the media and the reading public. He was cremated amidst genuine tributes paid by fellow writers, his wife and admirers. A few months after his death, a New York magazine revealed that Dorris seriously abused two of his daughters: one of them repeatedly at night, when his son would hear his sister's screams from the adjacent room. She was not a stepchild as in Woody Allen's case.

There are revelations galore of daughters and sons recalling in adulthood how their fathers in many instances and the mothers in some, sexually abused them in childhood. The doctors trained in Freud's psychology are making hay, destroying in the process the families, with the accused parents ending up either in prison or cemetery. None, barring a few scholars in psychology, is questioning whether Freudian psychoanalysis is a science robust enough to yield definitive evidence on parental abuse of children.

The saga of sex in American society has now reached schools and day-care centres. In the mid-West, a perfectly happy young housewife, with an affluent husband and two toddlers, seduced a 12-year-old boy in the school where she was teaching, and gave birth to his child. When arraigned, she confessed and promised not to repeat the performance. Sure enough, she was back at her game and carried the young boy's second child. Innocent children in a day-care school, run by a couple, were systematically sexually abused by them—the man assaulted the girls and his wife the boys.

Sociologists have been trying to seek an explanation for this depravity shaking the very foundations of American and western societies. Hunger and sex are legitimate needs of all humans. Hunger is almost banished in these societies; and one would have believed that an appetite for sex has enough scope to be satiated in this permissive society. In countries like India, where sex is taboo and open indulgence is frowned upon, it is understandable if not justifiable, to attribute sexual repression to lack of opportunity for sexual indulgence. Why then should sexual perversities, incestuous relations and child abuse abound?

One hypothesis is the ennui that pervades affluent societies where basic human needs are well met. With easy access to both food and sex the mind gropes for unusual ways to satisfy desire, and in so doing it goes berserk. The second, and perhaps a more convincing hypothesis, is that the break-up of family due to rampant and ravaging divorces seems to have undermined the biological relationships between father and daughter, mother and son, and sister and brother. In a remarried family with children from previous spouses, the parents and the children do not look upon each other as belonging to the same flesh and blood. Oedipus thus has come to rule supreme. Or does the scatological chaos betoken the extremity of individualism combined with hedonism, which turned society's value system upside down? What I do is what matters, and whether it impinges on the interests of others is no concern of mine. This is no more than the 'negative freedom' of Isaiah Berlin running amok. So does the doctrine of hedonism signify. My pleasure is what I seek. And if it becomes the pain of somebody else it is his problem. Is this society doomed to be a Gomorrah?

Business Standard, 16 June 1998.

30

A cage seeking a bird

JUSTICE seeks truth; and truth is sought to administer justice. But when they choose a judge, justice turns topsy-turvy and truth is made to stand on its head. Justice, that strange abstraction, can only be articulated in the person who delivers it. Yes, a judge has to be judged before he becomes a justice of the High Court or the Supreme Court. But who can be the judge of judges?

The judicial committee of the US Senate is the repository of wisdom which questions the nominees of the President for the Supreme Court. The committee votes on his choices. In normal times it has probed into the credentials, academic and personal, of the candidate, his character and record. But all that changed with the defeat of Derek Bork four years ago. On being questioned about his philosophy, he held forth on natural law, abortion rights, affirmative action—all of these issues which have shaken up American society in the last few years. Bork, as was his wont, let out the truth; he did not hold back, did not prevaricate, did not budge. Yes, he was turned down for telling the truth. The truth was not important so much as whether or not he was a conformist or a nonconformist; he was laid to pasture.

David Souter came close on the heels of Bork. Wise, wily and tutored as a primary schoolboy, he told the Judiciary Committee everything except what it did not want to hear. For him 'justice sans truth' was the new logo of the Supreme Court. With Souter's elevation, caginess became a hallmark of the Supreme Court.

And now comes Clarence Thomas as President Bush's nominee on the Supreme Court—a black with a distinguished record, high legal qualifications but a 'white in black sheeps clothes' as many derisively called him. He followed Thurgood Marshall who distinguished himself as a liberal judge with a social conscience and a caring disposition for the disadvantaged. He lived up to his name—'Thorough Good', a name he chose for himself—and conscience. It is into his shoes that Clarence Thomas was asked to step.

Thomas is not Bork as he is black, Thomas is not Souter who started with a *tabula rasa,* not having published his views on any of the controversial issues. Thomas could not tell the truth as he did not want to court the fate of Bork; he could not prevaricate as he had already articulated his views on several controversial topics during his earlier bureaucratic and judicial mutations. He chose the strange course of a 'confirmatory conversation'—putting his views in as unambiguous a way as he could so that the judicial committee could be convinced. But he had a peculiar infirmity as a black man who had come to the top by using the rope of affirmative action, but not without realising its limits. At once he became the target of his community for his betrayal of the class, and of feminist groups for his rather vague pronouncements on abortion rights.

The judicial committee consisting of doubting Thomases doubted Thomas, asking him about his intellectual position on this issue and that. But they themselves don't want to be doubted. If their cheques have bounced, it is just a case of amnesia or just that they were overburdened with affairs of the state. If some of them had told untruths in the name of truth or had remained in ideological closets or had cheated at college examinations—these were just the pranks of naughty children of naughty rich parents. Anyway, these are all permissive acts in a permissive society. If a member of the committee had plagiarised the speech of some British politician it was merely an act of eclecticism. But to be a judge and that too of the Supreme Court, which not only interprets the constitution of the American republic but also legislates it, he should stand in all his nakedness before the august judicial committee. He should be transparently truthful and above all reproach.

Clarence Thomas stood before the bar as an honourable man, well tutored by his Republican mentor, John Danforth, having rehearsed his answers on questions on which his views were well known. Of course, he evaded some answers; he did not tell lies nor did he tell the truth. But through the rigmarole of the confirmation process, Thomas told the persistent doubting Thomases that he was his own self and if he had changed his opinions it was for good reasons. The world was changing, not static. Any man who thinks had to change with the times, but changing one's view was not the same thing as changing one's conscience. Thomas declared he had not been guilty of the latter when a member of the judicial committee recalled his views when he had been a policymaker and an advocate. "I am a person who did not hide from the problem. My past record is relevant but, senator, I am a member of the judiciary now and I think it is a fair question from me to you to see whether or not my policy positions have tainted my role as a judge."

Thomas was grilled again on his approach to affirmative action. He was asked how he could reconcile his opposition to a 1986 Supreme Court ruling upholding an affirmative action programme with himself having benefited from an affirmative action programme at the Yale Law School. He was also asked how he had criticised a Supreme Court ruling in a case supporting the hiring of a woman in preference to a better qualified male candidate. Unflapped, he replied that he saw

> no similarities between the problem in the Supreme Court case and affirmative action. The problem in the Supreme Court case was that the federal statute explicitly prohibited discrimination in any form. But at Yale where I was educated, the issue was not about two people competing for one job. It was a case of an institution being very subjective in its selection process.

Perhaps the most revealing views expressed by Thomas, and which belied his image as a conservative, related to the law and order issue. He said,

> You know, in my current court I have occasion to look out the window that faces C Street, and there are conducted buses that bring in the criminal defendants to our criminal justice system, bus load after bus load. And you look out and you say to yourself, and I say to myself almost every day, but for the grace of God there go I. So you feel that you could have the same fate as those individuals, you could be picked up and put on the chain gang for just standing on the corner.

Is Thomas committed to natural law? When asked how he would interpret the Constitution he snapped back: "One starts with the text, looks to history and tradition and to the precedents and to notions of what liberty means, how it evolves in the country and moves with our history and our tradition."

The whole confirmation procedure was Manichaean in character. During the first part, until the judicial committee voted to transmit its decision to the full Senate, everyone was avoiding the truth—the committee members, the outside lobbyists and even Clarence Thomas. All that changed when Anita Hill dropped a bombshell with an accusation of sexual harassment against him. The confirmation hearing then took on the appearance of an indictment procedure. Earlier the truth was chased away, now the truth was desperately sought. Some old friends of Anita Hill were mobilised. Everyone swore that Thomas had molested Anita, talked about vile obscenities, the past was made to look like an X-rated film. Some others, bevy of girls who had worked closely with Thomas, said the opposite. What was deposed as truth indicting Thomas equally appeared to be truth indicting Anita Hill. Thomas, wreathed in pain, shattered in spirit, shamed in appearance, choked with emotion, and seething with anger, could say the only thing a black could say—the tragedy of Clarence Thomas was made the tragedy of all blacks in America and the world. "What I am accused of doing to Anita is what the world has accused the blacks of doing to womanhood." A black is stereotyped as a sexual dynamo, a predator oozing sex. "This has been the view of the black race, and it will appeal to all. I cannot fight it, I don't want to fight it. If you Senators want to reject my nomination in your wisdom, do it. It is your choice, not mine. I have suffered ignominy enough."

Who was telling the truth nobody knew, but someone was telling a lie. But lie telling is not new here or anywhere. Some members of the judicial committee have earned that honour, even some presidents of the United States have graced the ranks of prized liars. But what was new about this so-called confirmatory conversation is the ferocity with which Thomas' whole career was assaulted. This man, of humble origins, growing up in poverty, enjoying the benefit of affirmative action, has the gumption to aspire for the highest judicial office. It would have been all right if he was only poor; they might have become temporarily colour-blind if he was only black; his views on abortion, natural law and law and order would have been consigned to the dustbin. But unforgivable and unforgettable was his crime of disowning his past when he had used the rope of affirmative action himself to climb up in life. He ought to have been singing praises of affirmative action for his fellow blacks. You can make an enemy of the white, that is the natural law in the warfare of the races. But an enemy in your own family, tribe, group is the deadliest sin. You should deaden your nerves by remaining backward. Even if you come out of the dirt, ignorance and misery, you must glorify in it. Thomas was not prepared to do that. He had rediscovered himself during his transition from the black ghetto to a freer space where he "could think by himself." He had realised how crippling it could be to be permanently beholden to special favours. He was trying to be a black individual who can hold his own in any community or amongst the whites. He was articulating the ambitions, aspirations, pride, self-confidence and abilities of a resurgent new class of black intelligentsia.

But the collectivity of blacks is different from the individual persona of a black. The self-assurance of the few is a source of desperation for the many for whom special privileges are a means of submerging their insecurity and mediocrity. It is these groups, and others who hang on to them for petty gain, who launched the war on Clarence Thomas who could courageously deny affirmative action to his own sister. "Human beings are perhaps never more frightening", says Laurence van der Post, "than when they are convinced beyond doubt that they are right." Thomas, in one of the sombre moments during his appearance at the committee hearing on charges of sexual harassment of Anita Hill, ruefully referred to his as a "Kafkaesque situation"—bizarre, scary, and claustrophobic. It is a situation where a cage was seeking a bird. The Democrats tried to cage Thomas in his judicial views and, when they failed, Anita Hill and the anti-abortionist and feminist groups set up a moral cage to entrap him.

Economic and Political Weekly, 21 December 1991.

31

Doubting Thomases gun for Justice Thomas

THERE was a throw back to the history of nine years ago when Clarence Thomas, a black judge of the Supreme Court, locked horns a few months ago with the National Bar Association, a black lawyers' body. After going through a process of intermittently being invited and disinvited, Justice Thomas eventually got his back at his detractors at the meeting of the black lawyers by reasserting his views which had created a raging and personally bruising controversy during his confirmation hearings before the Senate committees.

To them Thomas gave a clinching reply. "I am a member of the judiciary now; I think it is a fair question from me to you to see whether or not my policy positions have tainted my role as a judge." Thwarting the opposition he made his way to the highest court in this land but the ghosts just did not leave him in peace. They haunted him every time there was an occasion—an invitation to speak at the universities or an association of blacks—he was humiliated by withdrawing the invitation or by a fusillade of vituperative attacks on his persona and family. Though all this made him a maverick, shunning publicity, refusing to be interviewed by the media, he not only stuck to his conviction as tar to his shirt and became even stronger in holding his beliefs.

His innards came out in full fury and force when he addressed the assembly of black lawyers. He started with a frontal body blow by holding a mirror to the hypocrisy of the black social interest groups and their leaders. "There now seems to be a broad acceptance", Thomas intoned,

> of the racial divide as a permanent state. As we once celebrated the things that we had in common with our fellow citizens, we do not share our race, so many now are triumphant about our differences—indeed, some go as far as all, but define each of us by our race and establish the range of our thinking and our opinions, if not our deeds by our colour. I for one see this in much the same way I saw our deal of rights: as nothing short of a denial of humanity.

His denigrators, contrary to their pretensions, do not occupy a high moral ground in holding on to their affirmative action programmes. The black community has not remained in the same backwater as it was some forty years ago. A resurgent middle class has emerged with high-profile intellectualism and self-confidence among the blacks, who would like to give up the crutches of affirmative action to stand on their own accomplishments and abilities. There is an academic like Professor Shelby Steele, a Fellow at Stanford University, who has excoriated black leaders thriving on the racial divide and black discrimination.

He said recently that "there is an awful lot of conservative sentiment in black America but at the moment the party line is enforced." He characterised the self-serving black lobby as espousing a flawed foundation of victimisation. There is intolerance amongst the majority of blacks towards the other view. Even Jesse Jackson had to face the same music as Thomas and Shelby, when he came under intense criticism for his remark that "There is nothing more painful for me at this stage of my life than to walk down the street and hear footsteps and start thinking about robbery, then look around and see somebody white and feel relieved."

But what is so tragic is not merely the opportunism and venality of the black leadership but its assailing the fundamental right of an individual to say what he wants to say. It is tragic because it is this right which the great black leaders like Du Bois and Martin Luther King used as a great weapon against the degrading white supremacy in America. When the blacks had no power, no wealth, it was this inalienable right of man which had both the power of money and a lethal weapon to fight injustice and racial discrimination. By denying this right to Justice Thomas, the blacks and their self-absorbed leadership are doing a greater harm to their own well-being.

The words of Justice Thomas should, therefore, resonate with humanity the world over.

> I have come here today to assert my right to think for myself, to refuse to have my ideas assigned to me as though I was an intellectual slave because I am black. I come to state that I am a man, free to think for myself and do as I please. But even more than that I have come to say: Isn't it time to move on?

Thomas was almost saying that doubting Thomases should doubt themselves, not him.

32

Neither mosaic nor melting pot

THE story was told to us long ago about cultural absorption, which keeps popping up every time the problems of immigration are discussed in the industrialised countries inundated in recent times with a rising wave of immigrants. A village yokel, wanting to have his son elevated to the higher cultural echelon of society, approached a well-educated high-caste Brahmin teacher in a city to board his son so that the boy would imbibe the sophistication of the teacher and his family in language, manner, and social etiquette. The villager returned six months later to see how far his son had progressed. The teacher, when he saw him, greeted him not in his own language and manner but those of the son! Max Weber theorised about lower culture being overtaken by the higher order. In this case the theory was made to stand on its head.

The old metaphors for immigrants slowly submerging into the host countries' mainstream values are changing fast, as dramatised by Australian parliamentarian Pauline Hanson's stringent tirades against immigrants into Australia, which have spawned a serious political crisis. Her battle cry is that Australia is in danger of being swamped by Asians who have their own culture and ethnic and religious traditions, form ghettos, and do not easily assimilate into society. Australia is not changing the immigrants, they are changing the Australian polity. Though the context is different, Hanson's outpourings strike a sympathetic chord in the breasts of the populace in other western countries like Holland, the UK, the US and Canada—the last two countries that are basically immigrant nations.

For Canada the analogue is not a melting pot but a mosaic—brightly coloured bits of ethnicity, culture, racial identity and language embedded side by side. They may contrast with one another, but together they form a portrait of the nation in the same way the dots on a pointilist painting convey a coherent image. But no longer, with large-scale immigrants who are non-English and non-French speaking, who constitute a fast growing segment of Canadian society. These now are around 27 per cent of the Canadian population, twice the corresponding American average. The gallimaufry of languages, ethnic differences, and cultural diversities is striking. Had it been merely that, perhaps, a mosaic could have been sustained but the immigrants' colour and the money that the Canadian government has to pour into improving their language proficiency harden and cement the anger and prejudice of the Canadians against immigrants. The infirmities of the immigrants are, of course, exaggerated; Canadian scholars point out that they quickly adjust to the democratic, liberal and cosmopolitan values of the society and whatever odd traits they inherit hardly remain beyond a second generation. Yet the strictures find a ready audience.

America's favourite metaphor has been the melting pot which is now being threatened not by the immigrants sticking to their inherited culture and other differences. The reasons are complex. The founding immigrants of America were Europeans, apart from the blacks brought from Africa as slaves, and though they came from different countries and religious sects, they were basically white and their umbrella religion was Christianity, so that the immigrant population did not take long to assimilate to make America a melting pot. But the inflow of immigrants since the 1960s has been from countries in Latin America, mainly Mexico, with languages of their own, competing for a place in the sun with English, the national language of America.

There has also been a wave of immigrants from Asia on a scale never before seen. In their case though language did not pose any serious problem their educational level has remained far higher than the average of native Americans. The highest university degrees in hard sciences are earned by the Asians, mainly the Chinese and Indians. Even more strikingly, the demographic map of America is changing so radically that in the second half of the twenty-first century the immigrants—first and second generation—would dictate terms in elections in certain states like California, Texas, and New York. In that event, the whole definition of the melting pot would change beyond recognition. The society that would emerge is one with predominance of the tradition and values of the immigrants, with local American values playing second fiddle.

The western societies face a Hobson's choice. Immigration, like the flow of capital, is an intrinsic and integral part of the process of globalisation. The underdeveloped world is short of capital and rich with labour, while the industrialised world is flush with capital and in need of labour, so for a dynamic equilibrium immigration and capital flows have to move in opposite directions. The difficulty arises because labour is not a homogenised entity like capital and it has non-economic ramifications. There is thus reason for lament. The structures of local economies fundamentally change with capital inflows in the same way that the local societies would change fundamentally with the inflow of labour. All this is a non-zero-sum game.

Business Standard, 15 February 1999.

[illegible]

[illegible]

33

Theatre of the absurd

NOTHING like this has ever happened in history, not even in the mythology of any religion. There is an eerie surrealism pervading the political scene in America, the most powerful nation at the acme of prosperity, a marvel of democracy, a custodian of moral values philosophised by the soaring prose of Thomas Jefferson.

Imagine a man accused of unpardonable perjury and obstruction of justice standing in the dock, coming out of his confinement into the majestic and glittering well of the supreme law-making body of the nation, holding in thrall his accusers, jurors and even the presiding judge, who all greet him with rapturous waves of ovation at every drop of a sentence or rhetoric. The Chief Justice of the Supreme Court, arbitrating over the prosecutorial presentation, dutifully comes in to occupy the front seat to listen respectfully to the accused. The jurors, who hold the fate of his presidency, troop in as meek supplicants, and the managers of the House, who forked out a long and boring litany of charges against him, sit like lambs, though with glum faces, wearing a stick-in-the-mud kind of expression and willy-nilly rise at times to clap tirelessly.

Surrealism resided in the juxtapositioning of the two scenes. The first, Congress, where the accused stands before the bar. His defence lawyers dismissed the charges against him as "witches brew", "conjecture", "prosecutorial fudge-making" and "shifting sand castles of speculation" and the other, at the other side of the venue, where the jurors who are 100 Senators along with the presiding judge, listen to the pontification of the man, no one knows whether he is a man on the lam or lord of the earth, couched in lofty prose, emotive summoning of American patriotism and a tantalising list of goodies for the next millennium.

There was an impeachment of the President before, but not like this where the impeached is coronated as soon as he emerges from the impeaching forum. The defence brief of the President is a curious amalgam of *mea culpa* in a garb of convoluted prose and a challenge to the House managers to dare to throw him out of his presidency. The defence lawyer, Charles Ruff, began in an apologetic tone to describe Clinton's behaviour as "morally reprehensible" and admitted that his client violated his "sacred obligations to his family and betrayed the trust of the American people." He then indulged in a strange but legally justifiable quibbling that "Clinton was evasive during his deposition in the private suit against him but he was truthful nonetheless." But this was just a politely disguised prelude to the venomous attack on the prosecution. He argued that the case against the President was constructed "out of sealing wax and string and spiders' web" and so it was, in essence, nothing more than "tenuous extrapolation without foundation." More tellingly, he picked holes in the prosecution's argument about the obstruction of justice by Clinton. By meticulously arranging details, he showed that the obstruction of justice charge, which if proven would be most damaging to Clinton, existed only in the imagination of the prosecutors.

And two hours later came the climactic scene of the virtuoso performance of the accused, President Clinton, in his State of the Union address to the nation. He knew too well his audience to craft his speech. Bipartisan, a word so bandied around in America that it has become a cliché. But Clinton, a consummate politician with subliminal instincts, knowing the mood of the nation, latched on to that as a defining doctrine of public polity. He began by saluting the Speaker of the House, John Hastert, who urged Congress to come together across party lines to solve the country's problems, and then said: "Mr Speaker, at your swearing in, you asked us all to work together in a spirit of bipartisanship and in a spirit of civility. Mr. Speaker, let us do exactly that." This was, of course, a double entendre. What Clinton was saying but not too explicitly was that bipartisanship should extend to this trial in the Senate as well, and if that happens it is a sure bet that he would be off the hook in this strange drama being enacted on American stage.

The actor in Clinton did not stop there. He appealed over the heads of the Senators and the Chief Justice to the higher jury of his countrymen. He did it sedulously with a flourish and usual dramatic gestures. He paid tributes to the widows, specially invited, of two security guards who lost their lives in defending Freedom's house, which roused the patriotic fervour to feverish heights. He then lauded a doughty black woman who upheld civil rights in refusing to vacate a seat in a bus in Alabama. And to climax it all, he unleashed some of the most revolutionary policy initiatives on the social security system reform and education, which drowned the audience in euphoric exuberance.

Thus at the end of it all, a moral wreck became a hero, a dynamiter of moral values became a dynamo, a perfidious person became a patriot. The whole political show in America turned bizarre as in the theatre of the absurd.

Business Standard, 10 January 1999.

34

The age of Milton Friedman

THE recent demise of Milton Friedman, the architect of a counter-revolution in economics, merits a reappraisal of the very core of economic doctrine and policy. Between 1930 and the late 1960s, the one economist who dominated economics, both in theory and policy, was John Maynard Keynes. The Great Depression played such havoc with the lives of humanity that governments were flummoxed about any practical and effective measures to bring the economies back to an even keel. It was the vision and ideas of Keynes which showed that there could be light at the end of a tunnel. A depression, according to him, was a consequence of a deficiency of aggregate demand, which could be raised through a well-designed fiscal policy; monetary policy would be powerless due to a liquidity trap. Thenceforward, economics came to be known as Keynesian economics, perhaps for the second time that economics became eponymous—the first to have that distinction was David Ricardo.

Keynesian economics held its sway for almost three and a half decades until Milton Friedman, with the intellectual stature and power of ideas similar to those of Keynes, challenged it to occupy an expanding space in economic discourse. If Keynes advocated fiscal policy as of primary importance for stabilising economies faced with economic disturbances, Friedman saw an antidote to economic fluctuations and the resulting instability in the use of monetary policy. If Keynes made a powerful case for discretion in policymaking and

The author is grateful to Anand Chandavarkar for his excellent comments on this paper.

its exercise, being sceptical of the vagaries of the markets, Friedman pinned his faith on rules guiding monetary policy, since he believed that discretion, being clouded with vested interests, would distort the behaviour of economic agents away from profit maximisation in their productive activities. For Keynes, a free-floating exchange rate regime was anathema as it would have adverse effects on employment and output. But for Friedman, freely determined exchange rate was a *sine qua non* of competitive efficiency and frictionless economic development. Consumption in the Keynesian system is a decreasing function of current income such that with a rise in income, consumption proportionally tends to decline; whereas in Friedman's schema consumption depends not on current income but on permanent income, comprising expected and current income, which is more stable. Keynes ascribed the great depression of the 1930s and other smaller ones to the inherent instability of the capitalist system, though his view of capitalism differed significantly from that of Karl Marx. In contrast, Friedman put the blame squarely on the policy of monetary contraction of the Federal Reserve, which precipitated the collapse of banks, and through it the enterprises. Thus, Keynes and Friedman figure as the lead protagonists in the great Discretion vs. Rules debate as also fiscal and monetary policy, respectively.

However, Friedmanian economics did not dim the lights of Keynesian economics until the early 1970s, when the US economy with a surging inflation plunged into a stagflation, i.e. coexistence of inflation and low employment, which rendered nugatory the famous Phillips curve rooted in the Keynesian tradeoff between inflation and unemployment. The effect of any stimulus in such a situation through demand management would only raise inflation without any impact on the level of unemployment, as workers would demand higher wages to protect themselves against a rise in inflation. In came (1968) the now famous Friedman's new idea of "natural rate of unemployment" which later morphed into the "non-accelerating inflation rate of unemployment (in short, NAIRU)" which suggested that a certain level of unemployment is unavoidable if inflation and inflationary expectations are to be kept under control. This pushed fiscal policy to stimulate aggregate demand for reducing unemployment into the background and gave a central role to monetary policy. Most of the central banks in both the industrial countries and emerging market economies first targeted money supply and have now switched to inflation targeting as a major tool for keeping inflation within a tolerable limit, and quite successfully. It seems that we all have become Friedmanian!

However, the tide seems to be turning again in economics with the emerging challenges to Friedmanian economics. His NAIRU is losing steam with rapid globalisation, which has weakened the workers' demand for higher wages as they face fierce competition from the augmented global labour supply. For this reason, inflation does not necessarily rise with a decline in the level of unemployment. In fact, a minimum level of unemployment at which inflation is supposed to rise has kept moving downward, particularly in America. Furthermore, there has been an exponential increase in productivity, which keeps the pressure on wages down, thereby affording more space for structural unemployment to decline.

During the last fifty years Keynes and Friedman were placed in the economic debate in two mutually exclusive camps. But this was somewhat exaggerated. At Keynes' centenary symposium held in Cambridge, England, Friedman lauded Keynes as the greatest economist ever born. According to Friedman, Keynes' greatest work is his *Treatise of Money, volume II,* dealing with applied economics, and not his *The General Theory;* and he drew some parallelism between his own monetary analysis and that of Keynes. At the same function he sprang another surprise when he gave a cogent and convincing rationale of Keynes' advocacy of state intervention in economic affairs. He argued that Keynes was right in his view of the state's role, if it is seen in the context of the economic and social milieu of Keynes' country, England, which, having gone through a prolonged process of democratic evolution, had developed institutions and social mores, ensuring an arm's-length relationship between functionaries of the state and the people they served. He also referred to the homogeneity of English society and the small size of England, which facilitated transparency and openness in governance, apart from the savvy and dedicated civil service, which went through fire with its time-tested code of conduct. Where Keynes went wrong, in Friedman's view, was when he tried to generalise from the British experience and to apply it to countries like America without the British traditions and culture. But Friedman overlooked that Keynes, in his Preface to the German edition of *The General Theory,* did acknowledge that much of *The General Theory* "is illustrated and expounded mainly with reference to the conditions existing in the Anglo-Saxon countries." Also, it is too easy to posit the polarity of Keynesian fiscal policy and Friedmanian monetary policy, given their basic complementarity, as so well captured in James Tobin's Common Funnel Theorem. Economic policy is seldom a matter of either or; rather, it is how much of each?

Friedman's involvement in India's economic problems was rather marginal, unlike many other western economists, as he was ideologically poles apart from Indian policymakers. Yet, by some strange happenstance, he was invited by the Planning Commission along with a few other foreign economists in 1963 for their advice. In a brief paper he prepared, he derived a feasible level of deficit financing without inflation on the basis of his own version of the Quantity Theory of Money. But it was totally ignored by the planners, deriding it as a Quantity Theory Theology. He was proved right in later years when the Fourth Plan collapsed with a serious foreign exchange crisis and surging inflationary pressures. Thereafter, it was B.R. Shenoy, his intellectual soul mate, who carried on the battle by using the armoury of Friedmanian economics.

Once, to a group of the Reserve Bank of India economists who were arguing strongly for planning, Friedman put a pointed question: "When would you say that planning has succeeded in India?" One of them, with a take-it-from-me air, replied, "When India will produce twenty million tons of steel, twenty-five millions of cement, and so on." Promptly came another bullet from Friedman, "Ask yourself whether India would not have achieved that quantity without planning." The questioner clammed up with a grump. Later history proved that Friedman was on the side of the angels.

Friedman, despite his eminence, never looked down upon young economists eager to make their mark in their field. A young Indian, rather euphoric about the first article on inflation in India he published in a refereed journal of the Chicago University, and thinking that he broke new ground in inflation economics, gave him an offprint of that article, expecting encomiums. Friedman was friendly, read the article with detailed comments, and discussed it with him as if he was his equal, complimenting him on some points. The young man was on cloud nine until Friedman showed that his analysis was no different from what the quantity theory of money would have yielded. When he saw him crestfallen, he patted him and said, "Young man, you should always read what you write after a time lag and you will know what wrongs you committed and that will make you do right next time around."

For all his fundamental contributions to economics and his fame, Friedman remained a down-to-earth economist, fully cognisant of the human foibles and vanity of scientists. The toast that he proposed in 1976 at the Nobel Prize ceremony clearly bears testimony to this. "As some of you may know", he said,

> my monetary studies have led me to the conclusion that central banks profitably be replaced by computers geared to provide a steady rate of growth in the quantity of money. Fortunately for me personally, that conclusion has had no practical impact—Else there would have been no Central Bank of Sweden to have established the award I am honored to receive. Should I draw the moral that sometimes to fail is to succeed?

In order to deprecate a common tendency of people to convert a Nobel laureate into an instant expert on all and sundry, he said in the same address that

> Somehow, we badly need an antidote for both the inflated attention granted a Nobel laureate in areas outside his competence and the inflated ego each of us is in so much danger of acquiring.

A classic example of this was Bertrand Russell. One can also think of many others among the newly crowned Nobel laureates.

Though Friedman, co-author with his wife Rose, of *Freedom to Choose,* considered to be a manifesto of market fundamentalism, was thought to be apathetic to social and economic inequality, he was in fact deeply concerned with myriad social and economic ills. This was borne out by his autobiography *Two Lucky People,* jointly written with his wife, where he confessed how he was appalled by the poverty he saw in India to the point that he virtually decided not to revisit the country. What he was averse to was the discretionary injustice that was dished out in contemporary societies by corrupt politicians and the debauched bureaucracy without any responsibility for the consequences of their actions. Realising that in a free market economy the poor will suffer, he proposed voucher and negative income tax schemes bereft of the discretionary element.

Friedman's thinking on the linkages between economic and political freedom remained somewhat fuzzy to the end. In his

Capitalism and Freedom, he argued that the two were intertwined but the experience of Hong Kong, his favourite economy, convinced him that although economic freedom was necessary for political freedom, the converse was not true. Also, Friedman overlooked that Hong Kong was a freakish *sui generis* economy whose experience could scarcely be generalised. Many wondered also how Friedman could reconcile his belief system based on freedom in all spheres of life with his association with the repressive Pinochet regime in Chile.

Be that as it may. Milton Friedman's place in the world of economics is well assured not only because of his concepts and theorems but also due to his demonstration that free market can be an instrument of social justice, too.

E-Social Sciences.com, 1 December 2006.

Part II

Indica

35

Nehru: The hero that was

ILLUSION, like happiness, decreases with age. The longer you live, you see your dear ones depart. Events and persons you loathe linger on to gnaw at you. You then lose your mental equilibrium. Illusions you harbour about men and women follow the same track, with time unfolding new facts and opening ajar the cupboards of skeletons hidden so long. Awakened suddenly to reality, you stroke your conscience and wonder if what you believed hitherto was not an illusion.

Stanley Wolpert's biography of Nehru, published recently, dilates on Nehru's homoerotic proclivity and furtive encounters with Edwina Mountbatten. The book invited the ire of Indians since it contained Wolpert's insinuation about Nehru's "passionate, icy cold and indeed numbing" love affair with a young Englishman. However, this was just a wild speculation based on inferential logic and no hard evidence. His sneering allusions to Nehru's flirtations with Edwina have been in public domain because of Nehru's other biographers and those of the Mountbattens. What could have made it titillating was the correspondence between Nehru and Edwina, which was denied to Wolpert by Sonia Gandhi. In any case, it is not for these fragments of Nehru's life that Wolpert's biography will be remembered.

In Wolpert's gushing but nugatory narration of Nehru's life, there are some seemingly innocuous snippets which diminish him as a great Indian, democrat and secularist. After completing his Cambridge education, Nehru wanted to spend a few years in Oxford because 'Cambridge is becoming too full of Indians.' The thoughts were echoed in what he told years later to John Kenneth Galbraith: " I am the last Englishman to rule India." What else could this be, if not the hubris of a born aristocrat? His democratic pretensions were torn to smithereens by how he systematically destroyed the line of succession to pave the way for his daughter. His private virtues became public vices, and his public virtues were camouflaged private vices. When Indira decided to marry Feroze, Nehru wrote:

> I wanted to help you personally and I expected you to help me—hundreds and thousands of young men and girls have wanted to serve with me as secretaries—I have never encouraged anyone and shouldered my burden alone, for I had always imagined you to occupy that niche ... no one could take your place ... with this idea ever hovering in my mind I wrote piles and piles of historical and other letters to you, I wanted gently and slowly but surely to train your mind in that wider understanding of life and events that is essential for any big work ... I wanted to give you some training which would stand you in good stead in later life ... so that when time comes you could tackle any big national job.

Thus his entreaty to Indira to dump Feroze, and to become instead his amanuensis, was to prepare her to take from him the guardianship of the nation. History, of course, had surprises. Indira might have temporarily disappointed him but once she smelt the aroma of office, she sacrificed her marriage and joined him. With hindsight, one can see that Nehru's annoyance at his acolytes' proposing Indira as president of the Congress was a contrived act.

His ambivalent attitude towards his sister Vijayalaxmi's involvement with Sayyed Hussain is equally revealing about his secular postures. Far from opposing his father in preventing her from marrying Hussain, Nehru in fact tried to dissuade her. Years later, when this lovelorn couple chanced to have a liaison in Delhi, Nehru shrewdly posted her as ambassador in Moscow than High Commissioner in London, where she wanted to go to be near Hussain. Vijayalaxmi's wry comment on her appointment summed it all. "For some still unknown reason, I was to leave for Moscow. If bhai... realised how little importance the Soviet Union attached to this day [Independence Day], we would have been permitted to celebrate it at home."

The same narrow religious and caste calculations figured in Nehru's opposition to Indira's marriage. Feroze was close to his family. At one stage, he had nursed Kamala Nehru during her illness. Also, Nehru's other sister blessed her decision. But Nehru stubbornly persisted in finding, through friends, a suitable match in his high caste. These episodes show how tinsel were his secularist commitments in matters close to him and his family.

Much has been made of Nehru's distaste for power by his coxcombs. Some time in the 1950s, Nehru thought aloud of resigning his helmsmanship of the nation. When beseeched by his party men, he stooped into their blandishments. This mask of false prudence he often wore and with telling effect. Once in 1929, he feigned reluctance to be Congress president, but when pressed, readily agreed. There was a repeat performance at the time of the Pethic-Lawrence mission. His close friend and supporter Azad saw through his game. "Jawaharlal is very vain and cannot stand that anyone else should receive greater support than he", Azad said when Nehru agreed to be Congress president, which was a stepping-stone to prime-ministership. He added, ruing his vote for Nehru: "I acted according to my best judgement but the way things have shaped since then has made me realise that this was perhaps the greatest blunder of my life not to stand myself or support Sardar Patel." The relationship between Sardar and Azad was marked by personal and ideological animosity and yet Azad felt that Patel was a greater statesman.

We are a nation of icons and have paid a heavy price for being so. It is time we avoided iconolatry in judging our national heroes and heroines. It is better to start with a 'null' hypothesis that no one is great or unblemished until the facts, as they emerge in the course of our search, void that hypothesis.

Business Standard, 18 August 1997.

36

When reason plays truant

WHILE trying to answer economic questions in India, we cannot but raise political questions. All economic issues, vitally though they may be affecting the daily lives of the teeming millions, have to be posited in a given political context if they are not to seem either irrelevant or irrational. It is thus necessary, as current events are unfolding, to traverse a political landscape, to define its shape and contours before charting out a course for an economic habitat.

A political maelstrom has broken out, blurring the boundaries between the economic policy domain and the political process by which economic issues are winnowed, clarified and eventually translated into implementable policies. The Rajiv Gandhi regime made a promising beginning. There was an aura of youth, a certain degree of freshness in economic thinking and an attempt, however fainthearted, to shake off the dead weight of history. At least for tactical purposes, if not out of conviction, all the political parties were involved in arriving at decisions on major national questions, both economic and political. A consensus was sought not so much to sweep under the carpet all the ideological differences as to seek middle ground, without political gimmickry. Halfway through, however, all these initiatives were jettisoned and the old games began to be played and political skulduggery held centre stage. Either the leader of the Congress Party did not know where he was going or the party, sensing that the direction in which he was going would erode the power concentrated in a small coterie of politicians, resumed a confrontational course with gusto and pugnacity.

The consequences are there for all to see. The economic liberalisation programme was stymied and there was a sudden throwback to populist slogans. The counterpart of backtracking in the economic field was reversal of the accommodating spirit in the political sphere. Soft options, whether in Kashmir or Punjab, were replaced by arm-twisting tactics, with conflicts being allowed to fester without countervailing action. Although some dissenting voices, mainly outside the mainstream political parties, were raised against the tyranny of power, the opposition parties without exception joined the chorus orchestrated by the Congress Party for relentless Army action as the only alternative.

The new regime of V.P. Singh came riding on the Bofors wave, and repeated almost the same economic policies of Rajiv Gandhi. If bank loans of the poor borrowers were written off and a hefty budget deficit incurred, jeopardising the viability of the banking system, it was only a logical culmination of the loan "Melas" celebrated by the Rajiv *Raj*. The Kashmir and Punjab policies were basically the same as those of the Congress party. But that did not prevent the Congress party as well as other parties from criticising the Singh government for not resolving the Kashmir and Punjab imbroglios. Elections in Kashmir and Punjab were ruled out on flimsy and undemocratic grounds. If military repression was a wrong policy, no one came up with an alternative other than still more repressive action. The Congress party, which in fact was instrumental in initiating the economic liberalisation policy, far from lending support to the Singh government, took potshots at it at every possible opportunity. And now the new Humpty Dumpty government of Chandrashekhar will continue the same set of economic policies, though with the populist rhetoric of socialism and poverty alleviation, perpetuate the same repressive regime in Kashmir, Punjab and now Assam, and will eventually meet the same fate, sooner than later, which Rajiv Gandhi and V.P. Singh met before.

There will be the usual gallimaufry of solutions offered by the know-all political commentators and the power-seeking politicians who change their opinion as easily as their party affiliations. Virtues will again be seen in political stability which the Congress alone will be credited with. The Janata party came and destabilised the nation; V.P. Singh descended and declared a caste war. So now is the time for the scion of the old dynasty to restore stability. But this phoney stability has proved as unstable as the instability of the Janata and Janata Dal governments. The Indira Gandhi-led stability between 1971 and 1977 gave us a gift of Emergency; a variant of her other 'stability', in 1980, engendered a Punjab disaster; the stability she bequeathed to her son through her sudden death converted India almost into a banana republic. The stability of the Congress brand is an emaciating stability of a geriatric ward and has been as great a curse as the instability of the coalition governments.

We the eggheads have exhausted the extant lexicon of political idioms and might do well to invent a new one. It is no longer this party or that or this leader or that who would emancipate Indian society from the labyrinth of decay and defunct political institutions. The malaise is much deeper in the body politic. The obsessive addiction to centralisation of power at the centre is what every political party irrespective of its ideological label yearns for. Proximity to that powerhouse inebriates them. So long as that power is concentrated at the centre, reducing the constituent states to impotency, no rational economic policy, be it economic liberalisation or decentralised planning, is likely to be on the agenda of any party nor will the insurgency abate in states like Kashmir, Punjab, Assam, and who knows where else. Blueprinting any economic policy has to have the architectural design of political institutions and political process. If the latter is in disrepair, articulation of economic policy will be as futile as lecturing in a classroom on rational expectations when irrationality abounds in society, or extolling the virtue of Pareto optimality in the midst of imperfect markets.

Maybe it is time now to organise a movement for reconvening a constituent assembly, with the sole mandate of transferring real power from the centre to the states. The power of the centre has grown, is growing, and has to be stemmed. Otherwise, there will not only be millions of mutinies as now but also mutinies by millions against other millions forever. Vidya Naipaul, drawing from the externals of his ancestral land, wrote from his innards,

> the present kinds of group excesses, sectarian excesses, religious excesses are the beginning of self-awareness. Indian union is greater than the sum of its parts and many of the movements of excesses strengthened the Indian state, defining it as the source of law and civility and reasonableness.

Naipaul should not have to expiate for his earlier harshness towards Indian society with this panegyric. It is precisely because the Indian union has become supreme by supplanting its parts that India has come to this sorry pass.

February 1991, unpublished.

37

A phantom of India

SOME years ago, the world of film craft changed to invent a new medium to portray the innards of a society. The images alternated between being sublime and droll, glorious and grim, profound and profane. Luis Malle's memorable documentary film of a few decades ago, *Phantom India,* depicted real people in Bombay being harangued and harried by the Left intellectuals residing at the luxurious Malabar Hill. Malle's commentary in French-accented English had a naughty throw-line: "Once Indians, adept in the language of their bygone masters, start talking, they never end." What an apt characterisation of us all!

Decades have passed, the world has turned upside down, countries far behind India in culture, history and economic growth have moved ahead but we as a nation have not given up our profession of talking *ad infinitum.*

India being faced with the enveloping economic crisis in 1990 changed willy-nilly the course of its economic policy. There has been, for the first time, a glimmer of hope that India after all might reach the potential its admirers had hoped for and India's bedraggled masses were vainly waiting for. But no, nary. The peregrinating prime minister, Narasimha Rao, frightened by the labels of being anti-poor fastened on to him by his political detractors, discovered a neologism and bored the hard-headed businessmen at Davos and the practitioners of realpolitik in the US Congress with his confused, convoluted and scatterbrained discourse on a "third way" to take India to the economic millennium. It was one of those verbal gymnastics which could have passed off as profound mysticism at one of the J. Krishnamurthy-type of enclaves. By doing so he pulled the rug from under the feet of his brilliant and honest-to-God finance minister. The reforms got stalled, costing him his place in the sun.

A politician is not a politician if he does not talk incessantly, while trimming his sails to the changing winds. Intellectuals who are supposed to live by their wits are a species of the same genre. Those who once adorned the corridors of power in government, some sun-tanned and some seeking limelight, feel cheated that their fig leaves are being taken away by upstart reformers. Harking back to the past they talk about how things have gone bad, poverty has increased, the country is going to the dogs, globalisation is an alias for new international tyranny. Have they stopped to think how poverty could be wished away in five years, while they or their policies could not remove it in forty years? Such questions are jejune and they don't want to answer them as they fear that their answers will not be any different. But their intellectual libido derives nourishment from their talk. They cite figures if they suit the readymade kit of their thoughts. If the statistics do not come to their rescue, they must be junked as they might have been made up by gnomes of the finance ministry or the Reserve Bank. Well, once in a while the foreign exchange reserves rise to the level of eight months imports. Oh, that is true, but it is a consequence of portfolio capital, which one day will bolt away. After all, portfolio investors are sharks, fair-weather friends. You should be Manichaean to understand them.

The old God of Communism not only failed but died, as Nietzsche would have said. The intellectuals then invented a devil—globalisation. One of them has propounded a theory that globalisation in the era of financial mobility dooms economies like India's to a perennial state of low and unstable growth. He has come out with his theory of how planning can contain globalisation, if not prevent it. Little do they realise that India changed its policies in 1991 not because its policymakers wanted to. Reforms were a *pis-aller* for India in a state of desperation. Use of the term "finance capital" in the context of globalisation as a historical anachronism is no more than a linguistic throwback to the era that has passed into history. Globalisation and economy of business is not something that any nation, however powerful or moral-laden, can order away like King Canute. Most countries in the world have opened up their economies to external influences; their trade as a proportion of GDP has grown and with it, the payments instruments mediated through banks have also increased in volume, diversity and speed. With goods the capital—short, medium and long term—has become more mobile. With opening of the current and capital account transactions in several countries, developing and developed, assets are moved across national boundaries in search of arbitrage, not only by institutions and industry but also by individuals with speed unthinkable a few years ago.

In addition, growing labour migration from the poor to the rich countries has enhanced the role of banks even from the common person's point of view. New financial instruments have emerged. All this, far from being a speculative indulgence, is a facilitator of transactions that contribute to the growth of industry and commerce. Even a country like Vietnam, extolled by Indian intellectuals as an ideal to follow, has been opening up its financial markets. Globalisation is going to rule the waves and it will be suicidal to get off the waves. India is not Louis Malle's phantom, but a real thing. Instead of wasting their lung power in talking *ad infinitum* and *ad hominem,* Indian intellectuals should get down to dealing with the consequences of globalisation to our advantage.

Business Standard, 27 May 1997.

38

Two riddles of India's economic growth

THE inefficiency of India's development process has been brilliantly explained in the work of Bhagwati-Padma Desai-Srinivasan in the past. Yet two riddles remained to be unravelled. The first is: why did the stabilisation policies, which India has pursued with a considerable degree of success, not lead to an acceleration of its growth rate until 1990? The second riddle is: why do Indian policymakers often shirk from maintaining the momentum of growth through unremitting structural adjustment, even when a conspicuous success was achieved in stabilising the economy in the latter half of the 1980s and in stabilisation-cum-structural adjustment since 1996?

Two volumes by Joshi and Little (*India: Microeconomic and Political Economy, 1964-1991*, Oxford University Press, New Delhi, 1994) (J&L) and a monograph by Ashok Desai (*My Economic Affair*, Wiley Eastern, New Delhi, 1993) between them have attempted to demystify these two riddles. The central thesis of J&L is that

> ... the style of macroeconomic policy, involving multiple controls, creates large price distortions that are at the heart of the problem of the inefficient use of resources. A fashionable view of Indian economic policy is that it was unsound microeconomically but sound macroeconomically, and further that these phenomena were positively linked—in other words, the controls that led to microeconomic inefficiency made it easier to attain macroeconomic balance. In contrast, one of our central conclusions is that India's control system was not only microeconomically inefficient but also macroeconomically perverse.

The reason is that the controls created in India a monster of a severe and stubborn fiscal adjustment problem, which attenuated the efficacy of other instruments of macroeconomic management such as exchange rate and monetary policy. They have also created "... opportunities for corruption, and the resulting payments or kickbacks raise the cost of both public and private economic activities, especially investment." The macroeconomic consequences of the control regime were most visible in the burgeoning fiscal deficit.

The legacy of fiscal imbalance has continued, perhaps with more serious consequences in the more liberalised and open economic system that India has created since 1991. The consolidated fiscal deficit of the non-financial public sector has hardly changed since 1987—hovering around 10 per cent of GDP. The question is how to rein in fiscal deficit without throwing the economy out of kilter. Some part of the fiscal deficit can be, and often is, financed by base money creation, which can take place at a certain rate without inflationary pressures, as the demand for money increases with GDP. Such monetary expansion is pure seignorage. The government can extract more revenue from higher seignorage than is warranted by the demand for money, at the cost of inflationary pressure which the economy could tolerate.

The relevant concept of fiscal deficit in this context is primary deficit, i.e. gross fiscal deficit minus interest payments. If primary deficit less the part of it financed by seignorage is nil, it implies that the existing public debt will grow with the interest rate paid, because the government is simply borrowing to pay interest. Hence, if the real interest rate exceeds the rate of growth, a primary deficit will be unsustainable. This is the case with India, which leads J&L to predict that "India is heading for another major crisis."

This brings us to the second riddle as to why India flatters with short spells of dynamic dynamism in economic policy only to disappoint by subsequent retreat into complacency and timidity in pursuing what has proved a boon. Ideas about how to change the political framework are hazy and ill defined. A blueprint of how to manage political change has been put forth with some daring by Desai. He identifies the ills of the electoral system with a disjunction between the monetary contributions to the politicians and the party which they stand for. In order that financial contribution must go not to the politicians for the jobs they do or get done but to parties for the policies they espouse, Desai suggests "elections based on lists and proportional representation. Every contesting party would have to put up a list of candidates containing as many names as there are seats in the legislative body. It would win seats in proportion to the number of votes in polls."

Many of Desai's ideas on political restructuring may appear quixotic to some of his critics, and utopian to his friends. The politicians as well as the parties have resisted simple reforms like restraining political corruption and preventing defection by elected representatives and to expect these revolutionary ideas to permeate the political arena is to ask for the moon. The remedies may appear to be the ruminations of a gadfly, but the issues are real and have to be faced sooner or later.

It is possible that if the economic reforms continue, even in their truncated form, without any reversal, they may tear apart the political straitjacket. The essence of economic reforms lies in the transfer of decision making from the top to the bottom. In the Indian context, it may mean that the Centre would tend to weaken, with economic decision making power shifting first to the states and gradually to the district level, and still further down. Political parties may look to the states as the primary theatre for attaining power, which in turn may lead to competition amongst states to outperform each other. As a result, the ownership of an enterprise is likely to be less important than its efficiency. Furthermore, the distance between the rulers and the electorate will be telescoped, providing greater scope for the voters to judge the economic performance of the parties, which is the ultimate guarantee for their welfare. Perhaps, such thinking is, to borrow Oscar Wilde's aphorism, a triumph of hope over experience.

Business Standard, 10 March 1998.

39

Nothing ages like a honeymoon

THE world hyperbolised about the miracles of the East Asian economies to an extent that the mystery was sought to be explained in terms of some values peculiar to those societies or some hidden but yet undiscovered economic laws. This honeymoon with the East Asian countries would have continued without loss of enthusiasm and the raft of superlatives but for the jolt these economies received during the last four months. What now seems to be a dismaying phenomenon was long in coming but few expected its sudden thud.

There have been two economists though who had, through historical parables and searching economic analysis, demystified the East Asian growth. Amartya Sen picked bones with Singapore's pontificating philosopher statesman, Lee Kuan Yew, on whether East Asia's economic achievement was due to the so-called Asian values which posited a positive relationship between economic growth and authoritarian governance. Sen found, through an erudite survey of historical, political, and philosophical landscapes that "on balance the hypothesis that there is no relation between freedom and prosperity in either direction is hard to reject." Sen's strictures should put paid to the pretensions of those who worshipped surrogate idols when their God failed. Paul Krugman focused on the mainsprings of East Asian growth by arguing what then appeared to be unorthodox and provocative, that the East Asian economic growth could be simply explained in terms of an increase in capital and labour inputs and that productivity increase hardly figured in their growth accounting.

Now both Sen and Krugman have been vindicated in their own ways. There is no such thing as Asian values nor any magic economic laws that governed East Asian growth. It is only helpful policies like openness to competition, the use of international markets together with a high level of literacy and education that accounted for their growth. They could have achieved what they did even without the authoritarian state intervention, if those "helpful policies" were pursued. The Krugman thesis went further in divining the present economic crisis in East Asia.

If capital and labour are the two factor inputs contributing to growth, sooner or later the economies would reach their frontiers. The saving rates have been high over a long haul and they are at a stage beyond which they cannot go. After all, there is a limit to which consumption can be compressed. Without productivity growth, however, growth was in some way inefficient. On an average, capital-output ratio in East Asia is around 5, which is way above that in the industrial countries and even higher than in a country like Vietnam. Labour's contribution was well sustained until these economies almost hit full employment or near full employment. In Malaysia, Thailand, and Korea, the unemployment rate was between 2 and 4 per cent; below which it could not fall without causing a bottleneck in production.

If capital domestically produced has reached its apogee, it can be supplemented by foreign capital. This is exactly what is happening in the East Asian countries. However, even with foreign capital, these economies ran intc problems because of competition in their export markets. Until 1995 most exports from East Asia were labour-intensive. With labour supply shrinking and consequent wage pressures, labour-intensive production no longer remained profitable.

On the other hand, in the exports market, countries like China and Vietnam, with abundant labour, fiercely competed with the advanced East Asian countries. This meant that unless the East Asian countries embarked on capital-intensive production, their level in the export market would shrivel. Growth of productivity thus has become the main desideratum, as Krugman rightly predicted.

The much-vaunted Asian values applied in an authoritarian direction of the economy created inefficient financial systems and a real-asset bubble. In the early stages, most of these economies used non-market institutions established through authoritarian methods to create market incentives. While that worked well initially, the residue it left spawned special interests in industry and finance. The weaknesses did not surface since the growth rates, spurred by an increase in capital and labour, continued over a long stretch of time, but once they slowed, the micro-distortions suppressed so far became more dominant, particularly in the context of growing openness of the Asian economies.

Domestic investment financed by foreign capital led to mounting foreign liabilities, which were not hedged, the exchange rates being anchored to the US dollar.

The present currency crisis in East Asia, thus, is not a product of a conspiracy hatched by some finance gnomes like George Soros; the laws of politics and economics have at last come into their own. There is no such thing as a miracle or Asian values, except in the puerile imagination of the success-inebriated East Asian statesman.

Business Standard, 30 December 1997.

40

Carrying bricks to the Tower of Babel

Arthur Koestler once said of man that he is compelled to shape facts and data into hard bricks, stick them together with the slime of his theories and beliefs, and carry them to Babel—even though he knows that the tower will never be completed. Many of us have been manufacturing such bricks for many years in economic policy. Several propositions were constructed as unassailable truths. They were used as foundations for building up the Indian economy. The economy did make impressive progress initially but it never reached the expected level. But those propositions were never abandoned, and they are likely to be used as the rationale to scotch reforms on the anvil.

The first of these propositions is that devaluation is harmful when the economy is partially planned because it distorts planned investment through a rise in import prices. It does not raise exports, lowers export prices, and thus benefits foreign buyers. Besides, the argument goes, protectionist pressures in industrialised countries will rise if the exports of a country depreciating its currency flood their markets.

Experience is to the contrary. Imports as a result of devaluation will no doubt be costlier. But it does not follow that investment will be upset. The new price structure rationalises investment allocation, making it more efficient. Greater efficiency means saving of resources spent. The economy benefits to the extent that resources saved are expended on additional investment. The same is true of exports. Devaluation raises the profitability of exported goods and to that extent improves their ability to compete with similar goods produced elsewhere.

This does not mean that protectionist measures by the rich countries are to be ignored, but our country is not the only victim. So long as protectionist policies are neutral between various developing countries, no particular country suffers though developing countries as a group might. India's experience during the last five years fully supports the policy of steady, crawling devaluation of the rupee. Exports increased at a rate never reached before in the previous forty years. The benefits would have been even larger if only the fiscal deficit had been reined in.

Another brick to Babel is the sanctity of the public sector. The intentions with which the public sector was promoted were no doubt noble, idealistic, and had some rationale in the beginning. There was also a consensus in its favour across the spectrum of all political opinion. However, the consensus by itself is not a justification if it is not yielding any profits year in and year out. The way it is managed in India, the public sector does not respond to market signals. Its losses are routinely funded through market borrowing; hence, it has no compulsion to streamline its operations. It is highly politicised, and often overstaffed by 30 to 40 per cent. It is the people at large who pay for its inefficiency through either higher taxes or higher inflation.

Before banking was taken over by the State in 1969, it was operated with some sense of responsibility and accountability to shareholders. There were no doubt bad debts, but within limits, because of the prudential control scrupulously and rigorously exercised by the Reserve Bank. With all this, there did occur some bank failures. With the nationalisation of banking, prudence and management were thrown to the winds and politics took over completely.

Today, Indian bank portfolios have gone sour to the extent of 40 to 50 per cent, and but for government ownership as a guarantee most of them would have gone out like the savings and loans associations in the United States. The state of the Indian banking system and other financial institutions has convincingly demonstrated that government ownership and the consequent lack of competition among banks has benefited neither the users of financial services nor productive investment.

The propositions arguing for import control to insulate domestic industry from foreign competition are of the same genre. Imports can be regulated either through limits on quantity or by raising their prices. The former is a palliative only in the short run as an emergency measure. However, its use even as a short-term remedy is questionable in today's context. With the curtailment of imports, domestic industrial capacity remains unutilised to a larger extent than otherwise. The domestic substitutes for imports are high-cost and low-quality not because domestic producers are incompetent or lack necessary skills but because they have nothing to fear from foreign competitors. They can continue to produce shoddy goods and reap profits they don't deserve to earn while consumers are unabashedly exploited. The argument that imports of capital goods would threaten domestic capital goods is equally specious. Some public sector firms have been producing low-quality high-cost machinery, and even after three decades of protection have not gone beyond adolescence.

Perhaps the greatest myth is the belief that a controlled economy is resented by the private sector, which incidentally is a beneficiary of a regulatory regime in India. Proliferation of regulations permits them to operate in a sheltered market and opening it to competitive forces is not to the advantage of inefficient firms. That is why their support for deregulation is lukewarm at best and hostile at worst. If deregulation comes at all, the industrialists with vested interests would welcome it only in the internal market, so that by clever manipulation and collusion a few producers can corner the market. For this reason the economy should be opened simultaneously to internal and external competition.

With the firm and defiant pronouncement of the finance minister to open the Indian economy one hopes that all these cobwebs of outdated economic thought will be swept away. The government, however, should not delude itself that the results would be quick or that the knights in socialist armour will lie low. It is going to be a long haul, with lots of trauma and disharmony.

The Times of India, 7 August 1994.

41

A dream of an optimist

WHEN there is little joy in the present one often is prone to leap into the future—to imagine things one could never possess, to reach elusive ideals.

Present-day India drowns you in gloom. The economy is in shambles, with a bleak future for the young and those yet to be born. Just pulled back from the edge of a precipice, it is chugging along. A set of economic policies—new for our government and to our intellectual hermits but old to many outside—is being unleashed. Tax policy is being revamped, trade barriers pulled down, the behemoth of the vast and sprawling public sector cut to size.

But these policies are not having an easy passage. Battalions of critics are up in arms. The Cassandras have been warning that disaster is round the corner. Wait for the day when devaluation will increase the payments deficit. You rein in the public sector and the rapacious private sector will be at your throat to destroy all that the nation created through the planning process. The elimination of tariffs on imports and import quotas will sink domestic industries in a flood of imports, leading to veritable de-industrialisation of the country. What will remain would be a Stone Age. Unemployment will reach a level where anarchy will abound and the poor will inhabit not a green land of hope but a cemetery of the dead.

In the midst of this deluge of prophecies, a Micawberian Indian has no choice but to keep his fingers crossed daydreaming, about what could be ten years later. He sees no virtue in the recipes doled out by the present critics of government policies. He has had his fill of these over the last forty years without reaching a millennium. In this torrent of conflicting cross currents of thought, he just decides to pin his faith on the future of his country and hopes that somehow his world will know no bounds at the end of the next decade.

Come the year 2001, clearly a full decade after a scholarly, dedicated Dr. Manmohan Singh started rolling out his new policies of economic reform, India will begin to see light at the end of the tunnel. What a dreadful crisis it was in 1991 when India had a horrid fiscal deficit of 10 per cent of GDP, a domestic public debt constituting 54 per cent of GDP, and foreign debt service sucking away almost 30 per cent of export receipts. The high unemployment rate—nobody knows what it was, though guesstimates were thrown around—was a millstone round the neck of the young, overpowering the employment market. And the poor multiplied in geometric progression with the completion of every five-year plan.

And then the miracle began to happen. Fiscal discipline became the guiding principle of economic policy circa 2001. In the span of ten years the fiscal deficit, a real fiscal deficit not a synthetic one, was reduced from 10 per cent of GDP to first one per cent and then converted into a modest surplus. Inflation, which tyrannised bank balances, was brought down from two digits to a modest one to two per cent. This outcome was made possible through a reduction in useless public spending, tax reform, and divestiture of public enterprises.

You may wonder how the deficit would be reduced. In 1991 the government owned some 3000 companies, accounting for 40 per cent of the investment. Their number was pruned to about 100 or so and the sale proceeds were used to cancel domestic debt which was eating away almost 26 per cent of the current expenditure of the Union government. The ratio of domestic debt to GDP was brought down to 15 per cent of GDP, though amortisation and some part of the sales was set aside to finance some contingencies that might arise from external shock.

Privatisation was not confined to the sale of companies; the private sector was permitted in activities that used to be reserved for the public sector. At the same time, the tax system was radically reformed to make it an efficient instrument of resource mobilisation. Corporate income tax was lowered from 55 per cent to 35 per cent, personal tax from 45 per cent to 35 per cent, and value added tax at a uniform rate was introduced. Tax revenue boomed in real and nominal terms, to reach 15 per cent of GDP. But the government did not shirk its responsibility; it simplified judicial procedures to expedite tax cases and put tax evaders in jail.

The government reduced import tariffs from 600–700 per cent to a modest 20 per cent. All subsidies were abolished, and the rupee was made fully convertible. The financial system was totally liberalised, while strengthening the supervisory apparatus, through elimination of selective credit controls, privatisation of banks, and introduction of new financial instruments designed to help against inflation and exchange rate uncertainty. When, with all these measures, the government found that the rate of growth did not increase, it sought to reduce external debt by using aggressively the Brady debt reduction plan. Capital flight was not only arrested but actually reversed. The balance of payments turned into black. A finale was reached when the government increased its expenditure on social services to 51 per cent of the current expenditure of the Union government, representing a rate of growth in real terms of 66 per cent between 1991 and 2001. The pared-down bureaucracy was engaged in doing what it could do best.

Could this be a pipe-dream of a Quixotic Indian idealist, a gullible citizen or a cock-eyed intellectual? Many in India would feel that way until their minds are opened to the world of Mexico of 1992—that overpopulated land which until recently was in stagnation and bankruptcy. All that a patriotic Indian would like India of the morrow to be is what Mexico of 1992 has become—confident, vibrant, fast-growing, and caring for its downtrodden masses.

The Times of India, 9 September 1992.

42

Economic astrologers no more

LOOKING at the outcome of economic forecasts from various sources—private business, investment bankers, commercial banks, government agencies, and international organisations—one is not sure whether economics as a science and economists have come of age or gone out of age. Economists, with their array of econometric tools and statistical sophistry, joined in large numbers businesses and banks in the heady days of the 1970s and 1980s. They constructed models fed with well-sifted data and cranked out results by using omnipresent computers at homes and offices. The world of business and bankers basked in the sunshine of profits when the forecasters predicted, or their masters thought they predicted, the outcome of their risky activities.

That euphoria is over, with the downside of economies in the West getting the better of the upside of the economic smart alecs. If the economy is in bloom, as it was during the 1980s, a forecast could work in an upbeat fashion and all is then hunky-dory. If the optimistic predictions were off by a few notches, it did not matter a whit so long as the profits turned out were substantial.

Now, with the globalisation of markets for goods and factors, and cataclysmic changes in the social and political arena worldwide, no one knows how events move. No pattern in their behaviour is discerned; no regularity in their sequencing is observed; the past is not replicated into either the present or the future. These changes in the social, political and economic space have upset the cocky economists whose forecasts go awry with unfailing regularity.

The consequences are traumatic for a once-thriving tribe of economic forecasters. Many of them have been put out to pasture and forced to eke out their existence in fields in which they are ill suited. For survival, they have to work more for much less. Universities, which produced economists like sausages, have now to hunt for students for doctoral studies.

The business and financial world has been doing as well or as badly as before, without these highly paid economic wizards. The market for them has shrivelled and there is now no more place for conducting business through hunches, intuition and informed guesses.

While the market has disciplined economic forecasters in the private sector, those in international organisations go on merrily with their myriad projections without running the risk of losing their jobs, as their clients form a captive market. The *World Economic Outlook*, brought out by the IMF biannually, is taken seriously for what it says about coming economic events in the world at large and in individual countries.

The policies of industrial countries, influenced by these forecasts, shape the contours of international economic and trade policy, which guides the actions of a large number of economic lightweights. If inflation is forecast to be rising, monetary policies have to be tightened; if the fiscal deficit is going to be enlarged, expenditure has to be curtailed; if world recession is projected to deepen, interest rates have to be lowered; if current accounts of the major industrial countries are likely to develop imbalances, exchange rates have to be realigned.

It is, therefore, interesting to see the track record of these projections over the years. The latest *World Economic Outlook*, published on 10 October 1991, has predicted that world output would grow in 1991 by 0.9 per cent; and for countries like the US, Japan and Germany, the economic hegemonists of the world, the rate of growth would be 0.3, 4.5 and 3.1 per cent, respectively. For developing countries, the rate projected for 1991 is 0.6 per cent. The rate of inflation predicted for industrial countries is 4.5 per cent and 58.7 per cent for developing countries. Lest you proceed to design your policies on the basis of this prognosis of the world economy, the report focuses your attention on the differences between what was predicted in May 1991 for 1991 and what it has now done in October 1991.

And here is the scorecard. The world output predicted now is 25 per cent less than that projected in May 1991. For the US, the rate of output predicted turned from positive to negative by 60 per cent; for Japan it was higher by 25 per cent, and for Germany it was higher by 11 per cent. The forecasting performance for inflation is no different. For industrial countries, the inflation rate is now predicted to be 6 per cent lower and for developing countries higher by 43 per cent.

The story of this kind of *mea culpa* is, however, not unique to this report of May. It is a phenomenon repeated every six months and with the same air of nonchalance. In fact, at no time since the inception of the *World Economic Outlook* have the projections come out true. They were off the mark not by small percentages, which could be within a tolerable limit of statistical aberration. What is even more galling is that the errors are in both directions. The forecasters, too, may justify their predictions by insisting that plus and minus deviations cancel each other out over a long run, after the fashion of a quirky economist, who explained inflation as an adjustment to earlier deflation and a subsequent deflation as a reaction to preceding inflation!

And yet the exercise is continued, and the multi-equational model from which these results are drawn is constantly honed and refined, with all that it implies in terms of resources, human and material. If these statistical exercises were purely intellectual gymnastics, one would have been amused if not enlightened. But since these are purported to lay out a framework for studying interrelations among national economies in a global context, and for evolving fiscal, monetary and other policies, not only in nation-states but also for strengthening the surveillance process of exchange rate policies across countries, it is now time to question the utility of these forecasts.

In economics, there can be nothing like precision when the real world, which it tries to explain, is in a perpetual flux. What is arguable, however, is not the fallibility of economic forecasts so much as the take-it-from-me style of supreme confidence with which these forecasts are put out for public consumption. Knowledge is respected only when its limits are explicitly recognised, particularly when that knowledge is lapped up by men of practised affairs as inviolate truths. Economists need to be humble and follow the advice proffered by Lord Keynes long ago, that it is better to be vaguely right than precisely wrong.

The Times of India, 29 October 1991.

43

I.G. Patel qua economist and policymaker

I.G. Patel was one of the foremost new-generation economists who contributed to thinking strategically on post-Independence India's economic development and articulating the economic policy. Around the time he joined the ministry of finance, Government of India, i.e. in 1954, economics as a social discipline was in its infancy. Barring a few notable exceptions, old-timers like A.K. Dasgupta, B.P. Adarkar, V.K.R.V. Rao, J.J. Anjaria, D.R. Gadgil, Brijmohan, B.R. Ambedkar, D. Ghosh, etc., who produced meaningful analytical work and the basic data relating to national income, there was little theoretical work done by the general run of economists. Whatever passed off as economics was in the nature of adaptive research, often using non-relevant economic concepts derived from economics textbooks. In the main, the focus was on short-term period analysis based on Keynes' General Theory. It was little realised that India's problems were of long-term nature not amenable to the Keynesian policy prescriptions.

If economics was in a rudimentary stage, economic policymaking, which required analytical underpinnings and well-organised information, relied on hunches and rationalisation of what the ruling administration had already decided on political expediency. As one of the most enlightened civil servants with economic persuasion mentioned, civil servants as a class believed that "even the most difficult economic problems would yield to their brilliance even though their academic training might have been in classical Greek and Latin" (B.K. Nehru as quoted in Guhan and Shroff, 1986: 37). More or less the same view was espoused by a seasoned politician. "The civil servants", he wrote, "bring to bear on their work a body of experience acquired over their careers....Their knowledge is often rich in detail but restricted in scope. By training and temperament, they are used to the command system of giving instructions and having them carried out" (C. Subramanian as quoted in Ibid.: 26). Yet another civil servant who was involved in economic administration made a strong plea for the presence of economists in government by arguing that "the analytical grasp of economists needs to be combined with the pragmatism of an economic administrator" (Ibid.: 39).

IG, by virtue of his solid background in economics learnt at Cambridge and Harvard, filled admirably the bill as Economic Adviser as enunciated by Jha. He was trained both in micro and macroeconomics—the latter acquiring growing importance in Cambridge in the wake of Keynes' General Theory. But IG had also deep insights into the extension of Keynes' short-term analysis to the long-term time horizon, thanks to the dynamic analysis of Roy Harrod and Evsey Domar. He also imbibed development economics being shaped by Rosenstein-Rodan with a "Big Push" approach to industrialisation, Ragnar Nurkse with his emphasis on generating sufficient demand for realising economies of scale and Michael Kalecki who stressed the importance of a link between the capacity to invest and the capacity to meet the demand for wage-goods if inflation and balance-of-payments difficulties are to be warded off. However, IG never took those theories as gospel truth. His analytical mind tested them in economies such as those of Japan and Australia which were in different development phases. The Harrod-Domar analytical framework focused on raising a rate of saving for financing investment. IG questioned this strategy as the rate of growth depends not only on saving but also on how productively the saving is used (Patel 2002: 220).

IG's vision of development was multi-dimensional. He was not carried away only by economic facts or logic; he believed in cultural factors in development as well because of his findings in his Ph.D. dissertation at Cambridge. These perceptions came in useful in course of his tenure as a policymaker as he could take a broader view of his role, enabling him to accommodate or modify purely economic considerations in the context of India's history, sociology and culture.

An intriguing question that is often raised is why IG, with all his brilliance, rigorous training in the discipline and the intellectual repertoire, preferred the role of economic policymaker rather than a scholar, expanding the frontiers of knowledge. He himself mentioned in his memoirs that he made that choice because he wanted to operate in the real world. For him economics is nothing if not an instrument for "ensuring the well-being of the most deprived and downtrodden" (Patel 2002: 32). The knowledge should expand but also its harnessing for the larger social good. He displayed his high technical and theoretical ability in some papers he wrote while in the International Monetary Fund (IMF). But he was swayed by what Joan Robinson once told him. "An economic model", she said, "can not tell much more than what we tell it" (Patel 1986: 24). IG later on improved upon this by saying that "After all, it is not internal consistency but consistency with the facts of life which distinguishes an operational from a pedagogic or propagandist model of growth" (Patel 1986, p. 27). With this mental and intellectual make-up of IG, the advice of his first boss in the IMF, the famous international monetary policymaker, E.M. Bernstein, that he should be a practical economist and after the experience at the IMF he should return to his country, was promptly accepted.

IG's first stab at research was his Ph.D. thesis, "Foreign Trade and Economic Development", in which he extended the Marshallian short-period analysis to a long period with open economy. The central idea was that it is necessary "to infuse modernity, technological change and efficiency all along the line and not only in the export industry" (Patel 2002: 28). Though it was rich in insights, its framework was not fully worked out. His first analytical paper in the IMF was "India's Elasticity of Demand for Gold." He systematically dealt with the nature of Indian demand for gold, which then was a live policy issue in India, with whatever data he could gather. This was a pioneering study in many ways. He estimated the responsiveness of the demand for gold to prices and income. The innovative feature of this study was that IG used sugar consumption as a proxy for national income, in view of the absence of reliable national income data, and used the relative price of gold rather than its absolute price as an independent variable in his regression analysis. For reasons unknown, IG never published this seminal article with enormous policy significance, though it was officially circulated within the IMF.

Another major analytical contribution of IG to the understanding of economic development, particularly of India, was in the report he wrote with Bernstein on "Economic Development with Stability." This report, whose focus was more on monetary analysis than national income, was justly famous for defining the scope for "safe" deficit financing in the context of a country like India, though it was bastardised by the politicians in India. This was followed by another paper by IG and Bernstein on the significance, nature and effects of inflation. They traced the origin of inflation to the tussle of income groups in society to claim a larger share of national income than what other sections were willing to surrender without a fight. Control of inflation therefore would be effective only if this struggle for appropriating income was settled.

Another seminal paper of IG's was "Selective Credit Controls in Underdeveloped Countries." A case for selective credit policies rests on the argument that the financial intermediation process does not by itself ensure the socially optimum use of resources. IG's was the first attempt to present a cohesive, consistent and convincing case for selective credit controls on the basis of economic calculus. Though a great deal of work was done in this area in later years, IG's paper was hardly improved upon and remains a classic.

IG's article on "Trade and Payments Policy for a Developing Economy", presented at the conference of the International Economic Association in 1961 at Brissago, Italy, dealt comprehensively with the problems of balance of payments of developing countries. It showed that external imbalances act as a special and distinct constraint on the continuing growth of their economies. Drawing on the book *Accumulation of Capital* by Joan Robinson, which distinguished for the first time between the balance-of-payments gap and the inflation gap that emerges in the process of development, IG developed the gap thesis further to highlight its policy implications for trade. This idea was later formalised by Hollis Chenery as the savings and foreign exchange gaps which dominated the development debate for many years.

Though the reason for IG's preference for a policymaker's role is partly idealistic and rooted in his growing up in an impoverished country, it was by no means irrational or intellectually unconvincing. He wanted the economists in India to ponder over what his tutor and famous economist, A.C. Pigou, wrote in his classic book *Economics of Welfare*. "It is no wonder", he said, "but rather the social enthusiasm which revolts from the sordidness of mean streets and the joylessness of withered lives, that is the beginning of economic science" (Pigou 1932: 5). Keeping this in view, IG defined his mission in life "to provide practical answers to questions that arise in real life by application in a limited context of simple economic concepts, such as substitution or shifting of incidence or cost-benefit ratios" (Patel 1986: 32).

References

Guhan, S. and M. Shroff (1986). *Essays on Economic Progress and Welfare, in Honour of I.G. Patel*. New Delhi: Oxford University Press.

Patel, I.G. (2002). *Glimpses of Indian Economic Policy: Insider's View*. New Delhi: Oxford University Press.

———. (1998), *Economic Reforms and Global Change*. New Delhi: Macmillan.

———. (1986). *Essays in Economic Policy and Economic Growth*. London: Macmillan.

———. (1963). "Trade and Payments Policy for a Developing Economy", in R. Harrod and D.C. Hague (eds.), *International Trade Theory in a Developing World: Proceedings of a Conference of International Economic Association*. London: Macmillan.

Pigou, A.C. (1932). *Economics of Welfare*. London: Macmillan.

E-Social Sciences, 28 August 2005.

44

Jagdish Bhagwati—An economist ahead of his time

INDIA at last succeeded in shaking off its proverbial drift and has begun a well-orchestrated effort beginning in mid-1991 to reach its economic potential, which its admirers hoped for but its politicians and economists resisted over the last three decades. A mixed economy emerging from a belief in the 'Commanding Heights' philosophy served the intended goals for a while, but it remained immune from change even as the economy passed through profound structural transformation. There were faint efforts to change the policy framework during the 1966–1989 period, but they were thwarted by populist slogans, despite the fact that the earlier policies had neither accelerated economic growth nor contributed to national self-sufficiency.

Politicians with their myopic vision were, of course, the main culprits but "the economists' responsibility for India's failings cannot be dismissed lightly", as Bhagwati pointed out, time and again. The failure of economists reflects in a way the failure of Indian intellectuals as a class. Most of them chose the painless course of being close to the government instead of risking isolation from it through the formulation of dissenting policy views. Discussion of public policies by intellectuals thus became a mere ritual to rationalise popular and acceptable ideas, rather than a vehicle for a searching analysis of current policies and for developing independent and superior alternatives. Dissent anywhere is costly; the easier course is to go along with the fashion and be rewarded with approbation in the short run. In India this may have been particularly true as the government was important and pervasive in its patronage, largely due to the very policies that needed criticism but were thus safe from it because of a complacent intellectual class.

Bhagwati broke this mould quite emphatically. His first book on the Indian economy with his wife Padma Desai in 1970 and his second book with his soul mate T.N. Srinivasan in 1975 boldly and decisively attacked the Indian policy framework at its core, formally changing the way in which that framework was regarded earlier. They did this through rigorous economic analysis, based not just on abstract principles but also on an acute grasp of the concrete Indian reality. Besides, a deep knowledge of the comparative experiences of other developing countries was brought to bear on the analysis of Indian policy framework and its flawed nature.

These important contributions were, however, ignored to a point that Bhagwati had despaired of India undertaking the necessary economic reforms in his lifetime. He shunned returning to the theme of Indian economic policy for a while, as he felt that he would be kicking yet again against a "stone wall." To his great surprise and pleasure, the Indian economic and political landscape dramatically changed in 1991.

The first act of the government that came to power in mid-1991 with Manmohan Singh as finance minister was to announce radical reform measures exactly along the lines long advocated by Bhagwati and his co-authors. This time, "reform by storm has supplanted the reform by stealth of Mrs Gandhi's time and reform with reluctance under Rajiv Gandhi." Almost a quarter of a century after Bhagwati broke with the economists in India to urge reforms, a period during which he and his co-authors attracted opprobrium and disdain, Bhagwati is now the subject of adulation. Once marginalised and pushed to the periphery, he is now on the centre stage of economic debate. He is regarded widely as the intellectual forerunner and a theoretician of the on-going reforms. Finance Minister Manmohan Singh, spearheading the reforms, declared that India's misfortune was to wait too long to implement what Bhagwati had urged with clarity and foresight two decades earlier. The prophets are being honoured in their own lifetime, after all.

Too much was made in India of the need to alleviate poverty to the exclusion of growth. A result was that India neither had growth nor poverty reduction till the reforms got under way. Here, too, Bhagwati was prophetic. His term at the Planning Commission, where he began his India career in the Perspective Planning Division in 1965, had drawn him directly into evolving a strategy for minimum incomes for the poor. This had convinced him of the importance of growth as the key component of the anti-poverty strategy. He said in his remarkable book, known for prescience and perspicacity, *India in Transition: Freeing the Economy* (1993), that

> There was no dramatic alternative for raising the poor to minimum incomes except to increase the overall size of the pie. The inter-county differences in the share of the bottom decile where poverty was manifestly rampant just did not seem substantial enough to suggest any other alternative path....Growth therefore was indisputably conceived to be an instrumental variable, not as an objective *per se.* It is not surprising, therefore, that the assertion to the contrary by institutions and intellectuals who belatedly turned to questions of poverty in the 1970s have provided many of us who were 'present at the creation' to take the backward glance and then turn again to stare coldly and with scorn at these nonsensical claims.

These words may appear harsh, but considering what the critics and detractors have done to deter economic reforms directed at enhancing the efficiency of savings and investment, which would have raised the GDP growth rate and helped to make a major dent on poverty, the strictures are well deserved.

The real significance of Bhagwati's writings on India does not lie only in the relevance of the present Indian policy framework derived from them; it goes far beyond it. His leadership has broken the sterile mindset of Indian intellectuals, and given them a new apparatus of thought with which to look at things in a different way. It is this contribution of Bhagwati which is enduring and has already raised the level of intellectual discourse on public policy in India.

Extracted from the author's article "Intellectual Origin of Indian Economic Reform", *World* Development, 22(7), April 1994.

45

Manmohan as a *deus ex machina*

IF national elections result in change of government at the centre, which seems probable on present indications, a curtain may soon drop on one of the most remarkable careers in public life. Manmohan Singh, who by happenstance became a nonpareil finance minister in the worst of times of India's history, not only survived his full term—itself an unprecedented feat—but also surmounted all the odds stacked against him to lift the Indian economy from the rut in which it has been for a long time. During his stewardship of India's finances he transformed both himself and the economy. He came into government from academia, where his early work on Indian exports sketched but a faint contour of what he was to so resoundingly demonstrate during the last four and a half years. His baptism in economic policymaking was during Indira Gandhi's populist regime of the 1970s and the policies he pursued then barely deviated from the beaten track of the era. His bold initiative of economic retrenchment in 1975, just before the Emergency was promulgated, was an exception but it was a Hobson's choice in those circumstances, as no other policy could have saved Mrs. Gandhi's skin. The Five-Year Plan he was associated with at the Planning Commission was the same plan as before with a change in sequential order, as Raj Krishna would have put it. This was by no means his fault, as the Planning Commission has outlived its utility. His tenure at the Reserve Bank was much too short for him to make any dent on that slumbering and blundering behemoth. His stint at the South-South Commission produced only a massive tome which was soon lost in the sands of time. Manmohan could in those days throw a *bon mot* at the World

Bank Development Seminar that "the issue is not so much whether the prices are right as whether the politics is right."

When Manmohan took over as finance minister at the most critical juncture of India's history, the country saw a totally new man with a new agenda, steely determination and inner strength to discard the intellectual baggage acquired in his bygone incarnations. His journey across countries in the course of his work at the South Commission revealed to him a cosmic vision of development and causes of India's marginalisation in the world economy. He was honest enough, and smart too, to realise that some of his earlier beliefs did not serve the country well and he accepted his share of the blame. He no longer held to his early misconception that politics should be right if economics is to be right. He reversed the order and pursued right economics to correct wrong politics and in the process changed the terms of economic debate in the country. He lived dangerously with calm resignation among his power-hungry colleagues, in an ambience of suspicion, scepticism and cynicism. Yet he maintained high moral standards in his personal dealings. Facing total destruction of his policies, he dropped half, after the fashion of a proverbial wise man. He remained a pragmatist in the best sense of the term in a world of asseverative ideologues and staid bureaucrats. When he faced resistance from some recalcitrant colleagues within his vicinity, he was firm and unremitting in shoving them off to be replaced by economists and civil servants who had the same commitments as he to the reforms. He even inducted a stormy petrel among Indian economists who was ploughing a lonely furrow, being ignored for the advocacy of the very ideas which constituted the central features of his new policies. His effectiveness as the helmsman at the country's finances was his admirable ability to see a thing clearly and as a whole. That is why, despite the inevitable compromises he had to enter, not all of his own volition, he could maintain the main structure of his policies unfrayed. He was never a fortissimo in explaining his policies; he preferred to focus on the basic policy parameters in his own unassuming way and to communicate the major messages to his countrymen.

Perhaps for the first time, the Indian finance minister could be a major player on the international stage. In the Madrid annual meeting of the IMF-World Bank, Manmohan could call the bluff of the industrial countries on SDR allocation, which eventually led to the defeat of their proposal at the Interim Committee. The mantle of leadership of G24 countries fell on him without his seeking it. With all his sophistication and a formidable intellectual repertoire, he could not have succeeded but for the fact that he had behind him a strong economy largely of his own making. I.G. Patel, another eminent Indian, had in the past similarly dominated the international gatherings with the same *savoir faire* as Manmohan, but his efforts were in vain, because he was representing a supplicating economy.

Manmohan has, of course, a phalanx of detractors who would revile his policies on the ground that there is nothing new in his so-called new economic policy. This is no more than an *ad hominem* attack on his persona. Manmohan has not invented new economics nor does he make that claim. All that Manmohan did was to put a sprint in the muscles and bones of the Indian economy so that it could grow faster than in the past, thereby telescoping the distance between itself and the other countries in its neighbourhood. The leftists amongst his critics can learn from a Communist historian, Eric Hobsbawn, who said of China, "One Socialist country in the 1970s was particularly worried by its relative backwardness, if only because its neighbour Japan was the most spectacularly successful capitalist state." It is to the credit of Manmohan that he made politicians of all persuasions aware of this desideratum.

With his astute and imaginative leadership of the economy, Manmohan transformed India in a more fundamental way. The reforms he unleashed remained skin-deep towards the end of his tenure as finance minister; he could not build a solid institutional infrastructure to ensure their continuity without a dominating personality like his. In the initial stages, when the opposition was vulnerable and the political leadership of his own party was groping in the dark to find solutions to the complex economic problems, he had many degrees of freedom, which he could have exploited to the full to bring about a systemic change in policymaking. But a weak-kneed prime minister, steeped in the manipulative culture and opportunism of the Congress party, put the spanner in the running wheels of reform. There is *déjà vu* about the functioning of the finance ministry. Its officials still continue to micro-manage the economy; the Banking Division in the ministry, an anachronism, is still there. There has been no attempt to build a body of technocrats and policymakers who, through continuous and sustained staff work, can maintain the momentum of reforms and generate a flow of new ideas in an evolving economic situation. If any outsider is to be inducted, the finance minister has to go through the same rigmarole of recruitment procedures as before. When Manmohan and his few trusted colleagues leave the stage, there is no knowing whether the apparatchiks who were shoved to the wings will not be back at the helm to truncate the reforms. But one thing is certain: that the forces Manmohan has unleashed will carry the Indian economy onward to reach its long-cherished economic destiny.

March 1996, unpublished.

46

Let there be *tabula rasa*

THE new Prime Minister struck the right note, though self-servingly, both in his address to the nation and in his reply in Parliament before the confidence vote was passed. He espoused a culture of consensus, not conflicts; amity, not animus; bonhomie, not belligerence. Leaving aside for a while the question whether the term consensus, though sounding opposition-friendly, is an appropriate vehicle for putting through a cohesive and consistent programme of economic reform, the sentiments he exuded might do a lot of good and, in any case, could not do harm to the Indian polity.

The real problem is how one proceeds to avoid occurrence of conflict. Ever since Rajiv Gandhi came to power, one scandal or another has become the country's staple politics. Had it not been for Bofors, V.P. Singh would not have become prime minister. Without Narasimha Rao's skulduggery there would not have been the Humpty-Dumpty government of the United Front. If Jayalalithaa's treasure of ladies' shoes and sarees had not overshadowed Imelda Marcos' wardrobe, the DMK government would not have been enthroned in Chennai; if there were no fodder scam, the Janata Dal would not have been decimated as a political force. The present government could not have been conceived if that stormy petrel Mamata Banerjee was not fired with a mission to expose the incipient scandal of the CPM government in West Bengal. And finally, Madam Gandhi would not have entered into the political arena, thwarting the BJP's tantalising majority, if the needle of suspicion were not swirling towards her late husband.

It is, thus, common sense that the cause of conflict can be removed only if amnesty for all parties involved in corruption is declared.

Could it be a moral outrage to do so? Certainly not. The new government, in consultation with all political parties, should decide that the ghosts of all public scandals should be buried, with the assurance that from now on, new rules would bind all the parties to a common ethical code. With all the apparent mendacity of this suggestion, it is only a political equivalent of tax amnesty, under which chronic and habituated tax-evaders are protected from the arm of law. If we as a nation were not outraged with such frequently resorted tax amnesties, it is utter hypocrisy to claim a high ground when it comes to politicians.

An economist can justify such amnesty as a 'second best' alternative; a political scientist can invoke the fundamental law of the 'art of the possible' to support it. A philosopher does not have any hesitation in rationalising it as 'existentialism' in its pristine purity; a modern artist can find a parallel for this in his dictum that images reside in the eyes of the beholder and not in form. The pragmatist, whose credo is 'useful is real', will see virtue in it. So the Indian prime minister can be all these rolled into one, if he declares political amnesty.

The notion of calling truce in regard to all scandals is not as fatuous as it may seem. Whatever its moral connotation, it is pre-eminently sensible. During the last forty years of independence, perhaps only one (*mea culpa* if wrong) scandal has been promptly decided in court and the culprit sent to jail. That is Haridas Mundhra: and for a much smaller crime than any of the present ones. Otherwise, not a single criminal act—be it the massacre of Sikhs in Delhi or Muslims in Mumbai or the Harshad Mehta swindle or the fodder scam in Bihar, not to speak of Bofors—has been punished. Millions of rupees have been squandered, countless battles have been fought, and the upshot of all this is the unsettling political process.

Calling quits, however, should be followed by instituting a new code of conduct, which would be possible only if a new legal body, insulated from political influence, is set up. Appointment to this tribunal will be made by the President from a panel recommended by the Chief Justice of India, the Prime Minister, and the leader of the largest opposition group in Parliament. The members are to be appointed on a non-renewable basis, until the end of their stipulated tenure. In the event of differences in the panel, the vote of the Chief Justice should be binding. The government should give top priority to overhauling the judiciary at all levels, which is even more important than economic reforms, to avoid delays in justice and to put in place time-saving special procedures for political and economic offences of all types. The investigating agencies should be independent of the ruling party and their panel should be appointed in the same way as the tribunal.

At one stroke, the political and economic crimes, which are at the root of poor governance, burgeoning corruption and political chicanery would be taken out of the hands of politicians and left to the impartial bodies, which are best equipped to dispense justice impartially, transparently, and equitably.

It is foolhardy to believe that the political process would be purified overnight; but at least its parameters would be set out. No prime minister of the country, including Nehru, has taken such a revolutionary step to ensure a culture of amity and good-fellow feeling. With all this, the Vajpayee government may fall, but even a few months of honest rule are worth a decade of stable but debauching, debasing and demeaning regime.

Business Standard, 10 June 1998.

47

The static world of intellectuals

INTELLECTUALS in India are a strange breed. They are generally somnolent, and when they stir up it is only to harp on their well-entrenched prejudices. Barring a few intrepid persons of character and some persistent civil rights groups the reactions of Indian intellectuals to events in Kashmir and Punjab have been on familiar lines, not different from those of the general run of politicians to whom intellectualism is anathema, or those of professional patriots for whom anything that departs from the beaten track is treason.

But come new changes in economy policy or some moves by the Americans, and these intellectuals spring to life and react in Pavlovian fashion. A relaxation by government of its policy towards foreign investment is equated with a sell-out to rapacious imperialists, without caring to know whether foreign investment is good or bad or whether the foreign capitalist is willing to enter the Indian bureaucratic jungle to reap profits. No thought will be given to the sea-change in the world's capital markets and technology or the relative advance of India's competitors in the international markets. Those of the rightist mindset behave similarly. For them the private sector is a deity that needs to be worshipped no matter whether it functions efficiently or not. The same holds true about anything that concerns America, be it regarding refuelling facilities for US aircraft or the invasion of Iraq.

No one should condone America for the hubris of power and riches. Certain actions of America may not dovetail into a predetermined mould. The recent invasion of Iraq, spearheaded by

America, may have been distasteful but that by itself does not make Saddam Hussein a champion of the Arab cause. And yet many Indian intellectuals paraded Saddam Hussein as a folk hero and the American war against him was stigmatised as a war waged by the white race against all non-white races.

There was little analysis of the Arab problem and its historical antecedents. Consider the one Davis Price-Jones has done in his rightly acclaimed book, *Closed Circle*. He has documented chapter and verse how Arabs through the centuries have pursued a paradigm of shame and honour. They mouth democracy, socialism or anti-imperialism, but the organising principle of their polity is oppression, with every available strategy, of all those within reach. They have killed more of their own people over the last four hundred years than their western imperialist tormentors have. Witness how the hordes of Kurds and Shias trudging away from their co-religionist hero beseech the infidels for succour. Not that Price-Jones is always right or that Arabs are always sinners, but he has at least adduced historical evidence to examine the Arab question through logic and reason, which is what intellectuals are supposed to do. If the conclusions are unpalatable so be it.

Looking at Indian intellectuals since 1945, one is amazed how their view of the world has remained static. The aura of communism as a philosophy faded during the 1960s, prompting the communists in countries from Italy to France to Spain to question their beliefs. The capitalism Marx defined and condemned has changed radically both in structure and functions. Science and technology have changed production relations. Colonialism has lost its earlier demonic quality since post-colonial regimes have committed even more heinous crimes against their own people than their colonial forebears. But all these events have passed by Indian intellectuals. Their thesis and antithesis have remained the same. They have continued to be slaves of myriad defunct doctrines and defeated societies.

One cannot but contrast the reflexes of most Indian intellectuals with those of their counterparts in the West. Many from academia and research institutes were rabidly anti-communist at the beginning of the Vietnam War. But once the tragedy began to unfold even the conservative think-tanks started rethinking. They regrouped their theories, dipped into their inner conscience, revised their conclusions and, like Noam Chomsky of MIT, led the battle against the administration of President Johnson.

They have already begun to raise questions about the 'new world order' to the point of calling it 'new world orders' for armaments. They have hauled the Bush administration over the coals for placating Israel and ingratiating Saddam Hussein prior to August 1990. Their commitment to objectivity is not diluted by their ideological preferences. Even the Reagan conformists of the early 1980s have now excoriated Reaganomics for making the American educational system a wasteland.

In Margaret Thatcher's country, her former intellectual comrades, who were strong supporters of hands-off kind of social policy planning have discarded their earlier beliefs on seeing how pernicious these could be.

This raises a pertinent question whether many Indian intellectuals are at all intellectual. We may be highly gifted with intelligence but we need to perceive prevailing social and political reality in its interconnectedness and as a part of the historical process. This role places an onerous responsibility on intellectuals to tell the truth as they perceive it and to have the honesty to admit past mistakes. It is only when you have the courage to admit you could be wrong that you can hope to be right. Since truth-seeking is a major goal, the intellectual should see that his criticism, in Marx's famous words, "will not shrink either from its own conclusions or from conflict with the powers that be."

We had a rich intellectual tradition in the pre-independence period. Should we not then, as a class, emulate men like G.K. Gokhale, B.R. Ambedkar, M.N. Roy, who could analyse each issue on its merit, clinically subject it to scrutiny and come to a conclusion free from their individual preferences?

The Times of India, 17 November 1991.

48

Social research boondoggles

IN public debate on governmental fiscal deficit and the outlook to rein it in attention is often focused on expenditure on the size of the civil service and maintenance of policy. It is seldom realised that the government has been spending enormous amounts of money on the establishment of a large number of social research institutions, particularly those devoted to research on economic policy. These are funded directly by the central and state governments and a few parastatal bodies like the Reserve Bank, developmental and commercial banks. Their finance does not end with the initial grants. It is a continuing, self-perpetuating affair.

Such has been the growth of these institutions in the last forty years that it has outpaced not only the measly rate of growth of India's income but also its usually frowned-upon rate of population growth. And yet so little is known about the quality of research generated by them and the amount of public money expended on their nourishment. No questions are raised whether these institutions contributed in any significant way to the enrichment of economic, political and social policies and whether the benefits of research are commensurate with the enormous cost incurred in maintaining them.

Many of these institutions are supposed to be think-tanks but they often fail to think. The promises made in the beginning are forgotten once the infrastructure is in place. Except a few honourable research outfits which have made a name for themselves nationally and internationally and received accolades for their high-quality research, most of them have produced mediocre and puerile stuff. Some of them compile volumes that include out-of-date and indifferent articles published elsewhere or the instantly prepared seminar papers recycling trite and worn-out ideas. Of course, an impressive army of publications is brought out at times under their imprimatur. But most of them would not have been accepted for publication by either publishers or academic journals of repute.

Various gimmicks are adopted to make these publications attractive to the not-so-well-informed readers. Outlandish economic oxymorons such as 'moneyless monetary economy' or 'vertical industry in a horizontal economy' are used as titles to peddle them. There is, however, no fear of a lack of market for them. The institutions finance a publisher and guarantee the market through an arrangement under which they themselves buy the bulk of them. Thus, a lucky publisher makes a double killing—first, when he is awarded the contract and, second, when he sells them back to the benefactor.

Those familiar with academic and research institutions abroad know that there should be well-defined guidelines for judging the quality of research. Every institution worth its name assigns this task to internal and external referees who have specialised in the respective fields—the former screen research projects at the proposal stage and the latter decide whether the output is worth publishing. An extremely small number of papers prepared at these institutions are published in academic journals either in India or abroad. What little quality stuff there is in the country is produced by those devoted academics slogging away resolutely at the universities in Calcutta and Delhi and the Indian Statistical Institute—the traditional seats of learning.

Thus, the only way for researchers at these centres to leap into the limelight is to bring out pamphlets or books incorporating their low-valued, high-volume research. When research thus degenerates, these institutes engage themselves in organising some seminar or the other on some eye-catching topics, again sponging on the government. Here again the papers submitted are the free-for-all kind of stuff. The discussions are often at a level that makes even ignorant politicians look scholarly.

At one such seminar in Delhi attended by some foreign luminaries a researcher from one of these institutions made a profound statement that "public sector enterprises cannot be eliminated by the government because of unanimity about their need across all spectra of political opinions." Even better is a discovery in one of the seminars in Bombay that "devaluation is a tool of the imperialists to exploit the LDCs" or "exporting is bad when Indian people are starving at home." Yet another way that these so-called research institutions keep themselves busy is through conducting graduate courses for awarding M.Phil. or Ph.D. degrees despite the proliferation of such universities in every nook and cranny of India.

Several research institutions have become magnets for retired bureaucrats, diplomats, former government and semi-government economists who even in their heyday did not produce any worthwhile research beyond writing notes on office files. There are some diplomats with no more than a nodding acquaintance with economics who suddenly become economic policy wizards and occupy one of the chairs endowed either by the finance ministry or the Reserve Bank. They do not fail to bring their bureaucratic culture to the institutions. Peons must be there to carry their briefcases and secretaries should stand by to loyally serve them. These old minions attach themselves to the coattails of their migratory bosses and together succeed in giving these institutions the appearance of geriatric wards. At one of the international conferences a foreign scholar on seeing grey-haired researchers from India whispered within hearing distance of others that Indian research institutions are the wineries where research ability matures with age.

The *Economist* of London recently categorised the best and the worst research institutes in a number of countries, both developed and developing. The best, it said, "combines intellectual depth, political influence, a flair for publicity, comfortable surroundings. Such institutes are few in India. But the worst have qualities of pedantry, irrelevance, obscurity."

Most of them are like waiting rooms where the younger members entertain themselves with whatever fare is on the table until such time as better prospects are found. The retired wait for a place on some committee or other, of which there is no dearth in India. Is it not time that the public and government wake up to find out how public funds are being used in the name of social research? There is no audit for accountability. These institutions have become pyramids—a material structure built on a broad supporting base of perks and comforts, but with a narrow research atop.

The Times of India, 15 April 1992.

49

A malady of reservations

FOR those in India who were affected by former Prime Minister V.P. Singh's decision to set a quota of jobs reserved for the backward classes, recent developments in America about affirmative action may bring some sobering thoughts. The backward classes phenomenon or its significance for electoral politics is not confined to a traditional society like India with its baggage of caste and religion. It is an equally live issue in this most modern of societies with arguments not totally dissimilar to those raised in India.

Much emotion and prejudice is often invested in controversies in which real issues are totally sidelined. The issues are explicitly exploited for political ends and no one fights shy of it. In an open polity, where support for policy can be obtained only through political action, to do otherwise is to exhibit political immaturity.

Until 1961, the blacks in America posed a dilemma for American society, as Gunnar Myrdal pointed out in his work on the problem. Here was the race of slaves grafted on to an essentially white society. However, as the polity progressed towards democracy, it was soon realised that denial of elementary human rights to a large minority was inconsistent with its democratic pretensions. The blacks were, as late as the early 1960s, the drawers of water and hewers of wood. It was only during the "great society" that President Johnson projected through a wide-ranging affirmative programme that the blacks could break into the inner parts of American society.

They received all possible privileges in academia and workplaces to erase their oppressive past. They since then have been brought into the mainstream; the number of blacks in business, industry and the service sector has reached a point that a new educational and enlightened middle class has emerged with much greater clout.

However, the very success of affirmative action has evoked a counter-reaction from the white majority. A clamour has been raised about the alleged fall in quality standards in education as well as in government and other private services because of the quotas assigned to blacks. There have been legal battles galore and, in consequence, affirmative action has been weakened. During the Reagan era, the party in power attempted for the first time to reverse the process. The Bush administration first passed legislation about six months ago to limit the quotas at workplaces but was forced to back down when Congress opposed his action strongly and persistently.

In the nature of things, affirmative action is a second-best alternative and it is futile to argue that it denies the majority the opportunities which it would get on its own. The concept of merit and the criteria that govern its determination are relative terms and are not independent of the cultural background. The merit tests, often based on the cultural, social and educational background of the majority, discriminate against minorities like the blacks and the Hispanics in American society.

The National Academy of Sciences came out with its severe strictures on the unfairness of the test. While application of rank-order, top-down hiring based on test results produces some productivity gains, sole reliance on these tests spawns some brutal consequence for the minorities. The Academy asserted that the use of tests can be an engine for the exclusion of racial minorities more permanent and thorough than individual ill will. The racially unfair tests are the norm, not the exception.

Indians need not lament why such minority-related issues should dominate politics in India. Moves are already afoot in the American political arena to exploit these issues for the 1992 presidential election. The Republicans have seen these issues as the Achilles heel of the Democrats, particularly when there is a backlash from the white establishment in the south and mid-west.

But this is not the view of all Republicans. They see the workplace quotas and other forms of minority preferences as potentially more explosive issues that will enter in the electoral calculus and they are moderating the stance of the Republicans at the extreme right. Black interests can be ignored but certainly not their votes. Is it any different from the behaviour of the Indian political parties?

And yet what is different here is the attitude of the emerging black middle class, which is not sold wholly on affirmative action as an antidote to the ills of the blacks. Michael Williams, chief of civil rights enforcement at the US Department of Education, boldly gave a ruling against race-designated scholarships in federally funded educational institutions.

Though the decision was reversed by President Bush, the guts of this intrepid black administrator are widely admired. It is now increasingly felt by high achievers among blacks that discriminatory treatment of blacks as a community is castrating, both intellectually and psychologically. It demeans their legitimate achievements and degrades them to a genre of inferior human beings.

Shelby Steele writes in his book *The Content of Our Character*:

> We have as a race been very good at the exercise of collective power. On the other hand, it is not anti-black, it is not neo-conservatism, to say that we have not put enough responsibility on the shoulders of individuals. We are, therefore, in the odd and self-defeating position in which taking responsibility for bettering ourselves feels like a surrender to white power.

The blacks thus are coming of age, at least they are beginning to. While this is a consequence of the effectiveness of past affirmative action, its limits as a future policy are being reached. The collectivity of the black is different from the individual black person. If you are successful, you don't require crutches which go only with failure. That such consciousness is lacking among backward class intellectuals in India is as rank a failure of the way affirmative action is enforced in India as the rank opportunism of the political leadership.

The Times of India, 13 January 1991.

50

The Indian State corrupts absolutely

A few years ago, Milton Friedman, Keynes' intellectual and ideological adversary, justified, to the surprise of many, Keynes' advocacy of state intervention in economy on the ground that it held true in Keynes' small and homogeneous country. This unusual and fascinating observation of Friedman needs to be recalled in the ongoing debate on governance in the context of economic reforms. On either side of the divide on this controversial issue there is an iota of truth. A modern civil society puts premium on both positive and negative freedoms defined by Isaiah Berlin. The first of these implies an absence of any restraint on individual freedom. But this does not ensure that the unrestrained individual will not encroach on the freedom of others. For this negative freedom is necessary. State intervention acquires its *raison d'être* in ensuring these two freedoms—one, empowering the citizens to develop capabilities to exercise their choices in all spheres without fear of being prevented from doing so; and two, providing institutions, legal safeguards and property rights to forestall arbitrary action. When the State transgresses this limit, it impairs both these freedoms. However, the domain of the State is specific to the social conditions, institutional environment, cultural traits and political traditions. In some societies the State can extend its jurisdiction to a wider area of people's lives without any pernicious consequences. But what is good for the goose may not necessarily be good for the gander. There are other countries where public servants are incapable of maintaining distance from the special interests and connected people, thereby creating a space for rampant corruption and misuse of State power. It is, therefore, sterile to discuss the role of the State in isolation from the particular social and political characteristics of the countries, as Friedman argued.

One can find a parable for the role of the State in India in the anthropological observations of one of India's perceptive social scientists, Prakash Reddy. He studied a Danish village 'Hvilaager', registering with great care his impressions of its residents and the relationship amongst them over a period of a year. His findings are startling. Reddy was astounded to see that the villagers hardly knew each other; they did not exchange visits with each other often; and social contacts amongst them were almost non-existent; they had little information about what other villagers, including their next-door neighbours, were doing and evinced no curiosity to find out how they conducted their daily lives. Even the relationship between parents and children was not very close. When children reached adulthood, they moved out and visited their parents rarely.

Reddy then contrasted these observations with his experiences in Indian villages, where everyone is nosy in making affairs of others his own. Beyond the family is the caste or religion and the interrelationship amongst the members within each group is as intimate as within the family.

These contrasting pictures of two villages have important implications for the role of the State and the corruption that is bred by it. In the Danish village the public servants will not be able to keep a close relationship with others; that ensures more impartial decision making in matters of public interest. On the other hand, a society like the one that mirrors the Indian village creates a fertile ground for sprouting corruption. Those who know the functionaries of the State would ask for favours and be given without much ado. Those without connections will be left out on a limb. If some strong-willed public servant decides to break the web of interrelationships that allows personalism, cronyism and pecuniary gains, his behaviour will be taken as conflicting with the acceptable social and cultural norm that close relatives, caste and religious loyalties should come first. This means that an arm's-length relationship, that is of paramount importance for State intervention to succeed for the well-being of all citizens, can not simply be built up in a county like India. No wonder that with the pervasive influence of the State in the Indian economic processes over the years not only did India get economics wrong but also it got corruption right, bestowing on the country the dubious international honour of being the sixth most corrupt nation in the world.

Why then are our intellectuals crowding out their scarce time in singing hosannas about the benign State and lamenting that the reforms are undermining it? The reason is the same as Reddy discovered in the Indian village. There has been an incestuous relationship amongst intellectuals, bureaucrats, politicians, and even private entrepreneurs that has given them an access to unearned riches; and if the State is marginalised to be a mere facilitator rather than a custodian, they all will lose their rent which they so egregiously harvested during the last fifty years of freedom.

Business Standard, 16 September 1997.

51

Blossoming in a foreign land

AN American wag once asked me why India should not be plucked from its geographical location in Asia and transplanted to the American continent. Reading about India's inefficiencies in economic management and the poverty there, in contrast to what Indians have been achieving in industry, academia and science in the US, he reasoned that the whole country would do well in a different milieu. This hyperbole concealed the disturbing fact that Indians blossomed to their full potential in a social and economic environment radically different from the one in which they were born and have grown.

The other day, the *Wall Street Journal*, quintessentially waspish, carried a full-blown article on a soon-to-be steel baron on the world stage, Ispat's Laxmi Mittal. In a short span of some fifteen years, this dashing dynamo changed the face of every steel plant he touched, be it in Indonesia, Mexico, Kyrgyzstan, and now the US. He took over what to begin with were lemons, overhauled their organisation, introduced innovation and made them high-profile steel plants. The *Wall Street Journal* went even further in foretelling that Mittal now had few rivals and in the none-too-distant future he may well emerge as a new messiah in steel technology, surpassing even the best in Japan. The author of the article asked Mittal why he did not do in India what he did elsewhere. Mittal's reply was crisp and sharp:

> If I were to buy an existing steel mill in India, I would have spent more than half of my life in chasing the bureaucrats and the politicians. On the other hand, in every other country where I transacted my business, it did not take me more than a few months.

The inventor of Bose speakers, who wanted to set up a plant in the land of his birth, has his own tale to tell, and it is no different from Laxmi Mittal's.

Mittal, of course, has hogged the headlines in the western press. But there are hundreds of such young entrepreneurs blazing the economic horizon of western countries. A young couple, Raj and Neera Singh, has taken the high-tech cell phone business by storm. Some eight years ago, they landed in the US from Kanpur IIT with nothing but their brains. They worked their guts into in a small apartment in Virginia experimenting with an idea of evolving a new cell phone technology that would drastically curtail the cost. They sold the idea to a telecommunication agency for a pittance. However, realising the value of the invention, the agency provided them with financial wherewithal. Now, the Singhs have turned into billionaires, spreading their wings to the federal government and major industries. Sudhakar Shenoy, voted outstanding entrepreneur in the Washington area for 1998 for up-scaling information technology, is yet another star on the firmament. Coming from nowhere, how could these Indians dominate the foreign lands? It is not as if those who migrate are transformed into geniuses the moment they enter the western hemisphere.

It is not merely economic Darwinism that drives the human spirit in western societies. There needs to be an incentive-compatible system and the cost of transacting business has to be minimum for the enterprise and the entrepreneurs to thrive. Under the first, inefficiency is punished and innovation is rewarded, while under the second, the markets tend to function more efficiently. High transaction costs, as Nobel laureate Douglas North pointed out, are major deterrents to the flowering of individuals and advancement of nations. Individuals typically act on incomplete information, North argued, with subjectively derived models that are not infrequently erroneous. To overcome that, information feedback is a prior condition for efficiency of outcome which low transaction costs alone can ensure. Sadly, India is cursed by the political state and the uncongenial social institutions which tend to cumulate the transaction costs of doing business, and it is that which renders the enterprise nugatory.

What is true of Indians in industry and commerce abroad is true, as well, of Indians in academia. Just look at the luminous circle of front-rank Indian economists: A.K. Sen, Jagdish Bhagwati, T.N. Srinivasan, and Avinash Dixit, and their younger colleagues, Raj Sah, Dileep Abreu, or the management scientists, Pankat Gamavat, Amar Bide, and Prahalad. They have all thrived and reached the acme of their intellectual career in a liberal and competitive academic environment where no favour is asked nor given. For every step in the ladder of promotion in the universities, it is their achievement in the respective fields, acknowledged by their peers, which was the decisive factor.

Not that all Indians who adorn the western academia are a superior breed. Many in Indian universities are as gifted as those who have become world-renowned scientists, but their early promise is betrayed, as is evident from their minuscule contributions to respective disciplines. The reason is simple. There is no incentive structure in place which draws the best from the academic community. Once they enter the university as lecturer or reader, their progress to full professorship is virtually automatic. There is no anxiety about tenure nor any obligation to earn it. The great astrophysicist, S. Chandrasekhar, a Nobel laureate, once said ruefully that he could not have become the scientist that he is in India, what with its patronage system, familial bonds, governmental interference, and lack of objective standards of assessment, which patriotism, however abiding, could have exorcised.

Business Standard, 10 October 1998.

Part III

Lest India forgets

52

Manu Shroff: Economist with pride as his carapace

IN emerging independent India during the early 1950s, government service, particularly its highly competitive administrative echelon with its prestige, power and perks was the ultimate nirvana for young educated Indians, even those endowed with specialised skills in mathematics, natural sciences, and engineering, which had low employment value. The private sector had low esteem, being considered a habitat for money-grabbing 'Boxwallas.' It was also difficult for qualified aspirants to consider entry into it, since it was largely family based, where networking and nepotism were paramount virtues.

The universe of government service expanded significantly in the late 1950s with the onset of an activist State committed to planning and with a new perspective on what public policy ought to be in an impoverished country, aiming at higher level of economic development with a pronounced egalitarian bias. This changed radically the focus of the government on how to run the administration. A 'look back and go forward' attitude and its concomitant feature of the command system of passing orders and ensuring that they were faithfully carried out were out of tune with the demands of the new situation. Realising this desideratum, the government reprised its old ideas of governance, leading to change in the role of the finance ministry in regard to implementation of the new economic paradigm. Since this could not have been achieved by the outdated administrative system, the government redefined the requirements of some civil servants and started recruiting economists trained in high-valued economic discipline so that they would become problem-solvers rather than problem-creators through procrastinating the implementation of economic programmes, citing precedents and interpreting or misinterpreting the rigmarole of rule books.

It was at the dawn of a new approach to the nation's development and its instrumentalities that many Indians, specialising in advanced economics and quantitative techniques, trooped into the economic policymaking apparatus of the government of India, particularly the finance and commerce ministries and the Planning Commission.

Manu Shroff, who passed away on 29 January 2007 after a long and traumatic battle with cancer, was one of those stars who joined the finance ministry after an illustrious academic career at the Bombay University and the London School of Economics (LSE). Though he passed the Bar examination in England, he changed his mind to become an economist after he met some of the leading lights in economics at the LSE. On return to India, he found initially few openings for a career in his chosen field. He then joined the Associated Chamber of Commerce and Industry (Assocham), Delhi. He came face to face with India's stunted growth but also realised that the so-called captains of industry and trade had an ostrich-like vision of what needed to be done for India's rapid industrialisation. He was soon disillusioned and was thinking of switching to the legal profession. It was precisely at this juncture that the finance ministry started a recruitment drive for economists. It was the most exciting time in the ministry, with J.J. Anjaria heading the economic wing after his tenure at the International Monetary Fund (IMF) and the Reserve Bank of India and the charismatic and nonpareil I.G. Patel as second in command. With these at the helm, the intellectual milieu in the ministry underwent a sea-change, with intuition, hunches and the 'experience shows' culture no more the guides in conceptualising and operationalising economic policies. With a dream team in place, the foundations for a knowledge-based economic policy were firmly laid.

Manu's forte was going to the first principles, which enabled him to think clearly, without mistaking trees for the woods. When confronted with intricate problems, he looked at the broad canvas but did not overlook the warp and weft of irksome details. He was aware of short-term macroeconomics awaiting quick answers but rarely lost sight of the long-term developmental framework within which it had to be situated. This was evident in his work as a member of the Resources Working Group charged with determining a feasible level of deficit financing during each plan period. He was practical without being starry eyed; dedicated to the developmental goals without being economical on facts so that he would not hesitate to backtrack from commitment to unsustainable growth fantasies, if the facts on hand indicated otherwise; and punctilious without being a risk-averter. He never gave convenient advice to please his superiors but abided by the decision handed down to him even when it did not conform to his reasoning. Here he conflated academic discipline with the bureaucratic imperative. That was why he commanded respect from his superiors. At one of the Aid India Club meetings in Paris, which he attended as an Alternate Executive Director on the World Bank, he spotted an error in the export figures in the document that his bosses brought from Delhi. He was ignored by the chief of the delegation, who was his superior. The error was pointed out in course of the discussions by the World Bank economist, to the embarrassment of his colleagues. Manu had a quiet smile but without croaking.

Manu belonged to a rare breed of bureaucrats who never ran foul of his superiors, getting the sobriquet of 'Man Friday.' His association with I.G. Patel was legendary. There were many occasions when he presented the views of his office without clearance from Delhi for want of time. IG had confidence that Manu would never deviate from the general line of thinking of the ministry. They were intellectual soul-mates to perfection. S. Jagannathan, former finance secretary and Governor of the Reserve Bank, trusted his judgement on economic matters. At one of the consultation meetings with the IMF, the head of the Fund delegation made some offensive remarks about policymaking in India, using economic jargon. Jagannathan knew the hollowness of the strictures but before rebutting, he took Manu aside to check with him what he wanted to say, particularly its underlying economic logic. The same was true of Manu's relationship with that great economist, V.K. Ramaswami, who was the Chief Economic Adviser. In several meetings, whether in the Planning Commission or with foreign delegations, Ramaswami often directed the questions addressed to him for answers to Manu sitting behind him. So much was the trust and confidence reposed in Manu by his bosses.

Manu's amiability and self-discipline to work within the ambit of the labyrinthine bureaucracy without rocking the boat—many of his friends felt—contributed to the blighting of his creative talents and economic scholarship. He was widely read in economics and other subjects and had a flair for original thinking but did not allow himself to blossom intellectually, like his close friend and colleague V.K. Ramaswami. But whatever little he did was precious enough to be noticed. He once wrote a paper for an international conference on development, arguing that foreign debt-servicing burden on developing economies could be whittled down if it were linked with expanding trade among them. But his paper remained in the unpublished proceedings of the conference. A few years later, the same seminal idea with a little more analytical underpinning was put forth independently by another Indian economist and Professor R.N. Cooper of the Harvard University, which received wide academic acclaim. When a friend asked Manu why he had not published his paper in any academic journal of repute, his insouciant reply, somewhat redolent of Satyen Bose, was, "It does not matter so long as it is there in the literature." This was Manu—of original bent of mind without a desire for self-promotion and public adulation. The same attitude of submerging his intellectual persona unfortunately diminished his contribution to some policy issues. As a member of the committee on financial sector reforms appointed by the Ministry of Finance in 1991, he and another member, Mrinal Dutta Choudhari, did not go the whole hog in recording their minute of dissent despite their serious reservations about the main thrust of the report, which was a gallimaufry of 'running with the hare and hunting with the hounds' kind of arguments.

Perhaps, Manu's long-held belief system kept his originality dormant. He placed a premium on bureaucrats remaining faceless and impersonal. Many of his friends and family members often urged him to take to writing but he nodded away their entreaties. Anyone who reads his masterly article on globalisation, published in the *Economic and Political Weekly* a few years ago, would realise how much the subject has lost by his self-denial.

Unfortunately, his belief system, which came in the way of his writing, and his loyalty to the government he served received a jolt later in his career. He was an additional secretary in the finance ministry after his distinguished record in the World Bank-IMF

Development Committee and was senior enough to become either a Chief Economic Adviser or finance secretary. But all this went up in smoke when a paranoid and vindictive Indira Gandhi staged a comeback. Identifying Manu with her bête noire, Morarji Desai, she shunted him to the Planning Commission—that quango for geriatric and functionless bureaucracy. Frustrated but with his honour intact, he resigned, against the advice of his friends. He then joined the Indian Institute of Management, Ahmedabad, as a professor and soon after became the editor of *The Economic Times*.

As an editor, Manu distinguished himself as an editorial writer, with intricate arguments pithily put and succinct and subtle reasoning, avoiding journalistic mumbo-jumbo. He focused on the basic issues of public policy, which raised informed debate. He started a new feature for invited economists like Anand Chandavarkar and others to write on some great economists like Richard Kahn.

Manu's honour was partially restored with the departure of the Rajiv Gandhi regime. He was made a member of the Finance Commission and also offered concurrent membership of the Planning Commission, which he turned down, being never enamoured of that effete body.

Manu for all his misfortunes was blessed with a wonderful wife—an economist in her own right and a member of the Indian Administrative Service. She was a real life-partner, sharing with him both joys and sorrows. When Manu was denied his due in the government, she opted out of a post of secretary at the Centre and chief secretary with the Gujarat government as a sort of silent protest against the injustice done to her husband. She instead took up a junior post as a Gujarat government representative in Bombay to be with Manu.

Manu took his triumphs and travails in stride without rejoicing or remorse, a hallmark of equanimity. He had a horde of friends and admirers. He often went out of his way to help others. His altruism, compassion and genuine interest in people around him bring to mind the lines of Walt Whitman,

> I dream'd i-n a dream I saw a city invincible to
> The attacks of the whole of the earth;
> I dream'd that was the new city of Friends

Economic and Political Weekly, 3 February 2007.

53

B.S. Minhas: Prescribing rationality

ECONOMICS more than pure sciences is bedevilled by many methodological conundrums which lead economists like Kaushik Basu to assign greater weight to 'intuition and knack.' There was first a positivist *versus* normative controversy. It played out for some time, terminating in a sort of reconciliation of the opposite views, leaving yet some grey areas of non-consensus. In the second half of the twentieth century, this methodological debate is superseded by a new one of theory *versus* empirics. Does a theory set the stage for application of economics to solving the problem of economic well-being? Or is it the other way round that empirical findings dispel the priors and weave the strands of a more reliable theoretical structure? This dyarchy is not confined to economics as a social discipline but applies also to the cognate area of economic policymaking. It is possible to reconcile these conflicting methodological issues if one follows Kenneth Arrow's beliefs. "An economist by training", said Arrow, "thinks of himself as the guardian of rationality, the ascriber of rationality to others, and the prescriber of rationality to the social world. It is this role that I will play."

Bagicha Singh Minhas, who passed away recently, epitomised what Arrow set for himself and his mission qua economist. After he hogged the limelight at the Stanford University with his path-breaking and profound theoretical contributions, he returned to India around the time, i.e. the early 1960s, when Amartya Sen and Jagdish Bhagwati were blazing new trails on the academic horizon. He joined the Indian Statistical Institute in Delhi where he made, along with

T.N. Srinivasan, L.R. Jain, M.R. Saluja, etc. major contributions to improve the Indian statistical system. He remained there except for brief spells at the Planning Commission as its member in 1971–73, Johns Hopkins and Sussex Universities, and at the World Bank in 1970 and again in 1985. His tenure at the Planning Commission turned out to be stormy despite the fact that he lived up to his role as the 'guardian of rationality.' His exit from the Commission made him a pariah ignored by the powers that be. He paid a price for believing in economics which, as Robert Lakachman characterised it, "has commanded respect and influenced events because its ablest practitioners placed themselves and their societies in the stream of history." He was not one of those who, as Lakachman put it, "think small thoughts, condemn themselves to be intellectual hirelings, instruments of other people's purpose."

Few Indian economists have been as original as Minhas was very early in his career in his contributions to economics. Minhas is known in the literature for the concept of constant elasticity of substitution production function. Alternatively known as the SMAC function (SMAC standing for its four authors—Solow, Minhas, Arrow and Chenery), it dislodged from the throne the Walras-Leontief-Harrod-Domar assumption of constant input coefficient and the Cobb-Douglas (C-D) production function, which implied a unitary elasticity of substitution between labour and capital. In the formulation of the Heckscher-Ohlin theory of international trade with its refinement by Paul Samuelson, capital-rich countries tend to export more capital-intensive products and import more labour-intensive products. Leontief, however, found in his celebrated empirical study of Heckscher-Ohlin theory that capital-rich USA was exporting more labour-intensive goods. Leontief explained this phenomenon, famously known as "Leontief paradox", by arguing that the US labour force was twice or thrice as efficient as the labour of its competitors in international trade. Minhas showed in his book and associated articles, all based on his Ph.D. thesis at the Stanford University, that

> invariance in ranking of industries by factor-intensity, a necessary assumption for the Heckscher-Ohlin to hold was not valid. Under the CES characterisation of technology, factor-intensity reversals are implied and it was further demonstrated that factor-intensities are reversed in the empirically relevant range. Therefore, there should have been no surprise or paradox in the finding that the US exported labor-intensive goods.

The SMAC function thus revolutionised the empirical foundations of the theory of international trade. Since the early 1960s, when this function was formulated, 'it has been difficult to keep count of the number of times the CES hypothesis has been cited and repeatedly used in many branches of economics, whereas for over thirty years preceding the 1960s, the C-D function had its continuous run.'

The history of how the SMAC function evolved is as thrilling as its novelty and is redolent of Newton's discovery of the gravity principle. When Minhas arrived in America for his graduate studies, he was fascinated by two observations in new surroundings—haircut in a barber's shop and a labour force on a farm he visited. The first exposed him to a high-cost haircut despite new gadgets used by the barber unlike in India, and the second intrigued him because a farm as big as 450 acres was managed by only two or three persons whereas his family farm back home engaged large casual labour in addition to several family members to operate a farm of only 18 acres. He was provoked to think aloud

> whether the economist's representation of technology, particularly the beautifully simple C-D hypothesis was consistent with the sharp contrast between the business practices of the barbers of Illinois and Punjab on the one hand and the farmers of my village and the Illinois farm I just visited the other day.

Constant cogitation on these real-world cases and the expertise he acquired in the use of mathematical techniques enabled him to hit upon the 'concept of elasticity of substitution and the demonstration that the numerical value of this elasticity is unity in the C-D production function." While this intuitive judgement of Minhas provided the impetus for rejection of the C-D function, he was not sure about a possible alternative for it which might generate his empirical results. It was at this juncture that Arrow, whom Minhas called a maestro, played a vital role with his intellectual input based on his ongoing work relating to generalisation of the C-D function. Thus the eponymous SMAC function was born. Though the names of Solow and Chenery were associated with it, it was mainly the brainchild of Minhas, with Arrow providing the inspiration for its final consummation.

However, the established icons in economics like Joan Robinson and Leontief were upset as this innovation posed a challenge to their well-accepted theories. Robinson's forte was never empirical validation of economic theories, preconceived or otherwise. She seemed to believe that economists cannot draw a simple table of economic numbers without something to guide the empirical work. It followed therefore that if the empirics belied the theory, then one should go for new ways of verifying it. Since Minhas' CES function flew in the face of her deeply held theoretical beliefs, she dubbed Minhas' work as "a case of looking in a dark room for a black cat that we are pretty certain is not there" and said patronisingly that "a talented man from India was bamboozled" by the academic company he kept. To which he plaintively replied that "coming as I did from the strong empirical traditions in the biological sciences, I had committed a sin against Mrs Robinson's brand of economic theology." Leontief's critique mainly focused on the implications of Minhas' research for nullifying his so-called Leontief Paradox. If factor-intensities are reversible in a relevant range, there should be no surprise in the USA exporting labour-intensive goods despite being capital-rich. Leontief tried by statistical legerdemain to show that Minhas' factor substitution can be interpreted not as 'substitution between capital and labour but rather substitution between different grades of labour or possibly the combination of both.' In that case his paradox could be saved. In the end, however, Minhas' contributions survived to become a standard staple in all investigations and were assigned a central role in the analysis of economic development.

The way Minhas embarked on his research in economics bears out his methodological predilections. In the mid-1950s when he entered the field there was a great debate between the proponents of 'Measurement without Theory' and those of the 'Theory without Measurement.' Since Minhas came to theory through his investigation of factor cost and factor use in industry in a cross-country context, he was sceptical about the mathematisation of economics which

> uses some phrases from the vocabulary of economics but are devoid of any empirical implications that can be confronted against data or vice versa. Some abstract exercises may fascinate, nevertheless they do not illuminate the path of decision makers in real life and may, therefore, be regarded as 'Theory without Relevance'.

Though the jury is still out in this methodological controversy, Minhas' espousal of 'Measurement without Theory' has proved productive, enriching economics with his valued theoretical contributions growing out of his long and arduous journey through the empirical woodland. This was indeed the high noon of Minhas' creative talent and his genius.

On his return to India, he did not jettison the empirical mode of his research. Realising that airy-fairy notions of economics were pervading the academic and political discourse in the context of India's economic development, he embarked on the mission to bring the debate down to earth, by applying his mind to improve the statistical base of the Indian economy. Being in the Planning unit of the Indian Statistical Institute with first-rate statisticians and mathematical economists like T.N. Srinivasan, he well succeeded in collaborative work relating to construction of reliable consumer price indices, state-wise and a country as a whole, and a searching analysis of the validity of National Sample Survey estimates of household consumption expenditure, which improved the understanding about the measurement of poverty and income distribution in India, thereby setting a framework for the great Indian poverty debate during the 1990s.

Though during a major part of his life Minhas was engaged in academic and operational research, he entered the policymaking arena albeit briefly when he was invited to be a member of the Planning Commission. As in academic research, he had some deeply held convictions about the methodological parameters of economic policymaking. He knew too well that a search for Pareto-optimality in designing economic policy was a pipe-dream but as a practical guide to making policy, he believed, one could show a change in policy to be Pareto-superior to the status quo. But in the world we live, with knowledge asymmetry and the possibility of pervasive market failures, approximation to even a vague notion of Pareto-optimality is not possible, unless one sets a well-defined objective goal, which Minhas defined as a social welfare function. However, in the nature of things, such a goal, overborne with the subjective judgements of politicians or their agents is almost an impossibility, as he realised on joining the Planning Commission. He was confronted there with two problems immediately. The first was the drought in 1972; the second was determination of the size of the Fifth Five Year Plan. Sycophantic bureaucrats and venal politicians, in trying to read the tea leaves in Mrs Indira Gandhi's cup, plumbed for nationalisation of the wholesale trade in food grains. Minhas' advice was disregarded, though the government soon came out a cropper when it restored private trade. The same happened when the government prepared the draft Fifth Plan with unrealistic assumptions, again ignoring Minhas' sound advice. This time Minhas showed great courage in resigning from the Commission without signing the draft plan. In all this Minhas personified Oscar Wide's wisecrack, "On an occasion of this kind, it is more than a moral duty to speak one's mind. It becomes a pleasure."

There was one memorable episode in Minhas' career as Economic Adviser to the government, which justified as an exception his methodological belief in economic policymaking. Around the mid-1960s, the question of acquisition of Boeing planes for Indian Airlines came up. The secretary of the Aviation Department, Asok Mitra, had to decide the right kind of planes—reliable, cost-effective, versatile, etc. Since the amounts involved were huge, what with rampant lobbying by the aircraft companies and the vested interests among bureaucrats and the politicians, it was necessary to carefully appraise the issue. Mitra, a rare specie of bureaucrats—honest to the core, innovative, thinking type—asked Minhas to head a committee to examine the economic feasibility of the proposal. Minhas' findings were opposed by several Congress party functionaries and ministers. Mitra then obtained a special permission for asking Minhas to present his report at the full cabinet meeting—a practise never before adopted. Minhas held forth for three hours, during which many of the ministers either dozed or yawned. The proposal was carried. In this case what Minhas intellectually perceived did happen—that the social welfare function was not given by politicians or civil servants but was ferreted through the studied efforts of economists without being contaminated by the politicians' manoeuvrings.

For all the intellectual pursuits of Minhas in India, there is no escaping the fact that he never scaled the scholarly heights he did at Stanford with his effulgent theoretical contributions to economics. Many of his admirers always wondered why. But these thoughts never occurred to Minhas as he was more philosophical and detached from mundane affairs. Perhaps he mused, like John Ruskin, that "The greatest reward for man's toil is not what he gets for it but what he becomes by it."

E-Social Sciences, 14 January 2006.

54

I.G. Patel: An equanimous economist

WITH the passing away of I.G. Patel, close on the heels of the death of S.R. Sen, the era of the best and the brightest Indians in economic policymaking, that began immediately after independence, is on the wane. It is on such a sad and sombre occasion that one tends to look forward in the past—the past one shared with some of the finest men and women in India as elsewhere. IG, as he was even better known, occupies a unique niche among such friends, who gave so much joy, intellectual stimulus, wise counsel, unselfish service to his country and the international community at large, friendship, and that rarest of human virtues—unstinting kindness to people who happened to be in his proximity. IG was a virtuous man in the sense Bernard Shaw defined it: "Virtue", he said, "consists not in abstaining from vice but in not desiring it."

Very few attained a legendary status so early in their lives as IG did. He earned many laurels during his scholastic career in India, but his lustre was brightened when he topped the Economics Tripos at Cambridge—a rare feat in those days. He capped it with a pioneering doctoral dissertation entitled "Foreign Trade and Economic Development" which, regrettably, was never published. It plugged a conspicuous gap in the Cambridge tradition—the economics of the Marshallian short period in a closed economy. He emerged thereafter as a nonpareil intellectual, blazing a new trail in his chosen field. When IG came on the scene, economics in India, as one mischievous

---

I thank Anand Chandavarkar for his comments and suggestions.

young Indian economist used to define it, was a science abroad and art in India because the tomes written on the subject, with few exceptions, were more a labour of love than an exercise of logical reasoning. The emergence of IG along with a few others, like K.N. Raj, V.K. Ramaswami and Manmohan Singh, marked a watershed in the development of economics as a serious subject of discourse and application. IG was a luminous star on the dismal firmament of economists in those days. Things never remained the same since.

IG's career as a civil servant, economist, and economic advisor, national and international, spanned over four decades. But he did not allow himself to be mired in bureaucratic minutiae with notings on files and sanctimonious observations at meetings. He overcame the tedium and routine of the day-to-day chores to reflect on what could be rationalised on a broader scale. He displayed *savoir faire* in discourses and dominated international gatherings, though his efforts were often in vain because he was representing a supplicating country. Some of his ideas on aid links and deficit financing were novel and refreshing, coming as they did from handling practical problems and the way he sought to resolve them. His grasp of the issues was matched by his limpid and persuasive prose, and a turn of phrase. He never aged intellectually.

I.G. Patel's intellectual solistice was the tenure at the International Monetary Fund as a callow young economist, along with the maven Edward Bernstein, economic counsellor of the Fund. The two wrote their famous report on deficit financing and economic development, which put a favourable construct on deficit financing. He also came up later with a highly original idea of aid link. However, in the world of practical men, both these ideas were debased. To quote his teacher Joan Robinson, the ideas he originated were 'bastardised'—the first by the politicians in developing countries including India, who debauched the currencies; and the second by the Fund's blinkered bureaucracy, which transmuted the aid link into toothless Special Drawing Rights (SDR).

IG fits admirably a profile of an economist sketched by Robert Solow. First, the economist should not intertwine ideas and egos; and second, he or she should not let down the team he or she works with. The first aspect makes ideas fly; the second leads to a productive effort becoming a labour of love and enjoyment.

With all his eminence, he avoided the *ad hominem* in his discourse. He was a pianissimo in gently moving to the centre of an argument without harsh notes, even when he differed strongly. In small gatherings he was expressive without being condescending, homely without being inquisitive, and sensitive to others' feelings. He reminded people around him of what Augustine said: "If your lips would keep from slips, of five things have a care: to whom you speak, of whom you speak, and how, and when and where."

Yet there was a forbidding air about his persona. To many he appeared to be somewhat imperial, circumspect in his mien, reflective in his thoughts and remote in his feelings. But it was really his innate shyness which posed as a carapace to veer away the attention focused on him. He was impeccable in courtesies and social discourse. He did occasionally fancy a talk about human foibles but never indulged in solecism or innuendo about his colleagues and others, high-brow or low-brow, friar or pagan. IG as we knew him, was unworldly without being saintly, unambitious without being inactive, and warm-hearted without being sentimental. His friends missed his benign presence if they could not see him in critical phases of their lives.

IG was associated with many politicians but none of them could pierce through the armour of his integrity. A story that exemplifies his probity can now be told. When IG was Governor of the Reserve Bank of India, a report, at the behest of Indira Gandhi's government prepared by his upstart predecessor cast some aspersions on his character as Governor. When that report reached Indira Gandhi, she walked across to her then Special Adviser with the report and handed it over to him for examination but not before instructing him explicitly that IG was one of the great Indians and no harm should come to him. Knowing as we do how Indira Gandhi's vindictiveness destroyed many a career, this was indeed IG's moral triumph.

IG's economic philosophy was not undiluted and above dissent. He himself was aware that he was generally prone to balance 'pros' and 'cons', which lent a somewhat indecisive tone to his views. On the other hand, he was, mercifully, not an ideologue. He stated explicitly in his memoirs that "I was not a Marxist Socialist opposed to markets and private property. But I was not a card-carrying capitalist either...." His vision of economic policy was lofty without being impractical. So he said what can be his own epitaph for future generations of economic advisors in India as elsewhere: "So let us economists rejoice that economic policy is forever; nor any particular policy to be sure, but the search for a better one. The good will never be enough and the best is a contradiction in terms."

I described elsewhere another distinguished Indian economist, IG's colleague and a close friend, V.K. Ramaswami, as a beacon in the tempest. To many of us IG was a lodestar ever willing to guide those around him who go through a period of both turbulence and tranquillity, The world never ceases to need men and women of IG's ilk. The legendary A.C. Pigou, his supervisor at King's College, Cambridge, wrote a memorable two-liner testimonial for him: "I have known I.G. Patel. He is absolutely first rate." To which one could justly add "as an economist and as a human being."

Economic and Political Weekly, 23 July 2005.

55

Krishna Raj: Editor of eloquent silence

THE most spectacular, if unobtrusive, coup of the otherwise unsensational Sachin Chaudhuri was to induct—courtesy K.N. Raj—the young Krishna Raj fresh from the Delhi School of Economics. "But will he stay on?" the somewhat sceptical Sachin asked of Raj. "Rest assured", was the prompt riposte. Krishna Raj more than fulfilled the expectations of both his former teacher and Sachin Chaudhuri.

Krishna Raj tiptoed into the musty office of the *Economic Weekly* in the early 1960s. A man of humble origins with no assets and no friends in sprawling Bombay, he launched on his lifelong mission with a measly salary. Consigned to the corner of the office, he used to sub what was passed on to him. Sachin soon found it difficult to do without him. After the *Economic Weekly* folded up, some of Sachin's Bengali friends urged him to shift the *Weekly*'s office to Calcutta. Practical as he was and without a shade of parochialism, Sachin told some of his closest friends that the *Weekly* could thrive only in compassionate, cosmopolitan and collegial Bombay than in uni-cultural Calcutta. Among other reasons for his preference for Bombay the fear of losing Krishna Raj was a major one. With the passage of time, Krishna Raj grew in his job with distinction; but his lean frame and bashful expression, though hiding substance, never changed. He was equanimous in the true sense of the term: he took praise as a rebuke and rebuke as a praise and pursued unwaveringly his predestined goal, a living exemplar of Kipling's sage maxim:

This is written together with Anand Chandavarkar.

Beware of those two impostors, praise and blame. A professor of Rutgers University dedicated his book to Krishna Raj without his knowing; and when his friends drew his attention to it, he just smiled it away. He was honoured with the Ram Nath Goenka award of more than one lakh rupees for his editorial excellence, but the award money was quietly donated to the Sameeksha Trust, even though his need of money to buy an apartment near his office was urgent. Late in life, when he realised that five hours in transit to office affected his effectiveness as an editor, he decided to shift to a place nearer his office, but lack of finance came in the way until his children came up with the necessary wherewithal.

From nowhere he came and scaled to the top in his profession, assimilating the best of his two predecessors—the great Sachin Chaudhuri with the '*bhadralok*' charm and the compassionate Ravi Hazari with his conviviality and lack of ego—both of whom gave to Krishna Raj as much as they received from him. Yet he was not an epigone; he raised the art of editing to a high level, combining the knowledge-based part of the *EPW* with that dealing with social, economic and political affairs with shrewd commentaries. In the process, he developed his own brand of editorship, not easily matched in or outside India. In the last twenty years he made the *EPW* into a high-class journal of analysis, research and commentary. Krishna Raj refused to call it a weekly. It was bracketed with the refereed journals without being one. One has only to scan journals of repute like the *American Economic Review, Quarterly Journal of Economics, Review of Economics and Statistics, Journal of Economic Perspectives,* etc. to see at least three to four citations of articles from the *EPW* in every issue. To reach that acme of academic excellence the editor had to have that rare skill in judging the quality of articles and choosing the right scholars to consult without lowering standards. The *EPW* today is read widely in libraries of leading universities in the US, UK, India, and on the Continent, not to speak of the developing world. Partha Chatterji, who surveyed social research in India and Asia (a paper based on which appeared in the *EPW*) referred to the *EPW* as perhaps the most dominant journal for discourses on social sciences. Joan Robinson used *EPW* articles for her lectures at Cambridge. Michael Lipton (Sussex University) held it up as a model of its kind. Today, the *EPW* occupies a unique niche as a quality journal run by a non-profit trust. This achievement of Krishna

Raj and his colleagues is all the more eye-catching and admirable against the background of many academic journals of Indian universities and research institutes, which languished in the last four decades for one reason or another.

A heterodox editor, Krishna Raj never sought models. He was an eclectic and very much his own self, with an unerring instinct for focusing on themes like the caste system among non-Hindus, or that hardy perennial of religious conversions and the cultural aspects of natural resources. No wonder the *Times Literary Supplement* called the *EPW* "that enterprising Bombay periodical." The choice of contributors too, from an admiring and carefully nursed domestic and international constituency, was nothing short of uncanny, with author and subject perfectly matched. His editorial capsule introductions to articles were models of craftsmanship. His editorial stance lived up to the memorable dictum of C.P. Scott of the Manchester *Guardian*—facts are sacred: comment is free—and did not exactly endear him to the Left always-in-the-right brigade. His editorial style could on occasions be baffling but it always worked, and he delivered without fanfare or formality, as a distraught North American academic discovered. "It is months since I submitted a painfully researched article to the *EPW* but not even a bare acknowledgement. Do you know the editor? My research grant depends on its publication." A couple of weeks later the overjoyed author received a complimentary copy of the *EPW* carrying his article and was eagerly awaiting the precious reprints. That was Krishna Raj all over. A true 'original', a maverick whether as an editor or as a human being of rare texture. A consummate listener in a nation of compulsive talkers, he did not have a defined body language but morphed listening into an art form. His silences, like those of the Quakers, were intensely communicative. The editor who never editorialised. He had a rare gift for people in all stations of life.

Krishna Raj might have appeared diffident and self-effacing. But when the *EPW*'s high standards were at stake, he could be bold and decisive in his own mild way. As in the case of an article by an internationally renowned economist, which Krishna Raj thought could be improved by deleting a few obscure words and sentences. He approached the author with his suggestions. The economist not only accepted them but also paid him rich compliments for his perspicacity and judgement. This episode was as much a tribute to Krishna Raj as it was to that gracious economist.

Krishna Raj was not a scholar but he was learned. He reminds one of Robert Rubin, a former US Treasury Secretary who said, "You learn more by listening than by talking and I have had the opportunity to listen to many who had much of great value to say." He inherited Sachin's art of talent scouting. There are stories galore of Krishna Raj's harnessing new talent. But one which comes to mind is the way he spotted the brilliance of Pravin Krishna, a young trade theorist and professor at Brown University. Pravin Krishna sent a review of Jagdish Bhagwati's book on Trade Theory to the *EPW*. When Krishna Raj read it he was so mesmerised by the quality of the review that he asked some of his close friends in the US to persuade this young man to publish more in the *EPW*. There was considerable disputation about the concept of John Williamson's 'Washington Consensus.' Krishna Raj felt that the concept was like the Philosopher's Stone—everyone talks about it without knowing much about it. He then requested John Williamson, the father of the concept, to revisit his idea; and John promptly published the article on the subject in the *EPW*, which made great waves. A few weeks later, *The Economist* published a long commentary on the 'Washington Consensus', drawing on Williamson's article in the *EPW* but without any acknowledgement of the source. When Krishna Raj's attention was drawn to this, he only shrugged his shoulders with his trademark gentle smile. He was not a man to flaunt his achievements. The same initiative he showed in getting Robert Flood, a well-known economist, to review Joseph Stiglitz's book on *Globalisation and Its Discontents*, which is one of the most cited among all reviews.

The EPW Research Foundation is one of Krishna Raj's babies. He discussed the idea with several young economists and took the plunge by persuading Sadanand Shetty to join him. Shetty, being of the same ideological hue as Krishna Raj, sacrificed his brilliant official prospects to be associated with him. Today, the database developed by the Research Foundation is used by universities in India and abroad and international organisations like the IMF.

Krishna Raj, like his mentor, was ideologically left of centre when he joined the *EPW* and he remained that way until the mid-1990s. During that phase he was severely criticised for making the *EPW* a forum for political partisanship. Prominent among these was Dharma Kumar who, assuming that Krishna Raj would not publish the criticism in the *EPW*, contemplated sending it to another journal. But an economist closely associated with the *EPW* from its inception assured her that Krishna Raj would be fair and she should send it to Krishna Raj. To her great surprise and delight her letter was promptly published, generating a lively controversy. Krishna Raj bore the brunt of the attack but never lost his composure. The wheel, however, turned full circle in 1996, when Krishna Raj shed old ideological garments more out of conviction than opportunism. Now he was hit below the belt by the critics, left of the centre, accusing him of having swerved from the ideological path of the *EPW*, which they mistakenly believed to be the legacy of Sachin Chaudhuri, and that his pro-economic reform editorials predisposed him towards Hindu fanaticism. Krishna Raj took all this in his stride. He did change his views on Indian economic policy; he might have as well replied to the dogmatists as Keynes did, "When the facts change, I change my mind. And what do you do, Sir?" But Krishna Raj's persona was different.

If Sachin Chaudhuri was the James Wilson (founder-editor of *The Economist*) of the *EPW*, Krishna Raj was emphatically its Walter Bagehot, who built an enduring modular edifice on the foundations laid by Sachin Chaudhuri. That is the measure of his stature and contribution.

Farewell, friend. RIP. The *EPW* will remain 'Stet'.

Economic and Political Weekly, 6 March 2004.

56

Asok Mitra: One of a kind

HUMAN life is a perpetual tussle between a search for the means of survival, which the body compels, and a pursuit of interests impelled by the free spirit of enquiry. For a living one chooses a way which supersedes the quest for the finer things of the mind, and as time passes the success or failure achieved in terms of physical well-being becomes the sole criterion for judging the worthwhileness of living. While this is virtually a universal norm, some persons of exceptional talent and calibre in any society transcend it. For them a uni-dimensional life is not sufficient for what they consider their life mission. A chosen profession is taken by them as a springboard for flights of the mind and unfettered roaming in the stratosphere of knowledge. They never feel knowledge-proof and, as Thomas Hobbes said, "Their quest of knowledge is a lust of mind that, by perseverance of delight in the continued and indefatigable generation of knowledge, exceeds the short vehemence of carnal pleasure."

Asok Mitra, one of the last members of the hallowed Indian Civil Service (ICS) and a distinguished art critic, demographer and social scientist, who passed away a few months ago, epitomised these high virtues. He was an illustrious civil servant of integrity and ability, and one endowed with a rare sense of public service. Though Mitra was a civil servant of pre-independence India with aristocratic airs, he defined himself differently from the other members of his cohort. And by so doing he denied himself the plums of jobs which could easily have come his way.

Mitra was essentially a polymath constantly on the lookout for new ideas, be they in his own chosen field of public service or in the fields of art, literature or even demographic statistics. Since the interface between thinking through problems in the universe of knowledge and the management of humdrum activities connected with administration is hardly conducive to harmonious relationships in a hierarchical organisation, he often ran foul of his superiors, to the detriment of his career.

When he entered the service Mitra set before himself the goal of achieving excellence, as conceptualised by Bertrand Russell, particularly because the service was highbrow, placed in a cocoon to immunise it from public contact. Russell wrote:

> I find that, doubtless owing to early environment, it (excellence) contains many elements which have hitherto been associated with aristocracy, such as fearlessness, independence of judgement, emancipation from the herd and leisurely culture. Is it possible to preserve these qualities, and even make them widespread, in an industrial community? And is it possible to dissociate them from the typical aristocratic vices: limitations of sympathy, haughtiness and cruelty to those outside a charmed circle?

Mitra could maintain all the savoury aspects of Russell's utopia, but he struggled to discard the chaff of the culture in which he functioned, though the service itself telescoped the interstices between virtue and vices. In the end he despaired, declaring ruefully, "I began my life by clinging to Gods that I imagined had existed in the past. The ones in my times mostly failed."

Asok Mitra scrupulously observed the rules and the behavioural discipline of his service, but at no stage was he overawed by them. He used both his head—to innovate—and his heart—to empathise with the citizenry he was required to serve. Though he spent time at Oxford University as part of his training for the service, Mitra was not seduced by it. While at Oxford he imbibed the liberal and scientific values of western civilisation, which helped him to develop a cosmopolitan view of his occupation, his country and wider mission.

Mitra disproved the oft-repeated cavil lodged against his service that it was neither Indian nor civil nor a service by defining his work not in the narrow sense of maintaining law and order but in the wider perspective of understanding the subaltern and other forces fashioning social mores, economic relationships, demographic tensions, and political change. His abiding interest in literature and art carried him to such heights of intellectual attainment as few of his ilk ever reached.

Mitra's experience as an apprentice, as a subdivisional officer in a part of what is Bangladesh, groomed him for assuming the luminous persona that was eventually his—a man of letters, social scientist, demographer and, above all, a renaissance man who possessed the fierce independence of thinking, modernistic vision and spirit of enquiry that his somnolent country needed most during both colonial rule and the transition to independence.

Asok Mitra's intellectual attributes, administrative acumen and sensibility were seen at their best in the way he perceived the great famine of 1943, which took the lives of thousands of his countrymen, particularly small farmers, and handled it. As he was a man on the spot confronted with the horrendous spectacle of men and women dying in phalanxes, his analysis carried great credibility, greater than the pronouncements of the then Government of India and those of economists and public men who were not directly involved. The facts as he saw them convinced Mitra that the famine could be understood only in terms of British geopolitical strategy, not in those of the rationale of the economists of that era or the ones who studied the anatomy of famine later. For Mitra neither low income nor low purchasing power nor hoarding were among the real causes.

As he wrote in his three fascinating but somewhat chaotically organised autobiographical works:

> The 1943 famine was different from all the previous famines in the eighteenth and nineteenth centuries and the one that threatened India but was satisfactorily averted in 1966-67. My suspicion that the famine was part of a wider central strategy was strengthened by the telltale unanimity of tight-lipped pronouncements at all stages of its progress, and all down the line from Winston Churchill in London to John Herbert in Calcutta.

The 1945 Royal Commission failed to measure up to the unrelenting thoroughness of its predecessors of the last quarter of the nineteenth century. Accounts by individuals have often been studies in vitro of one as part of the famine or the other.

Scholars like Ramakrishna Mukherjee or P.C. Mahalanobis might have been limited by their being still too close to the event to have had the time for more research and access to sources. But I wish Amartya Kumar Sen's book, coming four decades later, had gone looking for more. After all, matters like pricing policy, allocation and entitlement, intra-family distribution in male-dominated households leading to differentiated morbidity and mortality between the sexes and among age groups are obviously so pertinent to famine slowly emerging from the interplay of natural causes.

Mitra's strictures on the prevailing mode of thinking and the retrospective studies on the 1943 famine are debatable. But his daring to go into those issues on his own and challenge the received doctrine, quite contrary to the conventions governing his duties as a district official, reflected his quest for knowledge and his disinclination to take anything on faith. His cogitation on famine, however, paved the way for his emergence as a demographer in later years.

Mitra displayed sterling character and uprightness in the way he dealt with the famine in Bengal. He assiduously planned reports on the ever unfolding situation and transmitted them to the district magistrate. But he was dismayed to see little activity and only hype from the government in Calcutta.

When H.S. Suhrawardy, then minister of civil supplies, visited Munshiganj, Mitra's station of duty, he expressed mortification at the calamity that had befallen the subdivision supposedly due to dereliction on the part of the officer of his duty to report the situation. He pompously told supplicants at a meeting that he would have poured far more resources to ameliorate their miseries if only he had been properly informed.

Already seething with anger at being ignored by his superiors in Calcutta, Mitra responded to Suhrawardy's one-upmanship explosively.

> I have not shed my 30 pounds of flesh for nothing in the last six months. I am shocked by what the minister just said. ... Someone in his office is a guilty person who kept back all my letters and telegrams from the authorities before passing on the buck to the subdivisional officer in the district.

That was the end of the meeting. A red-faced Suhrawardy stormed out, admonishing Mitra that he should not have spoken up. But the latter, unmindful of the consequences, retorted confronting the minister eyeball to eyeball, that he would do it again if the circumstances were repeated. Mitra thought he had become a non-person overnight—until the day he met Suhrawardy subsequently in connection with some other business. That day the minister admitted that he had been wrong and that Mitra had been right all along. Mitra, bewildered by this unexpected decency, thanked him. One wonders if ministers in independent India could have behaved in such a civilised manner.

Mitra was equally outspoken about the community development project, guided and piloted by S.K. Dey. The original inspiration for these projects came from American architect Albert Mayer, who had started a pilot project in Uttar Pradesh in 1948. But the idea and the philosophy behind it were modified by Dey and the Planning Commission. Mitra felt that the idea had been reduced to a travesty by Dey, who was taking the credit for this innovation.

> We have a genius for wresting defeat out of the jaws of victory, said Mitra, and...our government is like the cock who insists on breaking a dozen eggs one after another into a frying pan, throwing each away, before proceeding to cook at all. We have spawned no end of excellent ideas and the mechanism of executing them in whatever area of nation-building one cares to think of, but never had the patience or determination to pursue any one of them to its logical end. Other countries that limited themselves to one or two ideas at a time made enough success of them to leave us, who were the originators, far behind.

Mitra believed that Dey did not sufficiently comprehend the significance of the changes in the structure of political power in India, the fact that the rich landlords had become dominant. So long as this was the reality the community development project would remain a pipe dream—as subsequent events have demonstrated.

Mitra, who worked with Dey in the community development project, made his doubts known to him and all those around him. Dey, who could brook no opposition, took every dissenting note of Mitra's as a sign of rebellion. Since the criticism focused on vested interests coming in the way of community development it could be easily perverted those days into a communist-type diatribe against the

Congress regime. Dey used this strategy to charge-sheet Mitra, alleging covert communist leanings and activities that undermined his authority.

The charge-sheet resulted in demotion. Mitra was banished from Calcutta to the districts. The tragedy was not that Dey almost destroyed Mitra's career but that other senior secretaries, even though convinced of the injustice, were too timid to stand up to the authorities. Mitra did not cave in. Head held high, he took his ill fortune in his stride and moved on.

What some regarded as intransigence on Asok Mitra's part was a consequence of deep conviction and adherence to some deeper values. Mitra almost sacrificed his career opportunities by standing up to Indira Gandhi, who had the reputation of not forgiving and forgetting. Gandhi, who began her career in the central government as minister of information and broadcasting, chose him as secretary in the ministry. During an early stage of her stewardship the subject of how much freedom should be allowed to the media, including radio, came up for discussion. The Left politicians, who called themselves her guardian angels, wanted the freedom curbed drastically to muzzle critics of her policies. Disgusted with the sycophantic crowd, which included several former communists, Mitra argued cogently but firmly against trampling on the freedom of speech, drawing on both historical experience and political thought. To the surprise of her flatterers, Indira Gandhi overruled them, though it was difficult to know whether she had been persuaded by Mitra's arguments or was acting out of considerations of political strategy.

Mitra's fearlessness was again demonstrated when, as secretary in the civil aviation ministry he forced a reversal of an aircraft purchase decision taken by the minister. This time he did not rely on his own judgement, as it was a technical matter. He prevailed on first-rate economists like B.S. Minhas and his colleagues to study the proposal for its technical and economic feasibility and carried the team to explain matters to the full cabinet meeting. Again Mitra won hands down. The minister, who had considered the deal a foregone conclusion, was not amused.

In 1951, when Mitra was a relatively junior officer, he was inducted as Census Commissioner in West Bengal. This assignment challenged his ingenuity and his innovative qualities of enquiry. As Mitra saw it, the 1951 census "marked a great divide between the pre-independence era of the census as a tool for law and order and the post-independence era of the census as a handmaiden of planning for cultural, economic, and social development." He wanted the census to be a point of reference for subsequent census reports in regard to comprehensiveness, concepts and definition, and the coverage of a wide range of variables.

The travels Mitra undertook through the length and breadth of West Bengal and the insights he gained convinced him to break away from the old census format. In his own words,

> The departure in the 1951 report for West Bengal centred on a new theme based on my own perception of the requirements of planning. I decided on bringing out as clearly as possible regional varieties and differences over the last fifty years in the demographic, social, cultural, and livelihood characteristics of the population in the various regions and sub-regions. I kept to the five main divisions of the census questionnaire but decided to go through in-depth to identify trends and explore the pattern of changes in rural and urban, male and female attributes.

The result was a *tour de force*, singularly the product of his own labour, intuition, originality and judgement. The achievement of Mitra supports a shrewd and pertinent observation of economist Nicholas Georgescu-Rogen:

> Isaiah Berlin, Paul Feyerabend, Gunnar Myrdal ran against the current. By comparing their conditions with mine, after long years, I have concluded that for the results of one's struggle the place from which one runs against a current matters enormously.

However, the census report Mitra prepared and the innovations he introduced did not have an easy passage and he had to summon his inner strength to carry it to the logical end. R.A. Gopalaswami, Census Commissioner, expressed dissatisfaction with the report and the innovations, and asked Mitra to "cut out all passages critical of government policy, past and present." He also advised him on how to revise his approach to what would be left after the excision.

As was his wont, Mitra refused point blank to compromise. Politely but firmly, he told Gopalaswami that he would not change it. If Gopalaswami was so convinced of the wrongness of the approach, he should recast the report himself or ask others in his office to do so. In the end Gopalaswami relented. He allowed Mitra to bring out the report, but under his name with a government disclaimer of responsibility to the effect that the views expressed in the report were only those of the author.

But Gopalaswami did not forget to let Mitra know that he would have to pay for his intransigence, that he should not expect any assignment in the Government of India in the future. As always, Mitra chose to live dangerously. Subsequent developments confirmed his faith in his own intuition and judgement. His 1951 report is now considered a classical document of India's census history. The report blazed a new trail in the census methodology adopted by emerging countries. It remains a true memorial to Mitra's tenacity, scholarship, integrity and selflessness. It was also a watershed in his career in that it opened new vistas of his interest in population studies.

Unlike the demographic studies which were an offshoot of Mitra's official career, his literary and artistic endeavours reflected his aesthetic sensibilities, characteristic of the Bengali '*bhadralok*.' Mitra has written widely on Indian artists such as Abanindranath, Rabindranath and Gaganendranath Tagore, and more prominently on Jaimini Roy, whom he brought before the public eye. He also co-authored a critical essay on Picasso.

Mitra approached Indian painting from the viewpoint of a modernist and in his characteristic manner subjected the so-called modern Indian painting to a severe test, to the discomfiture of Indian artists. Here again, as in many other areas of his work, he swam against the current. In his essay on "The Forces behind the Modern Movement" Mitra argued:

> The modern movement in painting received its most powerful stimulus not from the urge to see differently and therefore to draw differently but from the urge to feel and act patriotically and bring painting to the service of swadeshi and nationalism. The path was laid not through a reconstruction of the contemporary way of seeing but through a patriotic, revivalist drill.

It was because of this conviction that he valued most the paintings of Ravi Varma, which represented, in his view, "a striving to achieve in Indian painting what the new learning of Europe accomplished in Indian literature and philosophy, elements that were pertinent only to the world of seeing, the world of visual image." Mitra wanted the standards for judging art to be different from mere obsession with nationalism and the country's ancient heritage. His literary interests, however, were confined to translation of Tagore's Bengali novels and the fiction of some other noted Bengali men of letters.

Asok Mitra belonged to a genre of Indian civil servants—like R.C. Dutt, an eminent economic historian, and Malcolm Darling, noted for his insightful studies on agriculture and the rural populace—whose interests transcended their immediate preoccupation. Such administrators were perpetually exploring new worlds of ideas which enrich human life. Not for Asok Mitra the conventional and mundane standards by which success was measured and applauded. The world of bureaucratic glamour left him cold. He shied away from glitter and glare when he renounced a gubernatorial assignment that Indira Gandhi offered him on a platter.

Mitra's value system was revealed by his joining Jawaharlal Nehru University after retirement from service as a professor of population studies. He devoted his leisure not to wailing for what he had lost in his long and chequered career but to meeting people—young and old, scholars and writers, philosophers and historians, performing artists and painters—who wanted to climb new peaks of the mountain of knowledge and arch over the valleys of experience.

Like the protagonist of Oscar Wilde's *Picture of Dorian Gray*, he was not too careful in "the choice of his enemies", but was sagacious enough not to get entrapped with the detritus of ill feeling. In contemporary Indian society, transaction-oriented, egocentric, and smug, Asok Mitra was an odd man out.

Economic and Political Weekly, 25 March 2000.

57

V.K. Ramaswami: A beacon in the tempest

ECONOMISTS who have made profound and enduring contributions to their science fall into two identifiable classes. The first consists of those who, schooled in their discipline, start with a premise of an abstract world of perfect competition and develop an apparatus of thought to construct general theorems which are used to explain real phenomena. The other category actually work in the real world, observe complex situations, and search for some common patterns before formulating theories. The most outstanding economist of the second genre was John Maynard Keynes, whose intellectual make-up and development was one of the best, if not 'the' best. From the beginning of his career, he was actively involved with India's monetary history. His contribution to the theory and practice of the gold exchange standard, formulation of a sophisticated version of the quantity theory of money, and liquidity preference in its embryonic form, were in one way or another reflected in his classic work on *Indian Currency and Finance*. Keynes was the rarest of his breed, proving an exception to the observation of Kenneth Boulding that "every sociologist is necessarily born in a family but few economists are born in a firm."

Among a recent generation of economists, both in India and elsewhere, V.K. Ramaswami would come closest to Keynes, both because of the way he started his career as an economist and the trouble he took to make his impact on economics, particularly in the area of trade theory and policy. When he joined the Reserve Bank, he had nothing to his credit in terms of publications. His stint at the RBI was far too brief before he moved on to the Taxation Enquiry

Commission, where he produced his first incisive paper on commodity taxation in trade and production. He soon gravitated to the ministry of industrial development and foreign trade. He carried out a rare experiment of constructing a theoretical scheme from the policies already formulated and implemented, which he used for modifying the existing ones. He, of course, had no easy passage in a labyrinthine bureaucracy. He had to face intramural fights, confront feckless 'experience shows' kind of arguments of civil servants, who eventually fell in line because—as Bhagwati, Johnson and Srinivasan pointed out—"His interaction of policy and theory often startled the bureaucratic economists and civil servants with the subtlety of his economic logic and insights."

Most of Ramaswami's contributions to trade theory and policy owe their origin to the practical problems he handled. His most outstanding paper, written with Bhagwati (some ideas of which were later refined in another paper with Bhagwati and Srinivasan), was on the theory of optimal policy in the presence of domestic distortions and it was a direct response to what he experienced with regard to tariffs and quantitative restrictions that India had imposed during his tenure. The paper created a stir in the academia and transformed the prevailing notions regarding policy response to distortions. It argued that tariff imposition was a right response when the origin of the distortions was foreign, for example, the presence of monopoly power. But when distortions originate domestically, only the domestic instrument of tax subsidy will be optimal.

During his tenure with the Government of India there started a regime of the most complex, senseless, and often misdirected maze of import entitlement schemes for export promotion. These led to overlapping regulatory systems. Ramaswami tried to make sense out of this rigmarole by working through a theory of trade in intermediate goods, which later took him to focus on effective protection and the problem of devising optimal trade policies to collect given total revenue, when some factors are imported. The results of this inquiry are presented in another paper on optimal subsidies and taxes.

For a country like India, where the main source of revenue is taxation of imports which contain a large proportion of intermediate goods, the optimal policy is not to tax intermediates going into exports. This was the rationale underlying duty refund on intermediates.

In his short working life of barely fifteen years, Ramaswami contributed much to the core ideas on trade and policy, which emanated from his rendezvous with Indian economic policy. But his razor-sharp mind, his abiding interest in the subject, and intuitive reaction to the complex economic landscape enabled him to come up with strikingly new ideas which changed some of the highly prestigious and widely accepted theories. He was the first to notice that Samuelson's factor equalisation theorem did not necessarily mean interest rate equalisation.

It is a wonder how he could crystallise dreary and physically debilitating bureaucratic chores into high-quality theoretical rumination. Admittedly, his theory evolved naturally from his experiences. Many of his ideas arose from his duelling with bureaucrats and politicians. He seldom talked at meetings unless he had something important to say, which earned him the sobriquet of "India's famous non-spokesman" from S. Guhan.

His association with Bhagwati-Srinivasan should mark him out as one of the intellectual progenitors of the reform policies. It is true that while in government he did not proclaim aloud his dissatisfaction with economic policies. That would have been suicidal, without serving any purpose in those uncertain times. Those who knew the crucial role he played along with I.G. Patel in the 1966 devaluation knew where his preference was. More importantly, he left a rich legacy of ideas which provided underpinning for the reform policies today.

It is tragic that he should have met his death the way he did, at the height of his intellectual prowess. What G.L. Dickinson said of Frank Ramsay, who died young, could also be said of Ramaswami:

> Men like the one who died but the other day with all his promise unfulfilled is a type, unworldly without being saintly, unambitious without being inactive, warm-hearted without being sentimental. The world could never be driven by such men for the springs of action lie deep in ignorance and madness. But it is they who are the beacon in the tempest and they are more and not less needed now than ever before.

Business Standard, 2 February 1998.

58

S. Jagannathan: A friend of man

THESE are days in India evoking nostalgia about the era gone by, in which persons abided by the rules of propriety to build their character after the fashion of Confucian philosophy. The debauchery of the politicians' corruptibility, the mendacity of the civil servants, and a general decline of civility and moral standards, only bring into sharp focus the lustre of the generation of men and women in positions of power and responsibility who, in the presence of revolutionary and unsettling forces unleashed in India during the last few decades, did not deviate from the norms of rectitude and integrity and remained true to their assigned mission. They could have been seduced by the lure of pecuniary gains and lust of power at the bidding of politicians and thereby destroyed the fabric of society. Their contribution to whatever India is today is immense, though silent and without public acclaim. Such foreboding had found expression in a prophetic address way back in 1926 by the great savant Srinivas Sastri. "I fear", he said,

> that our best men may fail in their duty in the presence of revolutionary and anarchical forces now afoot in the country. If we destroy the present fabric, which is by no means perfect but which is capable of continual adaptation to better, finer issues, and also destroy the jurisprudence for the understanding and practical elucidation of which our intellect seems to be mightily fitted, shall we ever out of our traditional aptitude erect a similar fabric on the ruins?

These reflections are spawned by the passing away last month of S. Jagannathan, one of the most illustrious civil servants with conscience, integrity and ability—qualities which could be the envy of the brightest and the best in India. His sojourn in pursuit of his career, until he became Governor of the Reserve Bank in 1970, was distinguished, though quiet and self-effacing during those placid days in a newly awakening India. Thanks to the sagacity of Nehru and Sardar Patel, the scaffolding of the steel frame of the Indian administration was not tinkered with. Members of the administration at a non-political level carried out their functions with savvy and a sense of mission and imparted stability to a new nation in its early troubled times. The political leaders set the agenda, which was articulated by the civil servants without currying favour of their bosses, and the relationship between the two was harmonious with reciprocal civility. But the crunch came with Mrs Gandhi's ascendancy to the helm of government in 1966. The existing societal fabric was stretched to the utmost and finally was broken asunder in 1969 with nationalisation of banks—a denouement feared by Srinivas Sastri. Many of the best men on whom the responsibility rested to be dispassionate advisors and executors of policy caved in, to be sycophants and apologists of their political masters. There were a few exceptions; and Jagannathan was one of them. He presided over the central bank, which was undermined by Mrs Gandhi to use it as an instrument of patronage to feather the nest of her clan and the party. It was a delicate balancing act for Jagannathan and some of his colleagues like Hazari and Chari, who tried to keep aloof from the skulduggery and follow a straight and narrow path of probity to guard the public interest. The task was Sisyphean, particularly because the Reserve Bank was overseen by the newly established Banking Department in the Ministry of Finance—a contraption created to use financial institutions to divert funds for political activities of the ruling party. It is not widely known that Jagannathan during this critical period deftly managed the Bank and its associated institutions. A missive was issued to him that the Bank should make a special case for loans to Maruti Industries, the enterprise of the son of the then Prime Minister. Jagannathan played the Fabian tactics by engaging in minutiae of procedures, and eventually made the IDBI vice chairman reject the proposal on some technical grounds. It was a touch-and-go affair, with his job and reputation on the block. But he displayed inner strength and spunk, and without indulging in any heroics maintained the highest standards of public service. By nature and culture he was a pianissimo, gentle in argument but firm in determination. Even after he left the Reserve Bank and Mrs Gandhi's regime came to an ignominious end, he refrained from seeking public approbation for what he silently did. It was not in his character to angle for spotlight, always preferring to remain behind the scene and close to his family and friends. In this respect he reminded us of his equally illustrious predecessor B. Rama Rau, who quietly resigned his job when publicly rebuked by the irascible TTK, without issuing any statement defending himself.

Though a man of transparent sincerity and dignified demeanour, he was shrewd in his judgement of men and affairs of state. He would ask innocuous questions of members of his staff and colleagues but those questions were the vehicles for him to assess their grasp of the work at hand or their intellectual capacity. But he always was gracious enough not to humiliate them if he found them wanting. He chose the right people for the right jobs and at times took uncharacteristically bold steps of superseding the entrenched persons lacking in merit.

Though a bureaucrat he was very unbureaucratic in his treatment of the staff. He did not allow his authority to come in the way of his compassion. He protected some of his junior colleagues, without their knowing it, who inadvertently committed procedural snafu. Once he learnt that one of his economists was writing anonymously in a financial weekly criticising the government policies. What he found even more galling was that he was accepting payment from the journal. He could have disciplined him, which would have meant ruination of his career. Instead, he let word go to the young man through a friend that in his own interest he should cease writing and accepting compensation.

Jagannathan, for all his serious mien, had a delightful sense of humour with soupçon of cynicism, perhaps natural to a man of the world. At his farewell function in Washington a bluestocking was trying to impress others by narrating stories to show how close she was to one of Jagannathan's contemporaries present there. The lady's friend, having a reputation of amatory indulgences, interrupted her by saying that she should be careful in detailing her association with him as she might reveal her age. Someone related this to Jagannathan, who was a few steps away from the scene. With a twinkle in his eyes he retorted, "May be he was referring to her mental age."

Jagannathan, alas, has tiptoed into the world beyond this one, and quietly, in the same way he lived his life. His going and that of others of his ilk marks the end of a generation of honest and dedicated public men who, in their quiet ways, did what came naturally to them, but without compromising with their conscience and hankering after the limelight. It would have been satisfying for him if the generation that followed his had the same dreams and idealism. Perhaps he would have mused along with James Davis, "Let me live in my house by the road and be a friend of man."

Business Standard, 5 December 1996.

59

C.D. Deshmukh: An enigma

THE story of C.D. Deshmukh, a distinguished civil servant, politician by accident, the first Governor of the Reserve Bank of India in pre-independence India, is the story of a man who, endowed with all that is necessary to acquire greatness, just missed it. As a district officer he wrote some of the most original reports on revenue settlements; as Governor of the Reserve Bank, his annual speeches addressed to the Board of Directors were a model of penetrating economic analysis which would have done honour to any economist of original thought. He had a prophetic vision, befitting a great statesman; he had the makings of a literary figure with sensitivity and a talent for brilliant imagery, being steeped in classical Sanskrit and English literature. He was at ease with English, Sanskrit, and his native Marathi. As Sudarshan Desai, who guest-edited a book on him with finesse and *savoir faire* of an accomplished biographer, observed about Deshmukh's mastery over the English language,

> The diction and style represent the quintessential Deshmukh, using the English language with the devotion of a lover, the accuracy of a scholar, the eye of a novelist and the ear of a poet. He makes every word count and contributes to recreating the ambience of his childhood and youth. With just a right phrase or idiom, he sketches the lineaments of a character, nuances of human relationship or the inner charm of the landscape.

His patriotism and love for his country and its ancient civilisation were seen in his actions and words. He was sounded both by the British and US governments whether he would allow himself to be nominated Managing Director of the International Monetary Fund in

1956 but he turned down the offer as he believed that he had much to do in his own country rather than in the international organisation with all its fame and rewards. The same Deshmukh could write an extraordinarily trite and vain autobiography, cataloguing with the enthusiasm of a schoolboy his achievements. He betrayed a lack of equipoise, dignity and decorum in expatiating on the trifles of his life, unlike many of his own service such as Malcolm Darling, Penderel Moon and Asok Mitra, who could write their classic memoirs encapsulating with brilliant insights, the social, political and intellectual history of their times. He justified his quixotic quest for the presidency of India on the ground that his being in that office would help his wife, Durgabai, to undertake social work. His body language when he announced his engagement and his exuberance and extravagance in writing about his wife were unbecoming of a man of his stature, erudition and age.

One may well ask why such a gifted man could not scale the heights of greatness. One plausible explanation may be that his marriage to Durgabai at a late age broke the carapace he so assiduously built around him during his youth and released the avalanche of his pent-up emotions, sweeping him off his feet. Being prince charming, intellectually gifted, and a member of the elite service was enough for him to be married to a woman of accomplishments and social graces. But an indiscretion that he committed marrying an intellectually inferior daughter of a landlady might have haunted him all his life. He stored up his disappointments by maintaining a distance from his own society and people. When he met Durgabai, a lady of distinction and someone to reckon with in her own right, he totally surrendered. He became loony and he was not the same Deshmukh he was before. This is revealed in his article on Durgabai with an exhibitionist title. He writes:

> Her nose was small and well shaped and generally pleasing physiognomy was set off by a mole on the right side of the chin. The whole ensemble was bright and pleasing, set off by a fair complexion of the shade of light yellow wheat with an almost golden glow. In an ensemblage of women she would have been voted as good looking.

Even the greatest admirers of Durgabai would not have countenanced this hyperbole. Durgabai herself was modest enough to call herself "rustic." Such lack of judgement and restraint characterised Deshmukh in the last stages of his life.

What a pity that Deshmukh's enormous talents were laid to waste! Note, for instance, his imaginative exposé of the different types of people in change management. He envisaged a dynamic partnership of politicians, administrators, technicians, statisticians and economists as involving "a voluntary assumption of additional responsibilities as well as self-imposed discipline regarding non-interference. It is in a way a supreme *panchajana* practising *panchashila* within a country." His perceptive mind and intellectual perspicacity are manifest in his strictures on the weaknesses of Indian society, which he identified as a law-and-order situation, the control of growth of population, and conservation of land surfaces. These are dealt with, in his view, in a lackadaisical manner and "with infirmity of purpose because the revelation of the maladies calls for patient and objective study, for which in the hurly-burly of politics there is no time or even honest inclination." He castigated his perpetually garrulous countrymen, and rightly, that "Unlike China we seem to have no capacity for mounting movements as distinguished from exhortative slogans, occasional brush of enthusiasm and ephemeral campaigns....The wain that we hitch to the polestar is indeed a bullock cart." His catholicity of taste was reflected in his description of Srinivas Sastri's speeches "delivered in a steady, unimpeded flow of chaste and choice English, unmarred by a shallow passion or any superficial logic." The generosity of his spirit was seen in his tributes to his immediate predecessor as finance minister, John Mathai, who "had a sobriety of judgement in regard to men and affairs, a rare concern for principles, a delightful sense of humour with soupçon of cynicism natural to a man of the world, scholarliness with its flame kept by regular reading." He characterised Sir James Taylor, who shepherded him to governorship of the Reserve Bank, as one "among the most remarkable men that it has been my good fortune to know. His intelligence was like a lambent flame which illumined everything that it touched and purged it of dross...." There are very few of Deshmukh's genre in today's India.

Business Standard, 17 March 1993.

60

D.T. Lakdawala: Man's truest monument

THAT was just the beginning for a new generation of economists, of the 'Bombay School.' Many of the earlier ones who had dominated it gravitated to new pastures. Others passed into history as serious economists. K.T. Shah, the first director of the school, was a pariah. C.N. Vakil relished his image as an academic administrator. V.K.R.V. Rao was in the orbit of international organisations, girdling the globe, advocating one cause or another on India's behalf. D. Ghosh bade goodbye to academia after his unhappy experiences at both the Bombay School and Baroda. B.P. Adarkar forsook the university campus after going from pillar to post in a vain effort to find a permanent berth as a professor. Anjaria had just moved to the Reserve Bank of India to join J.V. Joshi, B.R. Shenoy and B.K. Madan, who were trying to build up a pioneering economic research department in the bank. Only Dantwala, with his handsome presence, deep knowledge, independence of thought and insights into stagnant Indian agriculture, was around.

It was at this time, around 1947, that a new crop of economists was rising on the horizon of Bombay University. Young K.S. Krishnaswamy, first as a researcher and then as a teacher, thrilled his students with his esoteric flights along the slippery indifference curves of Hicks and into the macroeconomics of Keynes and Oskar Lange. Being a high-flyer who could talk about economics in a mathematical language to students who were fashioned by a curriculum which treated mathematics as an alternative to logic, he had a mystique about him. His limpid prose, easy delivery and captivating style of presenting the intricate subject of the theory of value made him the darling of his students who were in search of a hero. Soon, however, he went away to the London School. In came D.T. Lakdawala from Harvard, where he had been spending a year studying the international aspects of development. Simple in appearance to the point of being shabbily dressed, serious of expression to be forbidding to his students, and spartan of habit, he made his quiet debut on the scene.

Very little was known about him, until he started his lectures on the history of economic thought. Methodical, scholarly, endowed with an elephantine memory and self-effacing, he used to enter the classroom with a wad of notes, which he never looked at throughout his lecture. Notes for him were like a peg to hang his thoughts on. He took us through the physiocrats' circular flow, Adam Smith's invisible hand, William Petty's monetary theory, Ricardo's iron law of wages, Marx's organic composition of capital, and Keynes' then-revolutionary General Theory; not once did he falter. It was truly an awe-inspiring performance. Soon he switched to lectures on taxation. Though he wrote a book on *Justice in Taxation*, it was a mystery to students like us who believed then, as students do now, that taxation was basically unjust. Many of us then felt that his lectures, though thorough, were arid, prosaic and of a pebble-gathering variety. The received doctrine was well presented, but there was no scintillating stream of thought, no provocative idea, no challenge to your wits. Yet, in retrospect, those lectures appear to have been a model of clarity and precision. They opened up a fascinating world of logical thought to his students, which helped them prepare for enquiry into the mysteries of economics on their own.

In a way, his lectures reflected both the strength and limitations of Lakdawala as an economist. He used economics as a vehicle through which he could look at a problem that required solution to enhance the welfare of the society we live in. He believed that one should not shirk the consequences of a certain action if it was informed by economic logic; and if one did, one should be able to justify it. Most of his contributions have been in the area of public policy. His dissertation on taxation raised pertinent issues about equity and fairness and he kept those considerations at the centre of his concern whenever he spoke or wrote on Indian planning, fiscal and monetary policy or, for that matter, centre–states relations or foreign aid and investment. There has been, in fact, a remarkable consistency in his approach over the years. He was not in favour of *dirigiste* economic policies; he was relentless in his criticism of Indian economic policies in the 1970s and 1980s, but he did not swing to the other extreme of advocating a free market economy. His innate sense of fairness and justice tempered his views on economic liberalisation, as is evident in the last article he wrote on the latest budget in the *Economic and Political Weekly*. He was one of the few intellectuals who refused to run with new fashions, while not being immune from change if it was warranted by the facts before him.

His work as a committee man on various economic issues, be they centre–state relations, wage policy, etc., were of exceptional quality and purpose. His book on the former subject, which was an offshoot of his labours on the working group appointed by the Administrative Reforms Commission, suggested for the first time a mechanism to determine financial allocations—both Plan and non-Plan—which were free from discretionary elements. He followed this up when he later became Deputy Chairman of the Planning Commission. He was not an apologist for organised labour which appropriated to itself a share of the national product out of all proportion to its contribution to it. The report on wage policy, prepared under his guidance for the National Commission on Labour, set out certain objective norms for wage determination. The paramount objective of wage policy, according to him, should be fairness without violating the interest of society as a whole.

There is, however, no identifiable original economic contribution with which Lakdawala's name can be associated. This was, in no small measure, due to his disposition to view issues from all points of view. His fondness for giving equal weight to all sides of the problem imparted strength to his lectures but prevented his fertile mind from breaking into new areas. His critical faculties were rich. Indeed, that mindset of his helped his students and others who came in contact with him to think more creatively on the subjects they were working on.

Lakdawala had a rare ability to harness economics for social purpose and to organise institutions which could enhance understanding by the politicians as well as the lay public of the country's economic problems. Not by age nor experience was his wisdom acquired. It was through his infinite capacity to work hard, without expecting reward or fame, that he came to command authority in his field and the respect of his colleagues and countrymen. He was instrumental in setting up the Sardar Patel Institute of Economic and Social Research in Ahmedabad, which is one of the few centres of research in the country to earn its keep. He took over the helmsmanship of the Centre for Monitoring Indian Economy when its founder, Narottam Shah, died prematurely. Though conceptualised by Shah, Lakdawala in his own quiet and self-effacing manner moulded it in a way that it could organise a statistical base for the Indian economy free from the ideological biases with which its founder had burdened it.

In many different ways Lakdawala's appearance belied his true nature. Though of serious mien he had a subtle and impish sense of humour, which he exuded through brevity of language mixed with a trademark wink of his right eye. A student of his, intelligent and serious, was troubled by his one-sided love affair and sought Lakdawala's advice. When asked for an interview, Lakdawala knew well what was coming. "Sir, I can't study because I love her." Quietly but sympathetically, Lakdawala mollified him, "Then love her." The student, overwhelmed, reacted, "But sir, she does not love me." Softly came the professor's consoling advice, "Then don't love her." This ding-dong conversation went on for one full hour, guru and disciple chasing each other's tail. At one of the annual conferences of the Indian Economic Association someone asked him who would be elected next year's president of the association. Batting his right eyelid, Lakdawala replied, "Young man, look around for the man who wears the cringing look." When the young man spotted the winner, Lakdawala counselled, "So, this will stand you in good stead in future." At a UN conference, where he was one of the honoured invitees, he regaled some of his former students around him with amusing asides. About one of the irrepressible talkers at the session, he said, "He is most interesting when he is not talking." Referring to the chairperson, who was most of the time dozing through the proceedings, he whispered to his neighbour, "He seems to be more bedborne than chairborne." Even better was his description of one of the participants who harangued his audience with an incessant flow of words as a "Columbus who has mistaken phrases for ideas." Those fortunate to be his close friends relished his company for the harmless small talk that he indulged in and the delectable conversational combat.

While friendly in relationships and extremely generous to students in difficulty, he did not countenance laxity in the standards he set for them. He once noticed that one of his Ph.D. students was wasting his time getting entangled in a bundle of emotions. He knew his potential, but thought that if he was not pulled up in time he would go astray. He told him over a cup of coffee in his room in no uncertain terms that he would have to send him down if he did not get back on track. Years later the same student worked with him on some committee. When the report was ready, he pulled him aside, softly intoning, "You did an excellent job but, you know, if I had not been harsh to you in the past, I would have lost an excellent economist." Such was Lakdawala, compassionate, caring, consoling, but correct in his personal and social relationships. The same Lakdawala, however, could be browbeaten by some of his aggressive colleagues. At a seminar in Bhopal one of his admiring students brought some beer to guzzle after sundown in the Circuit House. But one of his killjoy colleagues, also a former student, sat sulking in a corner, upset that Lakdawala and others should be committing the sin of drinking. This made Lakdawala hesitant, until the student who had arranged the show tore into the self-appointed custodian of moral values and urged Lakdawala to ignore him.

It is a great tragedy that the Bombay School of Economics, the cradle of many economists in the period prior to Indian independence, has gone into the wilderness. The rot began during Vakil's time. For all his administrative skills and humane actions, he was essentially a paternalistic figure, putting a premium on conformism, kinship and obedience, which tended to supersede the weight attached to academic achievement. The Bombay School became the habitat for former students of the Bombay School and the resulting inbreeding emasculated its spirit and intellectual vigour. Alwyn Hansen, who spent a year at the school in the 1950s, had sounded a warning about the dangers of treating the school as the bailiwick of former students, but his advice fell on deaf ears. Dantwala and Lakdawala, two economists of sterling character, high academic reputation and social commitment, valiantly tried to break the legacy, but in vain. Today the school, which was once a verdant garden of blooming talent, has become an academic wasteland. Lakdawala agonised over this for a long time. Beyond saying that it was for the younger generation to carry the torch, he often fell silent whenever the question of the school came up in private conversation.

In the ephemeral journey of life, we are often vain in assuming the permanence of our achievements, real or imaginary. In the flush of momentary glory or the excitement of public acclaim, we forget that they are all tossed into nothings on the tides of time. What remains is only dedication, social conscience and nobility of purpose. "A man's truest monument", said Minut Savage in his "The Song of Man", "is man himself". Lakdawala was such a man.

Economic and Political Weekly, 11 July 1992.

61

B.K. Madan: A ruminating and humane economist

EVEN when the world is about to break into the twenty-first century, India continues to place a premium on age. In a country where traditions, received doctrines and inherited wisdom constantly cast shadows on upcoming youth, it is taken as axiomatic that the ability to offer balanced advice and maturity of judgement resides only in people in their late forties and beyond. We as a nation feel perturbed when youth by happenstance comes to the vanguard of ideas or occupies public office which influences important policy decisions. If someone cites the example of America where young men and women just out of their teens get on the staff of the President, our first reaction is utter disbelief, but on reflection we attribute it to the immaturity of the American system with a very short history and no worthwhile traditions. However, India of the past was not always like India of the present. There have been some periods in Indian intellectual and administrative history when, though somewhat exceptionally, bright young men have dominated academia and administration under the British. In the field of economics, D.R. Gadgil, fresh from Cambridge, became in the 1920s the first principal of a well-known college in Gujarat at the age of twenty-four; C.D. Deshmukh, a distinguished member of the Indian Civil Service, was inducted at the age of thirty-nine into the newly established Reserve Bank of India in 1936 to be trained successively as a secretary of the Board, Deputy Governor and, finally, its first Indian Governor at the young age of forty-nine. B.K. Madan, who passed away recently, belongs to this select band of Indians who rose to high positions early in their lives, and contributed so much and so steadfastly in their respective areas of specialisation. Madan, together with J.V. Joshi, laid out a fertile ground in the form of the Reserve Bank's Research Department, which in many ways was responsible for a cornucopia of economists and the flowering of economic research in the country in the last forty-five years.

Though Madan was not anointed with education in British universities, as many of his contemporaries had been, he had the self-assurance and industry to start on his own. He became economic adviser to the Punjab government when he was only twenty-nine. He had the good fortune to study under Professor Brij Narain and Lala Manoharlal, a highly respected member of the Indian Civil Service and a distinguished economist in his own right trained under Lord Keynes. But what really launched Madan on the high road to success was his work on Imperial preference, prepared for a Ph.D. degree. His contribution was both solid and controversial—controversial because it contested the prevailing nationalistic view that Imperial preference would damage India's interests. He devised a very ingenious method to measure the cost-benefit of Imperial preference both to England and to India and on that basis concluded that if anything, India would benefit from the new commercial policy. The book was admired greatly by academics, one of whom (not an Indian) was prophetic enough to say that it was "assuring evidence that India has at her command the services of economists who can render valuable help in advising on the way in which she should adjust herself to a new and, let us hope, better world." Even more important than these encomiums, his book showed that Madan could brave controversies if the data on his hands and the reason at his command could support his conclusions.

Transition from the Punjab to the Reserve Bank took him to a wider arena. He not only made his mark as an economic advisor in the national and international aspects of Indian economic policy but also built the Research Department, the first of its kind in the country. He was chosen by Governor Deshmukh to be secretary of the Indian delegation to the Bretton Woods conference, which set up the International Monetary Fund and the World Bank. Those who have read the complete works of Keynes and Anand Chandavarkar's fascinating book on Keynes and India would know how highly

Keynes thought of the contributions of the Indian delegation to the Bretton Woods deliberations. It was the trinity—Deshmukh, A.D. Shroff and the young Madan—which formulated India's positions at the conference. Though Madan was modest enough not to exaggerate his own role in Bretton Woods, his account of the conference proceedings, punctuated by humour and anecdotes, would reveal his subtle but valuable contributions, particularly vital to India's interests. Knowing as we all do now how dominant the Bretton Woods 'twins' have become in the world's monetary affairs, it is somewhat strange to learn from Madan's asides in his account that these institutions at their birth had been credited with a low life expectancy. When queried on this point by Madan, as a member of the Indian delegation, Keynes' reply was "Not less than five years."

Madan was not a theoretical economist by any means nor did he claim to be one. When he came on the scene, economics was in its infancy in India and there were very few theoretical economists around, among them B.P. Adarkar, J.K. Mehta, A.K. Dasgupta, D. Ghosh. But he left enough theory to relate his rare economic insights to issues of practical policy. Once he was discussing the limitations of interest rate in the saving-investment processes. In his somewhat periphrastic way he suggested that while interest rate may not influence saving one way or another, it would certainly determine the form it takes. This was in the late 1950s when a low interest rate policy held sway over the minds of development economists and policymakers. In retrospect, this insight of Madan could be considered a forerunner of McKinnon-Shaw's innovative analytic framework of financial deepening which came on the scene during the 1970s. In the same way, while working on some practical problems at the Reserve Bank or setting areas of research work for his staff, he hit upon the idea that 'term credit' could be extended by commercial banks if an appropriate liquidity mechanism could be put in place. Not that this was a completely new idea—the Macmillan Committee in the UK had first mooted it—but the way Madan conceived of it in the Indian context reflected his insights into the Indian economy.

His preoccupation with policy matters often brought him to the major questions of the day. When some of his junior staff were engaged on money supply analysis, he showed perspicacity to raise the work to the definition of deficit financing and encouraged his staff to come out with a monograph on the subject. Those who have read this report, published as far back as in 1961, and the Sukhamoy Chakravarty report on the Indian monetary system published in 1985, will discern how much of the latter report had been anticipated in the study which Madan initiated. The same holds true of the study of income distribution as well as estimates of saving and investment and tax evasion. Madan put two of his able young economists to study this question and the results were published as far back as 1963; the arguments and the statistical base of these studies were used as important inputs in the official report on income distribution prepared by the Mahalanobis Committee. The saving-investment estimates, first brought out in a systematic fashion by the Reserve Bank group of economists, set the stage for integrating financial planning with physical planning in the Five-Year Plans and the formulation of an indicative plan for private sector investment.

Madan was, of course, a first-rate economic adviser, but he was something more. He was an organiser par excellence. He assiduously built up the research staff and devised the organisational setup of the Reserve Bank's Research Department in such a way that the brightest and the average could be optimally enmeshed. He used to devote attention to minute details of staff deployment. While admiring and even rewarding the bright economists under his charge, he did not disdain the lesser ones. For he knew that he was not running a university department but a policy research department of a bureaucratic organisation. With proper delineation of functions and matching of the skills of staff with the requirements of the job, he could get the best policy advice, along with a steady flow of well-sifted, carefully checked statistical information, which staff with average abilities could competently put out.

Enamoured though he was of innovative, dynamic and gifted economists, he was not lax in disciplining them, if the situation so warranted. There was the case of a young economist in the Reserve Bank, rather careless in observing institutional rules, who anonymously published an article in a financial journal on the subject he was working on at the bank. Madan, on noticing the similarity of content, took a serious view of the breach of discipline and postponed the economist's confirmation by a year, despite the fact that he held him in high regard intellectually. For the next four years he systematically ignored the economist. That was his way of sending a message to all that impulsiveness and egocentricity in a bureaucratic setup, with its own norms and rules book, will ultimately demoralise the whole staff and eventually diminish the department. But Madan never showed any animus towards the economist in question. Later, convinced that the young man had learnt his lesson, he personally monitored his progress to high achievements and success.

The Reserve Bank, being the central bank of the country, has had to maintain secrecy as regards the policy thinking that goes on all the time. But secrecy carried to excess also stifles creativity. Realising this, Madan was perhaps the first amongst high officials of the Reserve Bank to encourage young members of his research team to publish in outside journals on various aspects of monetary and development economics. It was in his time that there was a profusion of articles published in international journals of repute on a wide range of subjects. It was this, along with the research work of the Department, which made it one of the leading centres of monetary economics research in the country. How important his stewardship was is clear from what happened after his exit. The drought of research which started after his departure still persists.

Both by training and choice Madan's forte was international economics. He served twice at the International Monetary Fund as Executive Director. Though he was not wedded to the 'Commandment' economics of the Fund, he always wished that India maintained fiscal rectitude by refraining from reckless deficit financing. He did not believe that depreciation of the exchange rate could always be a sure recipe for external deficit, but held very pragmatic views on this question. Though he belonged to the international establishment because of his involvement in the Bretton Woods Conference and the subsequent negotiations to define India's relationship with the Bretton Woods twins, he knew in the marrow of his bones the limitations of the Fund in particular. He had a pithy phrase '*bandobust*' (policing) for those who unthinkingly believed in stabilisation programmes. He had mastered the minute details of the Articles of Association under which the Fund conducted its business, and always used that knowledge to get the maximum advantage for his country. Few Indians know even today how Madan in 1968 exploited a loophole in the procedures of nominating permanent members on the Executive Board of the Fund to prolong India's permanent seat by two years.

Madan's serious mien was somewhat misleading. He used to regularly write so-called ESP (extra-sensory perception) letters to finance minister Deshmukh, full of wit and humour, a little innuendo, and a good bit of well-meaning gossip about money men and their wheeling and dealing, and an inside view of the deliberations on important international monetary issues. In one of the letters he narrated a delightful story. At that time an Indian, a former non-gazetted employee of the Government of India, was an Executive Director of the World Bank. His British counterpart had been his boss in Delhi in the pre-independence days. When he saw the Indian Executive Director for the first time, he whispered to him, "Eh, have you gone up or have I gone down?" Prompt came the reply from the Indian, "Both."

Madan was cautious by nature but it did not mean that he was timid or compromising. He was aloof from his staff without being supercilious. This was deliberate to keep away those who liked to ingratiate themselves with their bosses. He handled relations with his counterparts in the finance ministry and the Planning Commission—newly emerging centres of economic policy research—with a deft touch. Without sacrificing what was the Reserve Bank's due, he avoided conflicts. He was saddened therefore by the subservience to which the Reserve Bank was reduced after the nationalisation of the commercial banks and the creation of the 'super central bank' in the form of the Banking Department of the Government of India. This does not mean that Madan, if he were at the helm of the Reserve Bank's Research Department in the present turbulent days, could have prevented the downgrading of the Reserve Bank's policy role. The whole culture in the country has now changed. He was lucky to have been the man for the times; he would not have been able to dominate economic policymaking now in the same way he did prior to 1965.

None could have imagined from Madan's mild manner or cautious behaviour that he would fight for certain principles which he considered necessary to the holding of public office. This was illustrated by what he did when he turned down the Government of India's decision to appoint him chairman of the Gold Control Board in 1962. As the grapevine had it, the finance minister expressed his displeasure at his rejecting the post and indicated that Madan should not hope to become a Deputy Governor of the Reserve Bank. Some press correspondent asked him whether what he had heard in Delhi was true. Being cautious, he smiled and said, "If loss of the Deputy Governorship is the price I had to pay for doing what I did, I would rather not have it."

Though taciturn, tactful, and keen on avoiding conflict situations, Madan could reveal the steel in his character when the chips were down. Such was the stuff which the older generation of Indians who occupied high official positions were made of.

Economic and Political Weekly, 19 January 1991.

62

B.P. Adarkar: An economist whose present was in the past

IN present-day India there has been a cornucopia of economists who flaunt their sophisticated skills in almost all domains of public policy but who, with some striking exceptions, also take pride in investing their theses with apologia for the party in power. There has been an opulence of high-powered mathematical techniques and effervescence of abstract theoretical thought which the economists display with an aplomb characteristic of the best minds anywhere in the world, but which when measured in terms of their relevance for the country's myriad problems, are all of the second order of smalls. The country is rich in highly endowed research institutions, offering comfort to the body and mind of economists for pursuing their scientific avocation, but they tend to become ghost institutions once the brightest and the best who are supposed to be housed in them gravitate to the world outside in lure of acclaim, fame and wealth. If this India is not cognizant of the contributions made by some of the economists in the 1930s in the face of all adversities, it cannot be attributed merely to a lapse of memory or to the generation gap. It is in no small measure a reflection of the hiatus between economists as harbingers of social and political change with an abiding concern for civil society, and economists revelling in intellectually exciting adventures in theoretical abstraction, subtleties of logical thinking and philosophical rumination, all somewhat removed from mundane daily life.

B.P. Adarkar, who recently passed away, belonged to that rare breed of highly gifted economists of the 1930s who straddled various fields of economics, with distinctive contributions of their own to the discipline, and also influenced public policy of the time with force and persistence, even if they did not always change its course. It was an era when educated youth were either drawn towards the Indian Civil Service, being the most powerful magnet in terms of income and power, or the academia as the second-best choice.

There was D.R. Gadgil who, through the munificence of his father-in-law, blazed a trail in designing highly ingenious survey techniques to study Indian agriculture and, in course of time, illuminated the whole field of agricultural economics; there was V.K.R.V. Rao, who pioneered the construction of national income accounts along scientific lines, which provided the first concrete proof of the damaging impact of British rule on the Indian economy; there were Jahangir Coyajee and B.R. Shenoy unravelling the intricacies of currency and finance, focusing on the pernicious consequences of the exchange rate in what was then known as the ratio controversy. There were, of course, the two stalwarts, Radha Kamal Mukherjee and his brother Radha Kumud who, between them, embellished labour economics and added sociological and philosophical dimensions to Indian economics, not to speak of young R.M. Joshi who made his debut all too briefly before his premature death. The work of all these economists provided a rich menu of empirical work which imparted strength to the public debate on economic policy.

While the forte of these economists was applied economics, there were others—B.P. Adarkar, Parimal Ghosh, J.K. Mehta, D. Ghosh, A.K. Dasgupta and P.C. Mahalanobis—who enriched the field of economic theory. Dasgupta ploughed his lonely furrow and, unmindful of financial reward or power, even at the ripe age of 84 made some lasting contribution to economic theory. His extension of Keynesian thought to development economics and policy can be considered to be of major importance with its bearing on Indian economic planning. Mahalanobis' two-sector planning model formed the basis of India's planning experiment, which carved a permanent niche for him in development economics. J.K. Mehta's forays in economic theory and its philosophical foundation did not go unrewarded. His originality in marginal analysis was recognised and his theory of "wantlessness," though philosophical in content and abstract, was applauded for its synthesis of western thought with eastern philosophy.

Of these, B.P. Adarkar and D. Ghosh—P. Ghosh did not live long enough to make his presence felt—fell by the wayside in post-independence India, which was a great pity considering the basic nature of their contributions in the theoretical and policy fields. It is not a mere coincidence that both these illustrious economists faded from the intellectual scene without receiving any accolade in the profession or being offered the presidency of the Indian Economic Association. Their presence could have spurred the resurgence of economic thinking in the country, the sterility of which propelled Sachin Chaudhuri to found the *Economic Weekly*.

One could have perhaps understood the amnesia about the contribution of D. Ghosh, who did not pursue his work beyond his little gem of a book on population pressure and economic efficiency. But it is a real tragedy that Adarkar's basic contributions on monetary theory and policy, federal finance—his book on this subject is still a classic—and fiscal policy should have gone out of the public mind in contemporary India.

All of Adarkar's major contributions were made before he was forty, not an age to bid goodbye to his first love. His small note on "Fisher's Theory of Interest Rate", which was subsequently included in his *Theory of Monetary Policy*, was so insightful that the conclusions it yielded are valid even today when inflation is a more troubling phenomenon. Even more importantly, his *Principles of Federal Finance* is a classic work which had an important bearing on India's federal polity, though it was never recognised as such by the powers that be. His ideas on the ratio controversy of the 1930s, at variance with those of the majority, were acutely perceptive and stressed in a penetrative way that distress gold sales by poor agriculturists were not the cause of the appreciated exchange rate but, in fact, the reverse. His forthright exposé of the manipulation of the exchange rate by the government helped to restore some perspective to the debate on the subject. Adarkar traversed with ease the field of labour economics. He designed a comprehensive scheme of social insurance for industrial labour, which revealed his sense of social commitment, his appreciation of the administrative ramifications of economic policies, and a penchant for the nitty-gritty of a plan of action. Few of the modern generation of Indians know that, despite his mastery of economic theory, Adarkar's achievements were not confined to the academic field. He was actively associated with the National Planning Committee of the Congress Party, headed by Jawaharlal Nehru. Though little is known about his contribution to the committee's deliberations, he was perhaps not in tune with its thinking as his association turned out to be short-lived.

Such a distinguished mind, one would have thought, would have blossomed after India became independent. Instead, Adarkar quit the academic scene, so that today's generation of Indian economists is totally oblivious of the fact that he was once India's foremost economic theorist. It is true that he was already lost in the labyrinth of government bureaucracy by the time India became free, which may have dimmed his originality. But it could not have been the only reason for Adarkar's exit from intellectual activity. Some of his contemporaries like V.K.R.V. Rao and B.R. Shenoy, even when entrapped by administrative and political office, remained active and vibrant.

A.K. Dasgupta, despite being associated, though briefly, with government or the international organisations, not only maintained his eminence as an economic theorist but scaled new intellectual heights, with important publications after the age of 60. The interesting question is why Adarkar, with his enormous intellectual endowments and a rare ability to roam in the realm of abstract thought, abdicated the empire which he had once dominated, resorted to the unfamiliar pursuit of making money in the diamond business, and finally indulged in a quixotic quest for the office of the presidency of the Indian Republic. Perhaps, one can search for clues to Adarkar's unhappy metamorphosis in the struggles he had to wage to achieve his intellectual status. He waited long to get a scholarship to study at Cambridge, and when he got it he had to face other disappointments in his personal life. In Cambridge he made his mark as an economist, but when he returned to the country, he was sent from pillar to post in search of even a modest position of a lecturer in economics. He drew a blank at the Bombay University, his alma mater, and so went to distant Allahabad and Banaras in pursuit of a secure station in life. Eventually he became Reader at Banaras but professorship eluded him, when others with lesser abilities and talent were rewarded with that hallowed post. He then moved to Allahabad

University. Embittered by adversity, he could not reconcile himself to his less deserving colleagues at the university, which compounded his problems further. Perhaps, he thought that the security of a government job and the power associated with it might compensate for the lack of academic recognition, and he left his labour of love for the pomp of bureaucracy. However, government, and central government at that, was the last place for a person of Adarkar's talent and expertise. Those were the halcyon days of the heaven-born ICS officers, who knew all answers to all questions; and Adarkar's well-thought-out and logically derived nostrums could only arouse their hostility. By coming to the government, Adarkar escaped the arrows and slings of his mediocre colleagues at the university, but he now had to withstand the stabs of the omniscient bureaucrats. His failure as an adviser stemmed from his inability to recognise that acceptance of advice is determined more by the channels through which it is offered than its intrinsic merit. His stint with the government, therefore, did not carry him beyond the rank of joint secretary and his contributions to policy did not go beyond instant notings on government files.

Thus, the University and the Government combined to sap Adarkar's genius. However, instead of unshackling himself from the stifling chains of the government, Adarkar succumbed to them and, as a result, his whole attitude to life changed radically. He believed that there was no higher mission in life than to make money and enjoy the comforts of life. In 1953, when a young man full of idealism sought his advice on what he should do to make a career as a good economist, Adarkar's laconic reply was, "My dear young man, don't have illusions about becoming an economist. Just make good money, and then you will be both a good economist and a successful man the world respects."

It is tragic that such a gifted and distinguished person, whose contributions to economic theory and Indian economic policy were pioneering ones, should have drifted away from economics. But one should not be harsh on him for his frailty. It requires a different psyche, an uncommon ability to subordinate the pains of the body to the undefined pleasures of the mind, a value system of a higher order, and a strong sense of identity. Otherwise, how can one explain Sachin Chaudhuri, after graduating from Dacca University, working variously as a private tutor, journalist, manager of a film studio, and then founding the *Economic Weekly* with meagre resources and no support but strong faith—to make his countrymen think scientifically on the economic issues of the day?

Economic and Political Weekly, 8 October 1988.

63

Sachin Chaudhuri: A catalyst

WITH the death of Sachin Chaudhuri, editor of the *Economic and Political Weekly*, an unusual personality has vanished from the Indian intellectual scene.

His was no ordinary brand of financial journalism. He used it only as a medium to disassemble some of the most basic ideas about growth economics, planning, and a host of other economic problems that went with them. Nor did he interpret financial journalism to mean purely matters economic. He set his sights beyond these narrow confines, and roamed with equal ease and aplomb the fields of political institutions and politics, sociology and social anthropology. In fact, he made his journal a forum for the expression of new ideas in all spheres of intellectual activity in the country. In essence, he was an intellectual amongst financial journalists, in the sense that he deemed the outpouring of news and views only as raw material for moulding and purveying the more fundamental scientific thought. And he was a journalist amongst intellectuals in a manner that he forsook technical jargon in his columns to put across to the lay public unconventional and novel scientific ideas. In the process, he evolved a new standard, a new style, and a new medium.

The story of the *Economic Weekly* is as fascinating as Sachin's personality. He was a graduate in economics but his formal education did not arouse in him an interest in the subject of economics so much as his subsequent dissatisfaction with the state of economic knowledge and economists in the country. While on travel abroad, he and his brother Hiten ran into a highly placed senior Indian economist, and the conversation inevitably turned to some burning economic issues of the time in India. The economist displayed such an amazing degree of innocence that it prompted Sachin's brother to egg him on to start a journal to educate the Indian public in economic thinking along scientific lines. This accidental entry into independent journalism was the thin end of the wedge, and it eventually led to the ushering in of a dynamic era in independent thinking among India's intellectuals.

Every era has its ethos. It was typical of the pre-independence Indian society to be either overwhelmed by western thought or submerged in the legacy of ancient Indian philosophy. It was inevitable, therefore, for intellectuals to be imitative in interpreting western scientific thought and, failing that, to involve into shastri-type of scholarship. Nowhere was this tradition so pronounced as in the social sciences, especially economic science. The treatises that gushed forth were either descriptive in treatment or historical in argument. There was no attempt whatsoever at establishing hypotheses and then proceeding to their logical dissection. Admittedly, there were a few exceptions, but the totality of contributions in this sphere did not deviate from the general standard. It even led some cynics to define economics as "an art in India but science abroad." It redounds to Sachin's credit that he was one of those who rendered this definition obsolete.

Sachin's *Weekly* was a historical necessity. With the advent of independence, new forces were unleashed. The period of negativism had come to an end. The reconstruction of the nation called for a positive and creative approach to the problems of the day. But precisely, creativity was the desideratum. Sachin, through his paper, attacked relentlessly the meek conformism among his countrymen. He questioned every premise, made others around him do likewise, and provoked and prodded the younger ones to be restless and to seek answers scientifically to the questions of the day. It is this achievement which drew a galaxy of young economists, sociologists, anthropologists and political thinkers towards the *Weekly*. Many of their new ideas excited controversies, sometimes furious. Indeed, Sachin's paper was a crucible of new ideas which helped to advance the frontiers of economics, sociology and anthropology. That is why the *Economic Weekly* figures so prominently in the texts of many articles appearing in the learned journals of many a university all over the world. It is no mean achievement of an editor, considering that in the fifty years prior to 1947, the number of articles by Indian authors appearing in technical journals of repute rarely exceeded a score or two.

Though Rostow described Sachin's journal as the "*New Statesman* of the East", it was not on all fours with the *New Statesman*. It had, of course, the invigorating characteristics of the *New Statesman*, its youthfulness, a somewhat leftward slant, its capacity to attract the cream of intellectuals. And yet it was vastly different from the *New Statesman*. This was not surprising to many who knew Sachin well. To imitate was repugnant to his nature. In fact, it was to banish the imitative attitudes deeply entrenched among Indians that he waged his battle. His journal was testimony to his peculiarly Bengali inventiveness and Indian assimilativeness. The result was conspicuously striking. His editorials or weekly notes, which contained commentaries on contemporary events, were no more than a prelude to the creative discourses in the subsequent pages. More often than not, they displayed the theoretical generalisation based on Indian facts. This neat dichotomy between distilled news and the theoretical and analytical treatment of some of the economic and sociological problems was the hallmark of the *Weekly*; and all this was a result of Sachin's own genius. Hence, he used to take legitimate pride in the remark of Gunnar Myrdal that the "weekly notes" revealed the most essential facts about Indian society. This was also true of some of the contributions of Indian economists, both in the theoretical and applied fields. These ranged from the choice of technique, investment pattern, trade theory, marketed surplus to balanced-unbalanced growth, and they appeared first in the pages of the *Weekly*. If one were to write the history of economic thought in India since 1948, a place of pride has to be given to the *Economic Weekly*. This is no mean achievement of Sachin.

And yet, for all his signal achievements in initiating new trends in thinking, Sachin's was no original mind, though he was gifted with a rare perception and a capacity to look at everything analytically. The qualities required for sustained work were not there. He was constantly in search of answers to the myriad questions that assailed a restless soul like his. In this quest, he traversed frequently from one subject to another like a grasshopper. But his hopping was purposive, and he had the perseverance of a bee. In the rough and tumble of a hectic journalistic life, he had enough time to gather around him young minds in various fields. He provoked, teased, and even cajoled these men and women to think of new problems and think in a scientific manner. Some among them, who were richly endowed with a mental apparatus, would never have taken to writing but for Sachin's wheedling. His thought processes, like his attire, were sprawling, often loose, but none the less flowing and direct, and were founded on the rock of sound common sense. He could, therefore, raise the right questions which led to churning of the issues at a more fundamental level among his young contributors. That was the major reason why he spawned a new generation of young thinkers and social scientists whose contribution to the subject was internationally acclaimed.

Like all intellectuals, he too had his hobby horses. But he knew the limits up to which he should cling to them. Once he was convinced that some of his concepts had outlived their utility, he did not hesitate to reassess and jettison them with due detachment. The *Economic Weekly*'s birth almost coincided with the establishment of a Planning Commission. He firmly believed that planning of a comprehensive nature was necessary. He made no apologies for this view. But his beliefs were not dogma. He started with the basic premise as a value judgement, but subsequent thinking was directed in an analytical manner. He got contributions from economists, in the country and outside, on the various aspects of planning, the institutional changes necessary for it, the policy orientation and the model building relevant to it. In the process, he enriched our knowledge about planning and planning mechanism. With all this, however, he did retain enough respect for other views. He did not set equations between men and their theories, but between the needs of the prevailing situation and the theories required to tackle them.

With all his admiration for planning, he had come to a stage, in the last few years, where he had to reassess his views on the type of planning we had in the last decade and a half. Without offering any apology for his earlier views—and it was not necessary either as he was quite definite about some of the positive achievements during the Nehru era—he began, in his accustomed manner, to question whether planning in the existing form was not inadequate in a new emerging situation. In the editorial, appropriately entitled "Miles to go", in the very first issue of the *Economic and Political Weekly* which he brought out after he left the *Economic Weekly*, he wrote:

> The nation can no longer be activised by an incantation of Nehru's ideas and Nehru's policies. But the forces released during that era have by no means worked themselves out. The task before the country today is to free these forces from the dead weight which is holding them back.... To leaven the enormous mass of dough, the yeast has clearly not been adequate.

It was this spirit, the spirit of enquiry, which was written all over the pages of his new *Weekly*.

His death has come at a time when the spirit as represented by Sachin Chaudhuri is most required to set in motion new thinking. Sachin, no doubt, has done his bit in putting his journal on a more secure basis than before, through the establishment of a trust. But it is still a toddling baby which needs caressing and guidance. Though many of his friends were conscious of his failing health, they were fondly hoping that he would live a few years more to ensure the smooth functioning of the trust. If he had not left the scene so soon.... But it is these "ifs" which make life both tragic and triumphant.

The Economic Times, 25 December 1966; originally appeared under the pen name DS.

Part IV

The places in between

64

The struggle of memory against forgetting

THE moment past is not necessarily moment dead: it comes back disconcertingly in a new incarnation to haunt those who live by their memories. The sudden dissolution of an impregnable empire that once was Soviet Russia and oneirolysis of a socialist dream have triggered the primal instincts in 'soviet man' to differentiate by language, and stir an exclusionist ethnicity. A former Soviet socialist republic, Moldovia, has become the new state of Moldova—reasserting its Romanian heritage, paying homage to the monarch who founded the first Moldova state some five hundred years ago, and consigning to the dump-hill of history the statues of Lenin and Stalin installed when it was absorbed in the Russian empire through the Russo-German Treaty of 1940.

The country is struggling to dismantle the remnants of the socialist utopia which destroyed its literary traditions and linkages with its Romanian forebearers. But the dissolution process is as painful, perhaps more painful than a forced submergence to proletarian state as a salient of a large landmass with eleven time zones. The hammer-and-sickle has given way to the crowned eagle as the new nation's symbol; the capital, a Russian-sounding Kishinev became Romanian-sounding Chisinau. And yet the change is just symbolic despite all that the nascent democracy is striving to achieve. The Russian tutelage is thrown out but not the Russian presence. The Russians, 12 per cent of its population, have carved out a state within a state. The Transnistra region of the country—the left bank of the Dnister River—is under siege with the presence of the 14th Russian army. The Russians may have gone, but they stubbornly resist being forgotten. The most admired and loved is a Russian, the poet Pushkin. Among the ruins of the fallen statues of the communist apparatchiks, Pushkin stands serenely in the central square of Chisinau. The Moldovans embraced Pushkin who came to their region as exile during the czarist regime. The Moldovans breathe and live literature with Romanian roots. Pushkin embellished and adorned it, with Russian historicity. Though Pushkin belonged to the ruling class, he became one of the folk heroes in Moldova and continues to be so even after the communists have faded as minimalists of yore.

But the old system of opaque statism lumbers on. Privatisation is in the air—privatisation of the collective farms, state enterprises, houses and apartments. The patrimonial bonds, freely distributed to the people in proportion to the length of their employment with the state, entitle them to stake their ownership claims. There is thus a withering away of the state—a tragicomic commentary on the Marxian epiphany to usher in the communist millennium. Privatism, a new nomenclature for capitalism, has become an heir apparent to socialism. But the transition to a new era is facing roadblocks. For privatisation requires a market, market needs institutions, institutions require a civil society with its rights and obligations. They see the lodestar of new opportunities, a new world—*Nova Mir*, as the Russians would say. But a reach for it is a struggle of the past against the future; a battle of an individual against collectivity; a conflict between change and inertia; and a bout between interests and institutions. It is a long and arduous haul to reach the destination.

Chisinau is strewn with myriad monuments to the communist regime. There is a gigantic building with granite, stern in appearance like the countenances of the communists but with all the appurtenances for luxurious living. From there the command was to go from the communist party to all the functionaries of the Republic. It has long corridors, stretching as if to infinity, a typical Kafkaesque setting with its claustrophobia. Now this palace has become home for a parliamentary commission—a revenge taken by time on proletarian dictatorship. The communists too changed. The former first secretary of the party is Chairman of Parliament, and former second secretary is now President of the country. The Marxist dynamics may not have created a new society but it is shown to have a power to convert the former democratic centralist into a central democrat.

Though change is pervasive there is one constant in the equation of change. Cricova, Moldova's famous winery ensconced snugly at some hundred and thirty metres under ground—has been producing wines, come revolution or war, with velvety taste, flavour of black currant and cherry stones. This winery may be a metaphor for the regime that is bygone. It is in 'adit', which connotes for them darkness and dampness. And yet it is not a metaphor, as wine ages to taste velvety, whereas the regime aged to be hated. Memory, however, succeeds in its struggle against forgetting, an evocative phrase of Milan Kundera's, reflecting the trauma of a transforming society. A stack of wine bottles awaiting export still bears a label "The Soviet socialist republic of Moldovia of the U.S.S.R."

Business Standard, 21 April 1997.

65

The last laugh in Afghanistan

FIFTEEN years have gone by and yet very few have known what exactly happened in Vietnam that destroyed first the American armour, then the American army and, finally, this greatest nation's self-confidence. America had all the resources, all the manpower, all the support of its allies, but all in vain. They came a cropper; scapegoats were sought and also found. The media played foul, the students rioted, the draft dodgers' ranks swelled, liberalism sapped the very vitality of the nation. Hence America must go back to its roots, the roots of its bravado, its cruelty, its predatory onslaught on the Indians to make a nation. And when the memories of the ignominy were about to fade, there came the adventure of Brezhnev's Russia which sent its army of over a hundred thousand men into Afghanistan. At last, the Americans were gleeful. The same Russians had been smiling in their sleeves at the US predicament in Vietnam; and now they would meet their Vietnam in Afghanistan. Before their minds' eyes the traumatic saga of Vietnam resurfaced, only that this time the Russians would be the victims and they the gloaters.

And it almost happened that way. The Russians got sucked in till there arose a new star, Gorbachev, on the Russian firmament to announce the Russian withdrawal. Though superficially the Americans greeted the news with a sense of relief, deep down they wished for a Russian debacle. Aren't the Afghans great fighters? They would be on the Russians' trail. While the Russians were retreating they would be stewed in their own juice—as the Americans were in the final hours of the Vietnam War. The tales of wishful thinking went on long into the Arabian Nights.

The deadline of 15 February 1989 came and has gone. The Russian army is back in Russia and in the barracks. But the expected denouement has not come about, disappointing the Americans. The fib was floated that Najibullah's government would collapse the moment the Russians were gone. Were not the Russians defeated, as the Americans had been in Vietnam, and if Americans had been trounced why would not the Russians be? Are they superhuman? The Mujahadeen are strong, armed and supported by American dollars. But lo and behold, the Russians are out, and Najibullah is still there, deeply entrenched, even stronger than before and smiling with the newly acquired confidence of a victor. The Mujahadeen are banging their heads on the outer walls of Jalalabad, with their noses rubbed into dust and the rotting flesh of their dead comrades all around.

Hyperbolic reportage in American papers about the heroic struggle of the Mujahadeen, day in and day out, has destroyed the credibility of the so-called free press of the free world. The reports were managed by the American administration and the governments of other western countries in no way differently from the way the Indian press is. Blind anti-communism and self-serving analyses of Russian motives led them up the garden path, with made-up stories about the valour and bravado of the Afghan guerrillas. When the Najibullah regime survived for three months after the Russians' withdrawal, the truth began to emerge. The people here, as elsewhere, had been taken for a ride by the press and the western governments. The same press is now providing different tidings. Najibullah's party, the PDPA, is "now stronger than was supposed and it has indeed a strong base in cities and an indeterminate amount of support throughout Afghanistan." The Russians had left not because they had lost the war but because of a shift in their geopolitical strategy with Gorbachev's ascendancy. Russians have reached the point of what Paul Kennedy would describe as "imperial overstretch." It can no longer follow hegemonic policies internationally unless it resolves its internal social tensions, reforms its productive apparatus, and provides outlets to the people for articulation of their aspirations and hopes. In this grand power game Afghanistan is small change. True, the Russians did not cover themselves with glory in their Afghan occupation, but neither were they vanquished by the guerrillas armed by the Americans. In the Russian calculus the gains of exit are far in excess of the losses. There was thus no question of the Russians meeting their Vietnam in Afghanistan. Russia knows, as Americans and the world know, that Afghanistan cannot and would not remain beyond the pale of Russian influence. Geopolitical factors would never permit it.

What about the so-called brave Mujahadeen? They are riffraff drawn from squabbling and warring tribal communities. They have used American money for opium traffic and arms to mutilate and murder their own people more than the enemy. Selig Harrison, who is a pariah now in the American political arena, has been hammering home the point for months that the US government knows very little about the regime it has been seeking to overturn for so long and that the American press has fed the public cock-and-bull stories. He has produced the most damaging evidence about the American press. He has disclosed that "those few US journalists who got as far as Kabul and had the backbone to controvert received wisdom had their copy either rewritten or cut to ribbons. Most journalists just sat in the Intercon [Intercontinental Hotel] in Peshawar and did nothing." He knew of one journalist "who was eating his dinner when he was asked to file a story urgently to New York. He went out and made up completely phoney footage."

The cozenage was not confined to the realm of newspaper reporting but extended to portraying the Mujahideen as a patriotic band of Afghans, yearning for the liberation of their land. That they were the satanic errand boys of Khomeini was veiled, that they were a pipeline for heroin transmission to the western countries was pigeonholed, that they perpetrated the most heinous kind of crimes and atrocities on their fellow countrymen was swept under the carpet. Now everything has come out in the open. Thousands of prisoners were mutilated and women raped. Raza Anwar, an Afghan not by any means a friend of Najibullah, has written in his book that "to the Mujahadeen it is the observance of Islam itself to torture and mutilate the bodies of captured rebels." There have been several defections from the ranks of the Mujahadeen to the Afghan government, repelled by the cruelty of the rebels. By just being Najibullah's enemies, the Mujahadeen increased the ranks of the friends of the regime. Najibullah skilfully exploited the dark side of the rebels to prove his bona fides. He also offered blandishments to co-opt different tribal leaders in the government, destroying the unity of the Mujahadeen. Afghan society was never homogeneous; it has always been fractured with myriad tribal loyalties. With the passage of every day, the Najibullah regime is gaining sustenance and the hopes of Pakistan and America of toppling it are receding.

At the best of times the Americans are loath to remove their blinkers; the situation is now worse. They are still wedded to the belief that the Russian-backed government in Afghanistan will collapse and therefore they have turned their backs on a negotiated settlement. But Benazir Bhutto's Pakistan cannot afford that luxury. With so much on her plate, Benazir Bhutto wants to back out from the American policy and end the Afghan imbroglio. She does not want the Afghans to believe that they have traded one type of invader for another. A retreat now will be a victory later. Will the Americans oblige? Till then, Pakistan and Afghanistan will stand on the edge of a precipice. The Americans will see their greenbacks vanish in the valleys of Afghanistan, will provide arms to Afghans to kill Afghans and in return will get the dreadful scourge of heroin destroying American youth. In the furrows on Gorbachev's forehead at the time of signing the Afghan agreement, the Americans may have discovered the image of their own fate in Vietnam. Gorbachev did not laugh then, but he may be doing so now. Did they not say, those who laugh last, laugh best?

Economic and Political Weekly, 2 September 1989.

66

A waltz to war through peace

"POWER flows from the barrel of a gun", said Mao Zedong long ago, but his sayings, like his communist legacy, are slowly tiptoeing into the past. Its modern equivalent is that power grows from the womb of defeat. Look at Japan, now itching to be the greatest economic power, and it will not be long before it becomes a military one. And there follows West Germany close on the heels of Japan. These two nations, defeated in the last war, are back on the world stage as major players. Until recently, despite their economic power, they maintained low profiles in the international arena, be it international economic policy or East–West relations or positioning toward the third world countries. For the last three decades, they were satisfied with being mere coadjutors of the hoity-toity Americans. There is no need to keep these postures any more. The occupying powers have lost their occupation of being the victors. The defeated nations can turn their noses up to tell the Americans that they have grown too big for their boots. The world's greatest nation cannot be the world's greatest power. Japan has already begun to flex its muscles in international forums and in its bilateral relations with America, to aspire to beef up its defence capability by daring to produce fighter planes by borrowing American blueprints. West Germany has thrown down the gauntlet by questioning, for the first time, the NATO defence strategy in Europe designed to checkmate Soviet Russia. No more tutoring from Big Brother about how Germany should defend itself. Gorbachev has transformed the Germans by his charm, his charisma, his sleek footwork. When he addressed the United Nations, declaring that Russia would scale down the size of its armies, the United States played down the significance of the Russian offer. Maybe it is a ruse to lull the NATO allies into false security; may be Gorbachev is concealing his motives or buying time to reconstruct the Soviet economy before unleashing his secret weapons. The Bush Administration has been leisurely studying how the United States and its allies should match initiatives in foreign policy on a one-to-one basis. But the Germans have no patience with the Americans' endless search for a foolproof solution. In fact, they don't want any solution. They are in a hurry. Germany's chancellor Helmut Kohl and its foxy foreign minister Hans-Dietrich Genscher do not want to see short-range nuclear weapons on its frontiers, let alone modernising them at some point in the future. The western alliance is in disarray, with close friends breaking ranks slowly but inexorably.

What is in the German position that so much disconcerted the United States and caused anguish and anger to its President? Have Germans become war-weary or peace-mongers? If it is the short-range weapons system that the Germans would dump today, they would dispatch tomorrow the conventional land army back to the barracks, leaving the whole of western Europe exposed to the machinations and manipulations of a wily Gorbachev, so the Americans say. The cold country may have warmed up on design. Gorbachev will rule the roost and, sooner than later, Europe will not escape the death hug of the bad old bear. And yet it seems that the maturation of the United States' foreign policy is stalled, with all the vast resources of finely honed minds at its command. Foes remain distant in this game-theoretic foreign policy but friends who are supposed to be near are also distant. The minds of friends are a foreign territory, difficult to navigate, complicated to understand, and too enigmatic to be comfortable.

The tongues of foreign policy seers have begun to wag. Kissinger, who wears uneasily the mantle of Metternich, could not remove his blinkers. While asserting like an oracle that "the *status quo* cannot continue," he glories in the dream that "America will reshape constructively Europe's future." He still perceives the Russia of Gorbachev as a mirror image of the Russia of Stalin and West Germany as a likely victim of a Russian offensive. He pontificates that Germany should choose between "a new orientation to the East and the existing orientation to the West." And if it cannot choose the West, it would "lose the confidence of both." To him that is the historical pattern of German behaviour. Another expert, the ex-national security adviser of Carter, Zbigniew Brzezinski, is relaxed that the high noon of communism is over. For him war is banished if communism is buried and he would not care a damn if the Germans dump the nuclear arsenal into the Atlantic Ocean. Cyrus Vance, another foreign policy grandee, sees major changes unfolding in Europe but does not want America to flinch from "moving strong militarily, economically and politically." Listening to these prophets, one sorely misses Walter Lippman who knew how to shut up others, while shutting up himself faced with bewildering world events.

A fundamental tenet of science is that you cannot prove what is right but you can only prove what is wrong. It is not difficult to fault the American perception of German policy. Nobody is asking why Germany is deviating from the policy of the western world. Is it because it has suddenly discovered new virtues in Russian friendship? Is it scared that it would be the first country to be engulfed in a nuclear holocaust if war should break out? There are more complex reasons for Germany's behaviour. It is true that Kohl would lose the elections, with the electorate warming to Gorbachev's charisma and bonhomie. But the real reasons are deeper. Russia is fatigued and has lost its vitality to play war games. For the first time, internal tensions and conflicts have caused Russia to look inward. When such a formidable foe is in retreat, it is a Godsend for Germany to realise its dream of unification. It is deeply imbedded in the German psyche that their country is the Fatherland and it is the leader of western Europe in terms of economic power, human resources and defence potential. They are stirred by the vibrations of their history, glorious and hegemonistic, and agitated by their contrasting present, at once cringing and craven. Those who once occupied the throne do not relish being foot-soldiers of others, and least of all of those who are a spent force. Their impotence was manifest in their partitioned existence. If only they could unite, their power would rise like the phoenix, from the ruins of the Second World War. Two halves add up to more than one. The long-cherished unification of Germany will be a cathexis. Hans-Dietrich Genscher has told his countrymen, through his parliament, that the conflict with America is "really about weapon systems that can reach other parts of our Fatherland." The reaction is not confined to the politicians but is pervasive. A West German official lower down, when asked about

Washington's irritation with German disputation of NATO policies, shot back, "This is occupation mentality," and then bit his lips lest his inner thoughts break out. But this simple historic fact has escaped American foreign policymakers, as it has the British and the French. Even some of those foreign policy advisers like Brzezinski and Kissinger, who ought to know better, coming as they do from Poland and Germany, have not perceived this deeper significance of Germany's deviation because of their paranoiac attitude towards communism.

German reunification with a resurgent nationalism will threaten both Poland and the Jews, who suffered so much under Hitler's Germany. And yet they talk in the cold war idiom of stemming the tide of communism and gloat over it. Germany's "new orientation to the East", Kissinger laments, is in fact a Bismarckian vision of German power. Germany does not turn East or West, it moves only toward itself, its innards, its culture, and the historical legacy of power. Today its eastern orientation is not because it has developed friendship with Russia but because it can rediscover its soul lost in the labyrinthine chaos of 1945. Marx's divination that history repeats itself first as tragedy and then as farce has gone askew, like his divination about the evolution of human society. History repeats itself as tragedy not once but perpetually, as humanity never learns.

Economic and Political Weekly, 3 June 1989.

67

A new pharaoh knew not Joseph

THOSE were the days of animal spirits possessing the leaders and the followers; the devils darted through the eerie darkness of the age; it was the era of hatred and holocaust. The mills grinding millions of innocent Jews to their death worked overtime for their only crime of professing the faith of Judas. Until that cataclysmic event, they were part of the body politic of the civilised world—they were the brains and they were the businesses bringing material welfare to their fellow beings. But deep down the skin of the people of Christ was lurking the animus against the people of Judas, sanctified by the anecdotal myth of Judas's betrayal of Christ. There was left not shame but only sham sentiment. The conscience of Europe—the cradle of modern civilisation—went into deep slumber. The annihilation of people not for crime but for faith was the last straw which broke the back of the diaspora of Jews spread across all nations. You may belong to any nation but the definition of your nationhood is changed if you are a Jew. You are a citizen of a state in a season but not in all seasons. Even before Orwell's Newspeak there was a Jewspeak—language changed its meaning, nuances and words, when it came to the Jews. The frontiers of decency rolled back. The diaspora's days were numbered, so it was thought: Jews dreamed of their Promised Land for honour, security and peace. For them, life was a sum not merely of possessions but of their spiritual heritage and cherished beliefs. And the nation of Israel was born amidst the adulation of secularism through the midwifery of the statesmen of the western world and for Jews a time of Apocalypse arrived. They buried the ghosts of their sinning conscience, no matter that in the process they committed a new sin.

Forty long years have elapsed since the birth of Israel but the agony and trauma continue in its more intense form: Israel has lived surrounded by hostility. But when it is about to be recognised by its congenital adversaries, the whole concept of a Jewish state as a haven for the world's diaspora is being challenged, not by the dispossessed Palestinians, not by the Germans, their nemesis during the interwar period, but ironically enough by the nationals and rulers of Israel. If the dissipation of the diaspora was the coordinate of the new state, it has certainly not materialised over the years. Its history has shown that Israel, whatever else it might be, was certainly not a magnet for the world's Jews. Many from different lands who migrated to Israel in the first flush of their enthusiasm and religious fervour returned to their much-hated existence in the diaspora, particularly in the United States. Jews leaving Russia for Israel short-circuited their routes through deception to find homes largely in America but also in other countries in Europe.

After Gorbachev relaxed Soviet emigration rules, several thousands of Russian Jews are flowing toward America, so much so that the US authorities have diverted the asylum quota for the Vietnamese and others toward the Russian Jews.

An Israeli lady addressing an American Jewish congregation bluntly told the audience, "As an Israeli, I was brought up with the concept of the negation of the diaspora—we exist here and those over there are finished. For us to come to terms with the diaspora's existence is the theological equivalent of Vatican II." This is a very widely prevalent sentiment in Israel. They want immigration from other countries and the shrivelling of the diaspora in order to make that place the moral and political manifesto guiding the new generation of Israelis. But the Jews in the diaspora refused to oblige and now are branded as moral cowards with their love for their faith merely skating on the surface. There is a strong reaction from the orthodox Jews against the Jews in the diaspora, which is threatening the very foundations of Israel as a nation.

But the challenge thrown by the rulers of Israel is hurting the very Jews who did so much to nurse and stabilise Israel and to ensure its security. Jews are being rediscovered; the identity of Jews is being Xrayed. The question is no longer where the Jews are but who the Jews are. Who can you call a Jew? In the process of defining Jews, the whole relationship between the state of Israel and its loyal co-religionists in the American diaspora has been despoiled. The controversy arising from redefining who is a Jew is the most historic of disputes among Jews, originating in the parting of the ways amongst Christ's followers. But it has taken on a new dimension because it has fundamental implications for the Law of Return, the rock on which Israel is founded. Under this law every Jew, wherever he may be from, can become a citizen of Israel immediately after crossing its borders. The Law of Return, at one bold stroke, implicitly defined a Jew and thus rang the curtain on 2000 years of Jewish suffering in the world's diaspora. The new definition which the government of Israel, under the pressure of orthodox Jews, has been trying to adopt will, while embracing a vast majority of Jews—Conservative, Reform and unaffiliated who are born of Jewish mothers—reject those whose conversion has been sponsored by a Conservative or a Reform rabbi. This would most directly affect about 100–200 converted Jews every year, but far more disturbing is its impact on conversions by rabbis from the Reform, Conservative and reconstructionist branches of Judaism. Which means that almost the entire American Jewry will be delegitimised by the mapping of its close links with these three movements.

American Jews are being alienated, not only by the redefining of Jews but also by the insensitive acts of commission which are making them suspect in American society. The Pollard case, an Israeli operation where an American Jew was used for naval espionage, is almost putting Israel in the enemy camp. They fear that by this one act of stupidity, American society, which was the one singular source of strength to the Jewish state, will be alienated and the entire Jewish community's loyalty impugned. In the same way, Israel's South African connections have strained seriously the relations between Jews and the blacks—a growing minority with an electoral clout.

Even more important than these two issues, the souring of relations between American Jews and the Israelis is aggravated by the treatment Israel has administered to the West Bank Palestinians. The sagacious amongst the Jews have been saying, more frequently, assertively and loudly, that the policy to beat into submission the helpless, hapless and poor Palestinians has taken away all the moral ardour from the ethical foundations of Israel. "If they become like the enemy, then they are no different from the enemy." The guilt of the Jewish massacres in the Nazi era is already fading and if the Israelis behave the way they do, soon the people in America as elsewhere would find no difference between the killings of innocent Palestinians and the mass gas chamber deaths of innocent Jews in the Germany of Hitler. American Jews have realised this and they are trying to persuade the recalcitrant Israeli government to retrace its steps. It was the courageous and visionary American Jews who risked their all by talking to Arafat and the PLO. But they got in return the epithet of being renegades to the cause of Zionism.

If Israel does not wake up to this new reality, history will be cruel to it. Jews in America have been the staunchest, the wealthiest, and the most consistent supporters of Israel. It is their voice and persistence which provided the sinews to the American government's support of Israel. Jews in America do not reside in islands of their own. If the Jewish diaspora is strong in American society, there are also the diasporas of the blacks, the Hispanics and the Asians to boot. They compete with the Jewish diaspora for influence over American policy and they have their own ethnic, religious and cultural bonds with their old countries. In this crucible of conflicting claims, interests and loyalties, the Jews in America have to survive and succeed. The geopolitical and cultural winds can blow from all directions. It is for Israel, therefore, to recognise that the rules of the game have been changing if they have not already changed. It is not too late for the new rulers of Israel to know their loyal old Joseph.

Economic and Political Weekly, 22 April 1989.

68

Manila: The more it changes...

NOTHING changes in this archipelago of over 7000 islands. In fact, nothing can change. Seasons come, festivals come, presidents come; they remain for a while to amuse and to be amused but when they go they leave behind the debris, the muck and the scum of the earth to wallow in dirt. Everything that comes and goes is preordained, as it were. The Spanish usurped this land of beautiful people but left only their sonorous names, music of erotic exhilaration, and the devil-take-the-hindmost attitude. The democratic Americans took them over to become imperial and left the people to stew in their own juice but without any identity, debased by the seductive onslaught of Yankee manhood. The Japanese, dreaming of the grandeur of the co-prosperity sphere in Asia, made the interregnum traumatic and dehumanising. What remained constant in this perpetually shifting political landscape was the rubric—Philippines with three Ps: papacy, symbol of religion; pork, a national food; and a pregnant woman, a pro-life celebration of Virgin Mary.

Come the season as it has been coming from times immemorial. The Xmas aroma is in the air with choral music being hummed in offices, streets, shantytowns, stadiums and the Palace. With the mellow sun above, Kipling would have mused, as he did eight decades ago, that

> ... the Christmas day is breaking wan;
> they will drink our health at dinner—
> those who tell us how they love us
> and then forget us till another year be gone.

A little over three years ago, a new revolution broke, more by the stupidity of a loony president than by the awakening consciousness of the *hoi polloi*. A tyrant was banished and a gentle, docile woman, widow of a rival, martyred politician, took over. People here, as elsewhere, were elated. Oh, the nation was unshackled, they roared. In the true modern tradition of Asia, the widow was installed in the Malacanang Palace. Oscar Wilde would have naughtily described it as a "triumph of hope over experience"—a remark he made about a man marrying a second time. Then again, except for a different person of a different sex, nothing changed, as nothing would ever change. The widow is showing every promise of being like those who have preceded her in other lands in Asia. Perhaps widowhood is a sacrificial offering on the altar of power. The same concentric circles of families resurfaced: Marcoses are out, Acquinos are in; Romulos stepped out, Coyuangos have stepped in; Laurels bowed out but Monsods filled the void.

The same gentry from the latifundia, which have submerged the landless labourers into servitude, now in new attire and symbols, formed the cabinet and assumed the role of power brokers. For a while, some soothing sounds were made, egalitarianism was flaunted, inequality and injustice were declared to be fugitives. But the law of motion of social change is circular. All these slogans faded. The ranks of rebels still swell in the jungle of Davov; the military is at bay. The foreign military bases are still there and would be there till the cows come home. Who would otherwise pay $500 million a year for their use and bail out the faltering economy?

Every day, gossip columns are agog with gory stories of disappearing Filipinos. Benjamin d'Lazaro, a left-wing polemicist and lampoonist, was snatched away in the very presence of his wife by ISAAF, a code word for the military intelligence group, and such abductions are mounting. Marcoses may have gone to the nunnery but a rich harvest of martyrs is reaped. And why should the military base be removed? It is a source of a thriving business in flesh. Some doyen amongst the pimps in the adjacent region brazenly told newspaper correspondents that if the bases were removed, the employment situation in the region would gravely deteriorate. He gave out some mind-boggling figures of his own earnings from pimping.

The whole Philippine society is a contradiction. It is predominantly a Catholic country but catholicism is not a virtue. The small but pious clerics doffing the frock join the ranks of the rebels; the beautiful, shy and ever-youthful girls become strumpets for lucre and they have their rendezvous in offices, hotels and other public places. A coy woman has become a *femme fatale*. The taxi drivers have become depraved. You cannot travel in these vehicles without taxi driver's licence and vehicle numbers being noted in a diary by a policeman. The line between virtue and vice, prayer and pandering has almost disappeared. But vices don't stick as there is a Virgin Mary idol in all places conveniently situated, so that you can quietly confess your sins on the way to committing new ones.

With the society in doldrums, being swindled by politicians left and right over the years, administrators do not refrain from boondoggling, cranking out figures. A hoity-toity chairman of the planning board thundered at the time of the visit of the IMF mission that she would allow lowering of the economy's growth rate from 6.5 per cent to 6 per cent only over her dead body and the next day went on a foreign junket. It has become a habit among bureaucrats to be perpetually peripatetic on one excuse or another. The travel cycle of the bureaucrats has become similar to the life cycle of Solomon Grundy in the nursery rhyme. They leave on a foreign tour on Monday, dine on Tuesday, wine on Wednesday, do business on Thursday to leave on Friday for home for rest to be fresh to resume the cycle.

While the debate on the growth rate goes on—does it not have an echo in our ancient land?—resources are frittered away on one cockeyed scheme or another. Now there is a vision of a 'mini-Marshall Plan.' Filipino bureaucrats and politicians are sharpening their wits, tuning their ears and refurbishing their socialising skills. They will be on the hunt for new pastures. If in the meantime prices rise, inflation erodes social values and public misery abounds, there is a kindly and matronly president, with a mellifluous voice, to issue a hokum to the merchants to roll back prices and to the industrialists to reduce their cost of production. The next day the newspapers go to town announcing that prices have fallen by two pesos per kilo. The day after there is a rash of social amnesia and nobody talks about prices any more.

So life goes on in this sprawling archipelago with hurricanes, deluges, and the deceptions of politicians. But the future for the country looks murky. The country has lost its zest and elan, with the corrupt and debauched leadership entrenched for so long. The memories of their great heroes José Rizal and Manual Roxas are fading. Slavery may have overtly gone but the scars left by different conquerors have eaten deep into the vitals of national pride and identity. It is slowly sinking into the psyche of the people that geographic independence is not a correlate of freedom from want and decent livelihood with honour and dignity. And in that state of mind, they hear the voices of their consanguineous fraternity in not-too-far-away Hawaii which enjoys affluence and freedom from the tyranny of their fellow countrymen. What is wrong being one more state in a federal polity, the United States of America, which grows by acquisition? The Philippines one day may simply drop out of the cartogram as a nation state, though its name may continue to retain the three Ps but with different connotations—pomp, patronage, and passivity.

Economic and Political Weekly, 11 February 1989.

69

Sri Lanka: The Poya epoch

FULL moon day, called Poya day in Sri Lanka, is a holiday, but it is not like any other holiday. Lord Buddha was born, died and was reborn, all on a full moon day. It is movement in a circle—birth, death, and rebirth. Death is merely an interregnum. So do not bother about death and not at all about life. Birth and death are the variables as in a simultaneous equations system, which is what Sri Lanka's society is. You hoard credits by observing the Buddha's birth and death by fasting and praying. Fast you must when you are unemployed with no income or employed on a pittance. Praying is a correlate of fasting. If fasting cleanses the body, praying purges the soul of impurities. Poya day comes every month, twelve times a year. Was the Buddha born twelve times and did he die twelve times in a year? you may ask. But does it really matter if the Buddha was born, died and was reborn on the full moon day of May? If there is no food and there are no jobs, then it helps spiritual enrichment if you fast and pray, pray and fast.

Birth, death, and birth again: the cycle goes on. Elections are in the air. Political parties are coming back to life, touching concern for the poor and the downtrodden is being expressed, new slogans are being composed, socialism consigned to a lumber room is now being refurbished. The ruling SLFP's confidence is wearing thin. It knows that it is being stripped of its leftist garments. It is struggling to be reborn. The economy is stagnating and unemployment is mounting. But do not raise unpleasant questions in this Poya season. The ruthless terror unleashed on striking railway workers (does it ring a bell?), the killing of university students, the grinding down of the youth who rebelled in 1971, the unfolding of dynastic power—you should abandon all such thoughts. Didn't the late Prime Minister—the present one's husband, the future one's father and the father-in-law may be of the one after—in a burst of brilliance come up with the idea that led to industrial peace? Hadn't income distribution become more equal? Again the Poya syndrome, birth and death, and birth again.

A new kind of 'non-elective democracy' is being born. The people are so happy with the government that they are urging postponement of the elections. Or so the official news media make out. But Sirimavo Bandaranaike, true democrat that she is, says, nothing doing. Some say that these are all trial balloons to see if elections can possibly be postponed. This may turn out to be a futile exercise, partly because of what is happening in the neighbouring countries. The cognoscenti aver that the SLFP faces a 'prisoners' dilemma', that its own behaviour is being conditioned by what others are likely to do or will do. In the meantime, rumblings have become louder in the SLFP, threatening a split. According to the grapevine, parliament was consigned to hibernation till 19 May lest a large number of the SLFP members crossed over to the opposition.

The CPL's love affair with the SLFP has ended. It cringingly whispers its approbation of the government's non-achievements and defensively tries to explain its posture during the recent strikes. But the CPL is small change in a large population and is expendable. The LSSP, which is struggling to recover from the battering it has received from the ruling party, is a bird of the same feather. Extinction threatens these parties, once supposedly the vanguards of a proletarian revolution.

The UNP, too, is being reborn. It is not the UNP you and I and others knew before. It, too, has turned socialistic. The old socialism of CPL, LSSP and SLFP is dead and a new one without compulsion and force is being born. What is this socialism? If for SLFP left of left is right, for UNP right of right is left. Politics, like the Buddha myth, has become circular. There is no end and no beginning. Nay, the beginning is the end and the end the beginning.

It is wall-poster socialism—loud in colours, titillating, but various. Banks and plantations have been nationalised, prices are administered, the land ownership pattern has been reformed—the trappings of a socialist state. There is a naïve faith in the State though it continues to be the handmaiden of an entrenched elite. If you want to fight the bourgeoisie you must use its own means. Here in Sri Lanka they dutifully follow this dictum of Lenin but by misreading socialism for the bourgeoisie. Nationalisation, price controls, all these means of socialism are employed to atrophy it. Social amnesia, loss of a sense of history, blurring of the vision are all inescapable in this Poya season with its alternation of birth and death.

The nearly three decades of independent Sri Lanka may well be described as a Poya epoch. Everything is being born or is dying and is being born again. Fasting, which is a surrogate for starving, and praying, which is a euphemism for inaction, have been constant in Sri Lanka's history. Revolution has been described as arrested evolution. If there is a shining example of a stymied evolution, it is Sri Lanka. The feudal oligarchy of the British period has continued, and the more it seemed to change the more it remained the same. Feudalism was leavened by a liquor-plied, neo-rich mercantile class which doubled for a capitalistic class. The same few families or their progeny held sway; Ceylonese society developed only in retrogression. You have to traverse miles and miles to discover even a semblance of developmental activity; capital stock has been rapidly depleted; the people in whose name political shenanigans have been conducted have remained bereft of any future and are cynical. Even organised labour has languished and its political wings have been clipped by internecine quarrels. The educated youth have drifted into parasitic occupations like pimping for tourists. Once in a while the somnolence of the society was shaken and the peace of the elite in power disturbed, when the army of the unemployed became the army of the night. With raw courage and faith in the faith, they tried to make a tryst with their destiny in 1971. But bravura is no alias for a revolution. Then twilight set in. Now the young men and women are being released from the prisons, completely sterilised of any ideas of revolutionary action. Evolution has been blocked off all right, but where is revolution? Or is dissolution arrested revolution?

Sri Lanka glories in the ancient ruins of Anuradhapura, capital city of King Parakramabahu VI. The city had begun to decay in his very lifetime. Now the modern ruins of Anura are being heaped on the ancient ruins of Anuradhapura. Ruins beget ruins—the dilapidation of the economy and the crashing of morale are there for all to see. Hope plays truant and the land is rendered arid with cynicism. The Prime Minister dots the land with statues of her husband, heaven knows whether in celebration of his death or in perpetuation of his memory. The laws of a socialist state spawn not justice and equality but in-laws. Access to the Bo tree, supposed to be the oldest on the planet, is a correlate of access to the house of the Bs. In such a land you fast and pray, pray and fast.

Economic and Political Weekly, 5 March 1977.

Part V

Time's sweet revenge

70

Old grain breaks through new husk

GORBACHEV came, spoke, and was conquered by his friendly foes. With dignified mien, measured tone and serene face, he expounded on the evils that beset his empire, particularly during the Stalin era: with a few phrases framed in quotidian language, he de-ideologised the differences between East and West. He reminded the world that conflict between nations and systems betrays intellectual impoverishment and the world would be a decent and better place to live in because of the "objective commonality of our destiny." The basis of universal peace and prosperity, he said, "is the freedom of choice as an unexceptional principle and if we affirm our adherence to freedom of choice, then there is no reason for the view that some live on earth by virtue of divine will, while others are here quite by chance." His punch line, which startled the audience and the world at large, was that "no economic reform is possible without matching dismantling of the political infrastructure of the Soviet regime." This atheist, a banner-holder of communist society, was making a confession as it were before God, of the sins his predecessors in the Soviet land had committed in the last seven decades. In this speech, he swept aside all the contradictions of capitalism, which the high priests of communism had made the basic justification for a communist state. Gorbachev came as an apparatchik, a communist Mephistopheles from the cold, but bowed out as a prophet of a warm new world.

Has he made history stand on its head? Or has he just restored a history which was topsy-turvy? Exactly ninety years ago, the same cleavage of views haunted the Second International. The main dramatis personae were Eduard Bernstein, Karl Kautsky, Wilhelm Liebknecht, Ignaz Auel, and many others from south Germany who reinterpreted the Marx-Engels doctrine and argued that capitalism would not decline due to its inner contradictions; it would instead reveal a far more robust capacity to adapt, as capitalist production increased and became varied. They visualised that the general crisis that Marx projected as characterising the capitalist mode of production would simply evaporate. For these reasons the sound democracies should avoid political power and concentrate on betterment of the conditions of workers within the existing social, political and economic order. Bernstein went even further:

> It must not expect to institute socialism as a result of a political and social crisis, but should build socialism by means of the progressive extension of social control and the gradual application of the principle of cooperation. The final goal, no matter what it is, is nothing; the movement is everything.

Bernstein and others of his ilk were furiously attacked with the choicest epithets, which was a staple of communist debate; and the one who spearheaded this onslaught was the young Rosa Luxemberg earning her spurs in the communist movement. Can one hear the echoes of the same debate now in the speeches of Gorbachev before the United Nations? Yes, the husk is new, the grain that breaks through it is ancient.

Who is Gorbachev? Is he a mere technocrat seduced by western affluence, a political sissy who sounds the death-knell of communism as a philosophy that overlaid the poor man's struggles over the last hundred and fifty years for a new millennium? As Cecil Markham of the *New York Times* asks, is the whole ideology under siege? Or is Gorbachev a Russian Jeremiah who is transmitting a new message that the communist movement is exfoliating, getting invigorated? But Gorbachev is not alone; the whole communist world is in ferment. The 'thousand flowers' are blooming. Communists in different communist nations are singing different tunes. And yet there is a pattern in their differences. The great divide is between communists ruling in communist countries and communists in non-communist countries.

A communist politician in Yugoslavia, an early drifter from the communist camp, said of the communist regime there, "The political bosses received their big black cars as early as 1946. A differentiation was being created that was quite opposed to our ideals and all that propaganda. That penetrated deeply into a young person." A Hungarian economist, S. Berend, a member of the Central Committee of the Communist Party, learned the hard way that

> ... it is not easy for Hungary to bring about a sound change. It dropped into a Stalinist era with internal-external conservatism that blocked the road to radical renewal and reform. Communism cannot be achieved in our lifetime. It will take a long period. Perhaps it would always remain an idea.

A Pole, a Marxist theoretician and adviser to the Communist Party, renounced the virtue of the traditional communist movement and believes "in the plurality of the socialist idea. It is not the monopoly of the communist movement. There are different roads to far-away socialist ideas. The Scandinavian Social Democracy realised something from these ideas."

But George Marchais, a French communist leader, would have nothing of this recantation. "I have never lost faith in what I believe—that is, socialism. I have never lost faith in socialism despite problems and difficulties." Yet another, now an editor of a paper in Italy, Daniele Billi-Heri, has no remorse:

> I have suffered so many disappointments. But I think that having been a committed communist has given me something that no one will ever be able to take away from me, something that I believe is important for any person: a capacity for indignation and rebellion.

What do these exilic encounters between communists in the communist world and those in the capitalist world signify? Perhaps you have to be in a communist state to be a non-communist or an ex-communist, and in a capitalist world to be a communist: That humanity's quest is always for what is not than what is, is an eternal verity of human existence. Our life is not one-dimensional; it is a sum of so many tangible and intangible things; and pluralism, not monism, paves the way for achieving these diverse pleasures of life. This is realised only when one nears the goal for which the struggle had been so hard and long. This is why those who live under communist regimes realise its infirmities more than those who perceive it from a distance and dream about it.

If capitalism were to adapt, change and usher in a new era of social equality, economic opportunity and amelioration of the impoverished, why did humanity go through the traumas of war, revolution, and the gory happenings in the killing fields? Slaves that we are of some defunct political philosophers and social engineers, we believe, so it seems, in a simplistic mission of the world and social change. Power, we were told, flows from the ownership of the means of production. Then why not transfer the means of production to the proletariat, so ran the argument. The State is the handmaiden of the capitalists. Then why not make it an instrument of the proletariat, the hitherto exploited hirelings of the decadent society, and anoint them with dictatorship? The result was no different. The State, that embodiment of naked power and exploitation, remains true to its nature, whether the class which dominates it is the greedy and sleazy capitalist or the vengeful proletariat. Gorbachev's stirring summoning of courage and idealism reveals a profound truth—not merely an indictment of communist regimes or the vulnerability of the capitalist system. There is no single pole which sustains the human endeavour for peaceful existence. It is a multipolar universe where religion, culture, geography, the philosophical moorings, and the productive forces all work in unison. Harmony and cohesion are assured only if these diverse forces, alien to one another but not additive vertically or horizontally, are given free rein. Freedom is the copping-stone of any organised social order; it may sometimes be restrained, it may at times be feeble, it may even be irksome, but it should never be allowed to languish. And that can happen only if the forces that create are deliberately balanced against those which destroy. Not to countervail power is to let hell loose on earth.

Economic and Political Weekly, 18 March 1989.

71

Gorbachev: Prometheus bound

SEVEN years ago around this time, the entire social and political history of human society was cataclysmically turned around, by the demise of communist Russia. People still debate whether it marked the end of history or the beginning of a new phase in its long march. Adherents of the failed God make Gorbachev the villain who undermined the system, by becoming a stooge of the western-capitalistic regimes. On the other hand, to antagonists of communism, he was a Prometheus who, witnessing the evils of the system from within, consciously destroyed it, to begin a new era of freedom.

Gorbachev, we were led to believe when he first came to prominence in 1985 as the General Secretary, wanted to save the Communist party and the system by reforming it. When he left the scene in his sombre farewell address, he sang altogether a different tune. "The totalitarian system, which prevented this country from becoming wealthy and prosperous for a long time also has been dismantled. A breakthrough has been made on the road to democratic reform and a multiparty system has become a reality." These are not surely the words of a reformist, but a revolutionary or you may call a counterrevolutionary, if what he laid to rest was the Russian revolution of 1917.

From his own memoirs as also his biography by Archie Brown, the Gorbachev that emerges is one like a prince of serendipity who stumbled into transforming Soviet society without seeking to do so. His early childhood and subsequent career certainly bespeak for his hidden agenda. Son of a tractor driver, he was brought up in

Stavropol just north of the Caucasus. Steeped in poverty, overwhelmed by the onslaught of famine—not natural but made by Stalin's forced collectivisation and by ostracisation in the wake of the arbitrary arrest of both his grandfathers—he and his family were brutalised both by the Nazis when they overpowered his region and by the Stalin regime. During his student days, which Gorbachev has so meticulously described in his memoirs, he had serious doubts about the system; and it is easy to take this narration as credible as it is consistent with what Gorbachev did when he came to power.

As First Secretary of the party's Krai Committee, he was concerned about agricultural production. He was exposed to the shenanigans of the system, which always falsely exaggerated agricultural production, and whenever the final outcome was belied, the blame was foisted on this cadre of the party or that in Stavropol. He was disillusioned there by the bluff and bluster of the party functionaries about the output figures and he often asked himself why this occurred time and again. He describes one such episode with perspicacity: " ... the situation was taking a turn for the absurd; while the leaders proclaimed achievements, the real state of affairs was worsening. The centre expected positive reports from the field and rapid speculation results. Well, whenever there is demand, there will be supply." He was applying Say's Law in economics to Soviet politics.

Walled within the Soviet Union, the country had become knowledge-proof. This dawned on Gorbachev in the 1970s when he visited continental Europe. He says of his experience:

> My travels abroad taught me that my previous belief in the superiority of socialist democracy over bourgeois system was shaken as I observed the functioning of civic society and the different political systems. Instead of seeking ways to catch up with other countries and prevent the country from sinking deeper into a state of crisis, the leadership was primarily concerned with devising new artificial ideological concepts which would sanctify the existing realities and present them as historical achievements.

Gorbachev talks about his mentor Andropov, who really brought him to the centre stage of Soviet politics. He was convinced, however, that Andropov knew Stalin's crimes better than anyone else. And yet Andropov did nothing. Most surprisingly, he describes Andropov's weaknesses in words which fit him to a tee. "He realised the need for changes, yet Andropov always remained a man of his time, and was one of those who were unable to break through the barrier of old ideas and values."

When Gorbachev got his chance, he failed to translate his own conviction and vision into an activist policy, the same way Andropov did. He insisted that the Soviet society could be salvaged through reform and not a total change; he vainly believed that the Union could be preserved; he misread tragically the significance of the Baltic revolt, and instead of firing the clique of apparatchiks like Yazor and Kryuchkov around him, ignored to his peril the democratic reformers. So the Soviet Union collapsed, swivelling him as a leader to the side wings. Vision relapses into myopia, if the hammer of power is without anvil.

Business Standard, 16 December 1997.

72

Trading Marx for dollars

MARX is on sale these days in the land of Lenin and Stalin. It may perturb the Marxists in Calcutta and Calicut but not those who have seen opportunities of trade in the midst of a debacle in domestic production. They tried to remove the exploitation of man by man by abolishing capitalism, they sought to plan for a heaven for workers of the world who were expropriated through the centuries. They generated quantities in the belief that quality would grow sooner or later out of quantity. They wanted to plan with the facts of the real world, but ended up planning without facts—at least the facts their comrades were conjuring up for so long. They daydreamt to write a grand novel of idealism, model men and women and ethereal happiness that would last till eternity, but came up with a fiction without imagination. They wanted to produce without trade, the latter because exchange means an exchange of the blood and toil of the poor for the profits of the rich and the hated. They looked for a revolution and now are faced with desolation.

The unkindest cut of all is having to dispose of in a secondary market at depressed prices the precious image of Karl Marx for a mess of pottage. Gorbachev now has indulged, in a clever way, in blarney of capitalism and capitalists to salvage his economic perestroika. Yes, there can be as many perestroikas as you want, depending upon what you set out to gain from the western democracies. If you need aid, call it economic perestroika; if you are hard pressed for democratic reform, call it democratic perestroika; if you want to promote trade, call it commercial perestroika. But every kind of perestroika has a price tag. You pay for it, and you have that perestroika which you can call your own.

Gorbachev has set the ball rolling. Boris Yeltsin is making his life miserable by giving him an ultimatum to launch a free market economy in five hundred days. If not, then Gorbachev, caught in a vice of his slogan of Leninism and Marxism on the one hand and economic perestroika on the other, is asking for a sliver of aid from his western friends. Gone now is the pretence that he wore last year that money was not needed for sustaining his reform programme. At this time "Soviet Russia is going through an extremely critical stage of perestroika", he pleaded in his letter to President Bush on the eve of the Houston summit. "Without breaking the obsolete economic structures, a further renewal of our society will be impossible." So far Gorbachev tried to chug along on his own but now he seems to have come to the end of his tether. He has demonstrated that he can manipulate the levers of power but it no longer pays, as it once did. Without any tangible assistance he will be powerless to withstand the fury of his angry mass of people, who lost the security of the bygone central planning without gaining the freedom and wherewithal to exercise a choice in the market to meet the minimum requirements for survival. In this ongoing film of Soviet perestroika, there are more fadeouts—of Marx, Lenin, Stalin—than fade-ins of capitalism and all that it is supposed to shower on hapless Russians.

But the dumping of Marx and Lenin and the relearning of Adam Smith and Ricardo is not enough in this revolutionary phase. For many-faceted perestroika, Gorbachev and his cohorts have to pursue relentlessly their study of Aristotle, Plato, Burke and Tocqueville, those gnomes of freewheeling capitalism that Russia and the Marxist revolution tried to bury in 1914. Now Oleg Rumyanstyev, a member of one of Moscow's small informal political groups, is bandying on the streets of Moscow a sheaf of papers heralding Russia's new constitution. He wants to be the James Madison of the Russsian democracy. "The period of Gorbachev's economic perestroika is over," he is already writing the political obituary of Gorbachev.

"We had no democratic forebears as in the West. We had to search abroad and in other national histories. There is nothing peculiar about that. The US constitution was established by people who already had a respect for the Bible, for private property. We have precious little of that. But some Russian roots also helped us. There was a great deal of discussion, for instance, in the early nineteenth century and then before the Bolshevik revolution about the need for a genuine court system."

Rumyanstyev and Yeltsin unfolded their blueprint of a new constitution for Russia, to the constitutional committee, calling it a document "thoroughly without ideology." This is apostasy for comrades afar in distant lands. Some brave soul mustered courage to call the draft constitution "a capitalist document" and "pretext for civil war." These neophyte politicians debunked not only communism but also the feudal order that predated it. "Communism", Marx had said, "is an advanced stage of capitalism". With all that is unfolding in Russia, maybe Marx's capitalism has just met its demise.

But that is not all. The salt is being rubbed on the wounds inflicted on communists the world over. The feasibility of economic perestroika is bearing scrutiny by the IMF, which Russia refused to join in 1946 calling it the imperialist club. The Fund's emissaries will be the final arbiters along with the World Bank and the OECD, to decide whether Karl Marx is dead and buried deep down the ground never to be resurrected. On the dead body of Marx and Marxism would rise the phoenix of the democratic Russian polity. But do not ask whether any new facts will be unearthed by the sleuths of the monetary Interpol; Russian statistics are a metaphysics, which is like a black rat in a dark hole which is not there. But do the facts matter? The only fact that will determine the final decision is not statistical but philosophical. If Marx is dead, what other facts are necessary?

This is all serious stuff; you require experts in economics, political science and sociology. There is a hilarious side to this economic-political perestroika. Some bright worldly wise Americans figured out how the pace of perestroika could be quickened in Russia. Ah, if only the women of Russia could be exposed to glamour, glitz and fashion, all the rest could be persuaded to embrace the new change. The bra manufacturers Duchowny and Foley, emulating the example of their leaders who initiated the SALT talks for improving relations with Soviet Russia, started their own brand of SALT—Soviet-American Lingerie Talks—to promote the sale of bras in the Russian market. Is it not the shortage of consumer goods which is creating serious problems for the success of perestroika? They can lick that problem by telling the Russians how to manufacture bras which are "soft, elastic and comfortable" and not "stiff and dowdy and ill-fitting Soviet-made brands." Those frumpy and frowzy Russian ladies can get excited with these new wares and Gorbachev would be off the hook. Duchowny, inventive and highly innovative, thought "part of Gorbachev's plan is to get consumer goods on the shelf to the women in the country." If they have a good bra, and if their children have nice clothing, they will see there is something happening in a real, tangible, immediate way. And then the wife can turn to her husband and say, "You are getting us something and now your turn is coming." What a pity that Gorbachev's Raisa did not think like Duchowny, despite all that talk that Gorbachev consults her on important matters of state. It escaped all the revolutionaries in history that revolution, to be successful, like lovemaking, has to begin with a nod from a woman. Marx, if only he had known this, would not have been traded so cheaply to the hated capitalists.

Economic and Political Weekly, 3 November 1990.

73

History unmade

EVENTS have been unfolding in communist China with the ferocity of a typhoon. Is history being made, we may credulously ask. No, history is being unmade. First a trickle, then a flood, that swamped the human landscape of China. Students leaving their cloistered, suffocating campuses mustered in strength at Tiananmen Square, but unlike their forebearers in the era of Red Guards, they did not destroy the homes, make a bonfire of books, mutilate the bodies either of their elders or their peers. They stirred up the spirits of their countrymen, roused their conscience, impregnated their inner urges with a new message. But like the Red Guards of yore, they shook up the apparatchiks with 'fat bottoms'—that is the only graphic phrase of Mao Zedong that they mouthed approvingly. They left poor Marx far behind, even Hegel, but echoed Nietzsche's philosophical dictum that "God is dead, God remains dead, and we have killed him."

Certainly God was alive before—the God that monitored the progress of the fight against oppression and social inequity during the Long March could not have remained dead. What is true is that someone killed the God. Who could that be? Not the students of today who have heard about the Long March only through their leaders. Perhaps none would ever know. In the Godless world of China, the students have coined a new slogan, "Law and democracy, not food and security." We neophytes in the art of living and politicking cannot figure out the language, much less grasp its hidden message. Communism, we thought, gives you security and food which the depraved of the world clamour for. But who can understand what communism is? It is like mathematics, as Bertrand Russell said long ago, "a subject in which we never know what we are talking about nor whether what we are saying is true." The generation of Chinese students after the marauding Red Guards of the 1960s invaded their seats of learning may not have known what mathematics is all about, but they certainly understood its language and mysteries. They may have told themselves that they "have been with their people where to its misfortune their people were." They braved the army unleashed by Deng and Li Peng and almost co-opted it in their quest for a consciousness of freedom.

But who is their hero? Aristotle? Plato? Rousseau? Jefferson? Abraham Lincoln? No. It is Mikhail Gorbachev, until recently a cog in the mighty Russian apparatus. But why Gorbachev, who is a toddling babe in this game of democracy? Gorbachev is a member of their family, their fraternity, and what he says has a certain air of *déjà vu*. He is facing the same problems which the students want their leaders to face. You liberalised the economy, you may have increased output, but who is enjoying the fruits of this liberalisation? They are telling the puffed-up leaders, if leaders they can be called, that economic liberalisation without political reforms, giving them voice in determining their future, is hypocrisy without limitation. Gorbachev sensed it, by assaulting first the citadel of power. He may have figured out that by providing outlets to the inner frustrations of his people, bottled up over the last seventy years, he would take the heat off their grievances. Consciousness of freedom is for them more precious than consumption of goods. The students may have reckoned that if they want to learn, they should learn from someone like them, facing problems the like of which they face. Friends in adversity are true friends. The Chinese leaders did not discover this truth, perhaps because they could not get over their addiction to the world of Confucius, inscrutable, enigmatic, and devious.

And yet the enigma of arrivals and departures of rebellions across the communist world leaves one cold. A few years ago it was Yugoslavia; and now a long queue—Hungary, Poland, China, and finally the original crusader, Russia. What has gone sour? Did they take a detour to the communist millennium by skipping the stage of full-blown capitalism? Like a traveller on a train who is over-carried, these communist states may be retracting to the stage they skipped. The Russia of Lenin was a country of incipient capitalism in the

Marxian lexicon. There was no flowering of capitalism which could be a springboard for a leap to communism as a tranquil station in social evolution. Chinese society on the eve of the communist revolution was feudal and leaders like Mao were patri-familial, bossy, authoritarian. Many of the production relations may have been ill synchronised with the evolving social relationships in new societies. It is somewhat curious, if not inexplicable, that the two countries which so far have been immune to the revolutionary brouhaha are East Germany and Czechoslovakia, both of which had well-advanced capitalist modes of production before turning communist. Could it be then that capitalism has remained a forbidden fruit for generations born in communist societies, so that at the first symptom of overt opposition, the whole superstructure of communism comes crashing down?

Or else, could it be that the social and political institutions of communist societies were not in congruence with the enormous technological innovations that revolutionised the techniques of production, information network, and mass communication, thus negating the impact of the instruments of power wielded by the communist state? If you know what goes on across your frontiers, you crane your neck to see how you stand in relation to the one beyond. Fred Hirst apparently outwitted the mighty Karl Marx. Man as much aspires for 'positional goods'—what he is in relation to others—as for material goods. It is this information revolution that probably hastened the demise of a communist state with all its appealing egalitarian gospel. And yet Marx lives amidst the ruination of his empire. His vision that the mode of production determines the social and political relations remains valid. Only that the nature of those political and social relations and institutions eluded the lesser leaders of the communist states. In an age when, and in a world where, the technological frontiers are advancing so much and so fast, there ought to be matching progress in the design and concept of social and political engineering if both production conditions and social relations that surround them have to move in step.

Yes, democracy has outsmarted communism as a way of life, but not for what Arnold Toynbee divined some thirty years ago. In a great divide between monolithic communist society and pluralistic democracy, Toynbee presaged, in terms of his idiom of challenge and response, communist society would succumb not to the consciousness of freedom or to the insatiability of man's unlimited wants, but to the undefined virtues of Christianity. "The relationship of the other spiritual forces of our time would be the only effective response to aggression, and would be decisive in creating the future of our civilisation." But the challenge that the communist states faced is not a challenge posed by religions so much as by the libertarian instinct of humanity.

With these headlines and datelines galore on mass protests in the communist world, you now see the communists in the capitalist world making a beeline for exits. For them getting on in the world is the political equivalent of getting out of the world they have known before. Here comes a leader of the Italian Communist Party, Achille Occhetto, dead set to change the image of a communist in the western eyes. Visiting the United States to ingratiate himself with its politicians, he has been saying that his party and he are about to banish the word 'communist' from their party. He did not mince words:

> Our party is not a member of a patrician political-ideological camp. It is not part of the so-called communist camp. On the contrary, I maintain that there is no longer a real communist movement and the traditions we represent are our own. We want democracy, no longer as a means to achieve socialism but to achieve democracy as a universal and in itself.

In this great metamorphosis of a communist, Occhetto is not alone. The fever is catching. And yet what Gorbachev and Zhao and Occhetto are saying through the roar of the Chinese students is not new to many in India. The same clarion call was given by an Indian who was a member of the Second International, a comrade of Lenin, and first a comrade of Mao and then his adversary, Manavendra Roy. At the end of his long journey, forlorn and forgotten, he lived in lonely splendour ruminating that "Man is and should be a measure of everything."

Economic and Political Weekly, 15 July 1989.

74

Children of the God that failed

THEY call these people 'bozis'—people without any definite direction or work. Like nomads, they drift along in search of work and, failing that, drugs or discarded half-bottles of vodka. Women among them, alienated and forlorn, barter their bodies for a morsel of food or even a cigarette stub, to warm up in winter and to cool their heels in summer. But 'bozis' are also 'bomzhis'—people who do not have any definite place of residence. In biting winter, airports and railway stations are their abode, and in summer, open-air public parks are the only welcoming places, if the cops are not around to hound them out. Among these bozis and bomzhis is a man who once was an economist, who first lost his job and then his wife; a woman, who lost her charm before losing the means of livelihood which were co-related with her youth; a meandering vagabond, bored stiff with his life in a village and perpetually nagged by the pestering family.

If you guess that these bomzhis abound in some depraved and degrading backward country, you may perhaps be right; if you curse a capitalist country, say, wretched America or England, where the worker is alienated from the fruits of his labour, you may perhaps be revealing your knowledge of dialectical materialism in its pristine form. But if you are told that none of your inferences is anywhere near the truth and that these hordes of bomzhis exist in that land of communism, Soviet Russia, you may perhaps pull your hair in disbelief and brand it all capitalist propaganda. But strange things are happening these days in all parts of the globe. Whether it is capitalism or socialism, neither can escape social stigmas—

prostitution, depravity, black-marketing, homelessness, drunkenness, and goodness knows what else. A communist Russia and its cohorts could bandy the slogan, till recently, "To everyone according to his needs." Now the slogan has changed, the tune has changed, the ethos has changed, and the very foundation of their philosophy is tottering. To cavil at America for its expanding tribe of homeless, the Soviets, a couple of years ago, filmed a television documentary on a destitute sleeping on the pavements of New York City and paid for his jaunt to Moscow to attest to the cruelty of the capitalist system. Now the joke is being played back. Russia is hoisted with its own petard. The American press, momentarily deprived of new scandals at home, is replete with juicy stories about the homeless, the unemployed, and the drunken of the communist world. The number of homeless seen is small; their number unseen is large. With Gorbachev's new policies bankruptcies will spread and unemployment will mount. Yes, the reserve army of unemployed in a proletarian state. And soon, the reserve army of unemployed will become the regular army of the homeless.

Is this homelessness a new phenomenon or was it hidden all these years, only to surface now with the onset of glasnost and perestroika, Gorbachev's new buzzwords? The shortage of housing in Russia and other communist countries has been known for years. Its manifestation was contained by the vigilance of the state, which did not permit people from the hinterlands to move to the cities without a valid document. Moscow and, like it, other leading cities of Russia, have been notoriously short of living space, leaving no choice to its denizens other than to share tiny apartments and communal bathrooms and kitchens with their extended families and friends. Good housing and luxury apartments are for the privileged Communist party elite, the intelligentsia, and those with access to the seats of power. Private property may have been abolished, but not the private ownership of power which holds the lives of people in thraldom. There was not, until recently, a freewheeling press to ventilate this seething discontent. Gorbachev's glasnost has now changed all that by tearing down the veil of secrecy. The press—*Pravda* and *Izvestia*—are itching to air the grievances in public. People are stirred out of their somnolence. Scores of letters have been pouring into newspaper offices, impaling the erring officials for their acts of omission and commission. Calamities and social evils are no longer non-events. That is why homelessness, though pervasive before, is now becoming, along with drunkenness and truancy, a major issue in the deliberations of the communist governments.

There is an irony of sorts in all this. Communism may not promise freedom of thought because enemies of the people may undermine the edifice of equality and social justice, but it surely needs to ensure freedom from want. Now the process is reversed: freedom from want has evaporated and freedom of thought is reasserting. Are all these social evils—homelessness, dope, unemployment, and black-marketing—endemic in all societies, communist and capitalist? We, the generation of the bygone era, dreamt of a better world which Marxian philosophy was thought to usher in. But if we see around us communist societies disintegrating, should we stop dreaming? Is humanity's quest for equality a chimera? One is uncomfortably reminded of a cynical remark of a Pole, with a tinge of sardonic humour, that "Under capitalism man is an enemy of man; under communism, it is just the reverse." But human nature being what it is, one likes to dream of a better world, a millennium where man is civil to man. If dreams are not to be dreamt, what are dreams meant for?

Gorbachev and the others of his ilk have recognised the limits of the proletarian state. Whatever justification there was for centralisation of power, it has now outlived its utility. Concentration of power without promise of a decent life for the citizen corrodes both mind and body. But what Gorbachev, who has to respond to his constituency for his survival, has discovered has totally eluded his comrades in India. They still have the vision of an egalitarian Russian society where everyone has a place to live and enough to eat. They believe that Gorbachev and Deng of China are denigrating their societies, having been seduced by capitalist blandishments or intimidated by western military prowess. Being safely ensconced in India, where the Indian communist leaders have not to face the music of angry and rebellious citizens, they can hold forth on the virtues of their decrepit programmes. Perhaps, they have been inwardly haunted by the infirmities of their beliefs, but confessing them may mean disowning their entire past with its beaming idealism and unselfish sacrifice. For leaders of the party, it is worse than harakiri. They have been used to following the lead, always basking in the glow of Russia or China or the East European countries. That is why they may have figured out that it is better to go to their graves clinging to what sustained them in their youth rather than with a sense of failure. Their God may have failed; but in this time and clime, there is no other God left to worship. The failed God is better than no God!

Economic and Political Weekly, 4 March 1989.

75

Assassins of communism

FAILURE is an orphan, they say. But this adage does not apply to the erosion of communism from countries in recent years. The leaders of the western world interpret the passing away of the communist empire as victory of the doctrine of democracy. Some others claim the credit for its demise because they could stand up to the communist dictatorship through building up countervailing power in the form of NATO.

But the communists have a different perception of this defeat of communism. One strand of thought takes a simple-minded view that it is renegades like Yeltsin and Gorbachev who conspired with the capitalists in the West to bring the edifice of golden communism down. But more sophisticated communists, particularly those in India who are loath to admit that they could go wrong, attribute the failure of communism to the dissociation of the Communist party and its apparatchiks from the people. They lament the death of Soviet society which "had set up the most comprehensive educational, cultural, health and social security arrangements the world has ever witnessed."

In this mélange of views, one thing that fails to come out is why such a society, if it was so egalitarian and satisfying to all its citizens, caved in so easily and without a fight. Now the truth is out. Boris Yeltsin in his book, *Against the Grain*, has presented a shocking picture of this imaginary fair society. He reveals that the politbureau of the Communist party enjoyed a luxurious lifestyle, including marble dachas, an array of domestic help to satisfy their every whim, and access to special stores, tailor shops and health clinics. This manifestation of privileged living is no way different from that of politicians in India or elsewhere in hated capitalist societies.

If the communists' apologetic explanation of the decline of communists is sheer prevarication, that by the leaders and the intellectuals of the West is self-serving. If democracy is strong and enduring, why did communism survive for so long and so powerfully for over seven decades in the Soviet Union and for three to four decades in China and Eastern Europe? The real causes of the communist collapse are endogenous; sooner or later, the societies rooted in that doctrine would have come to grief irrespective of whether the Communist party got dissociated from the people or whether the western countries had raised their defence wall against the communist danger.

It is the monism dominantly imposed on communist philosophy and its application in countries by Lenin and his colleagues which eventually destroyed communism and its human side, which had captivated the downtrodden and the liberals the world over. About ninety years ago, socialists like Eduard Bernstein, Karl Kautsky, Wilhelm Liebknecht, and Ignaz Auer reinterpreted the Marx-Engels doctrine and argued that capitalism would not decline due to its inner contradictions; it would instead reveal a far more robust capacity to adapt as capitalist production increased and became varied. They visualised that the general crisis that Marx projected as characterising the capitalist mode of production would simply evaporate.

However, explanations for any historic event after its occurrence should be less reliable than those which precede it. From this perspective, Rosa Luxemberg, the great Polish communist thinker, for some time a colleague of Lenin, had hit the nail on the head of all communists holding the Lenin-Stalin flag. She said in a book she wrote on the Russian Revolution a month before her violent death in 1918:

> Socialism, by its very nature, cannot be dictated, introduced by command. Lenin is completely mistaken in the means he employs: decree, the dictatorial power of a factory overseer, Draconian penalties, rule by terror...Without general election, without unrestricted freedom of press and assembly, without free exchange

of opinion, life dies out of every public institution and only bureaucracy remains active.

When the foundations of the communist society were thus shaky, the party and its leaders would have gone the way they did, they could not have behaved otherwise. The dogmata of the communists ruled supreme. They ignored one great thinker among them and remained busy reciting the mantras of Lenin while their Indian counterparts remembered Rosa Luxemberg only to name their daughters after her. It is not the capitalists in the West but the communists themselves who are the assassins of communism.

The Times of India, 8 July 1992.

76

Forever embers

A revolution that spills blood seems to have lost its nature. What is going on in Soviet Russia, East Germany, Poland, Hungary and Czechoslovakia is more than a revolution. It has all the hallmarks of what a revolution connotes and yet without tears. The empire—the communist empire—is being reduced to ashes, not with curses heaped on the emperor but a shower of panegyric to drown him. That architect of American democracy, Thomas Jefferson, paid homage to volunteerism that overlays democratic movements, but believed that the blood of those participating in these movements is the fertiliser of freedom. "What country before ever existed a century and a half without a rebellion?" Thomas Jefferson pondered about a hundred and fifty years ago. "The tree of liberty must be refreshed from time to time with the blood of patriots and tyrants. It is the natural manure." The events in Eastern Europe and Soviet Russia have made not only Marx and Lenin dated but also Jefferson. There are masses of people milling across the borders of Germany, teasing the feared dictators of yesteryears, cocking a snook at them; the timid and the servile in Russia now openly honour Stalin's victims. A mass gathering in Warsaw observes a symbolic funeral of victims of the post-war era known as Stalin's Terror; the politicians in Hungary declare the dawn of democracy, burying their communist past as a horrible nightmare. And yet no guns were fired, no prisoners held, no torture, no razing of buildings. Instead, the stern-faced apparatchiks passed into the woodwork one by one and, what is more, they praised the leader of leaders, Mikhail Gorbachev, as a symbol of freedom. "The freedom of Russians", they rent the air with their slogan, "is essential for the freedom of all people in the communist empire." Whether history has ended or returned or changed its name, never before in the recorded annals was there seen such a tremendous upheaval without mayhem.

Let us begin at the beginning. Soviet Russia's foreign minister tells Soviet legislators that "the nine-year Soviet military rule in Afghanistan had violated Soviet law and international norms of behaviour." He also confessed with disarming candour that construction of a radar system near Krasnoyarsk was an open violation of the Anti-Ballistic Missile Treaty with the United States. Eduard Shevardnadze is not disturbed "by the growth of political rivals to the communist parties of eastern Europe." Imre Nagy's Hungary awakes asking the Russians to go home while at the same time thanking their favourite "Gorby", whom also the rebelling Chinese welcomed in the midst of the Tiananmen Square tragedy. They recalled the trauma of 1956 which ushered in democracy, but took caution "to maintain an undisturbed and balanced relationship with the Kremlin." Then Poland follows suit but not without anger over the slaughter of thousands of Poles by the Satan of Terror. At the same gathering, two communist members of the cabinet plead for mercy and entreat the crowd to produce more tangible evidence of terror so that the guilty could be punished.

The new Hungarian democracy claims its inheritance not from America, not from the French Revolution, not from the British parliament but from Gorby's Russia. Gyula Obersovozhy, a writer and editor who was condemned to death in the 1956 Hungarian uprising, remarked:

> History has taught us that as long as Moscow is not free, we cannot be free either. The silent revolution could not have taken place in Eastern Europe if Gorbachev had not beckoned it. The Soviet bloc's bloodiest uprising of 1956 was branded as a counter-revolution until recently. It was Stalin's henchmen then who turned the revolution into a counter-revolution.

It is an irony of history that the new leaders of that same repressive system of Stalin and Brezhnev have countered the counter-revolution. Did not that great revolutionary, Jean-Jacques Rousseau, father of the French Revolution, tell his fellow revolutionaries in sombre tones that "the body politic like the human body begins to die from its birth, and bears in itself the curse of its own destruction?" Marx, so it seems, thought that Rousseau's precept held true only for capitalism, which sows the seeds of its own destruction. Biology is no respecter of ideology. Men in tragedy and adversity have no religion, no nationality, no race. Around the same time 15,000 people in Moscow surrounded the KGB's yellow brick headquarters and in fond remembrance wept for their kith and kin who were the victims of KGB terror. A retired woman with auburn hair and huge sad eyes held photographs of the many people whom they were commemorating. Yet another man, aged beyond his years, could now say, "Only in my sixties can I stand here and even dare to talk aloud about our country's history. Maybe the most important part of standing here, even if for just a half hour, is to try to begin building a guarantee that these atrocities will never happen again."

The communist dominoes are falling one after another. But most sensational has been the total collapse, sudden and massive, of the whole edifice of the regime of East Germany. The people did not rebel, they did not fight, they did not throw bombs. In fact, they brought about a revolution without being revolutionary. They followed the path of the mythological heroes of the Orient. The people took to renunciation *en masse*. They left the country of their birth, their youth, their ancestors, their memories. Did any ideology motivate them? Did any blandishments seduce them? The apologists of the regime first blamed the younger generation but when the youth were joined by the old and the infirm, the regime caved in. Egon Krenz acted for Honecker. The cabinet was first reshuffled and then banished, yet the people said nay. The politburo was bundled out. The stubbornness became more stubborn. Only when promises of overhauling the whole system were held out did the people relent. Yes, revolution sans revolutionaries. The rulers learned their lesson, though belatedly. "Whenever any form of government becomes destructive to the pursuit of happiness and liberty, it is the right of the people to alter or abolish it." The eternal values spawned by the consciousness of freedom came alive.

In the midst of the turmoil in the eastern Empire, Gorbachev and his comrades are unshaken and even indulged in one-upmanship. At a celebration in Washington of the seventy-second anniversary of the October Revolution whose legacy is in a shambles, the Soviet Ambassador Yuri V. Dobrynin proclaimed, "Each country has its own pattern, its own manner to reform the lives of the people. It is that optimistic spirit we saw in the demonstration in Moscow [a reference to Moscow protestors about Stalin's victims]. But we have to be realistic and we must work hard." Referring to the drastic events in East Germany, Poland and Hungary, Dobrynin said, "Events are developing at a rapid speed. You can see them in every Soviet activity. We have five Soviet deputies from the Supreme Soviet here: and they expressed eleven opinions." If the scorpion loses its sting can it still remain a scorpion? The world seems to be going upside down and the emperor loses his empire with a smile on his face and a bouquet of flowers in his hand.

With the cascading of events like a forest fire, one is chastened. Revolutions without a shot fired have rarely been seen before; but would the world see similar revolutions again? Some sham historian in the US State Department has pronounced the demise of history. According to him, the ideological battles fought over the last two–three hundred years were all lost in favour of liberal democracy. But did not democracies fight among themselves before? If ideology were the sole *raison d'être* for wars, the world would have long become one world. In the euphoria, yesterday's cold war strategists and the leaders of the nation-states of Europe, founded and unfounded since the crumbling of the Austro-Hungarian empire, have been strangely gripped by amnesia. Getting out of communism is not getting into heaven on earth, where man ceases to be enemy of man. André Gluckmann, a French philosopher, has brought these nation-statesmen down to earth by warning them that "getting out of communism is getting back into history." That history has not ended. It may return with its old fury and devilry.

Hitler's Lebensraum wrought havoc in the 1930s and 1940s. Hitler may have been destroyed but the ghost of Lebensraum, like all ghosts, may still lurk on a distant horizon. One should only look at the cartographic evolution of Germany from the imperial Germany of the late nineteenth century to the Weimar Germany Hitler inherited, to Hitler's New Order, and finally to the divided Germany of the post-Second World War period. The exodus of East Germans to West Germany may be in quest of democratic freedom, but what they leave behind would soon be a part of united Germany. If ideology plays truant, there will be no reason for East Germany to exist as a separate entity. The revolution in East Germany is therefore different from what is happening in Poland, Hungary, Czechoslovakia, Bulgaria and Soviet Russia. All have ostensibly become democracies, but soon may become warring and feuding nations. Germans in Sudetenland, Silesia, Prussia, which were parcelled out to Poland, Russia, France, etc., did not suffer in vain. All their humiliation, hubris, will return. Already in West Germany there are rumblings about the American and Russian armies being occupation armies. Do they not echo the anger of the 1920s' Germany?

The Russians have disgorged their cold war baggage. The Americans are gloating that it was their strong defence policies which brought the Russians to their knees. Little do they realise in their celebration of the triumph of democratic ideology that the cold war baggage left behind by the Russians has explosives of enough destructive power to trigger a hot war in Europe. West Germany as it is now is a great economic giant dominating the European Common Market. United Germany will have all the more power to itself. The former communist countries may have hugged the democratic ideology but only a few among them have lost a lust for power—the opiate of the nation-state. What democracy does in practise in contrast to its hallowed glitz has been well epitomised by de Tocqueville:

> Not only does democracy make every man forget his ancestors, but it hides his descendants and separates his contemporaries from him; it throws him back forever upon himself alone and threatens in the end to confine him entirely within the solitude of his own heart.

Economic and Political Weekly, 17 February 1990.

77

Ostriches of our time

YOU call yourself a political philosopher, an intellectual who sets the pace for social and political change. A legatee of the Hegelian logical traditions, and harbinger of Marx and Engels' vision, passion and a sense of history, you ignite the idealism of the youth, conjure up their dreams, and spur them to action so that a better world of the morrow would emerge from the shambles of the existing chaos. Then you call yourself a leader. But halfway through, something goes askew. The world you knew becomes unrecognisable, the comrades you jostled with in processions, in struggles on the streets, and on the ideological platforms are transmogrified into armies of the night, speaking different languages, singing unheard-of tunes. Without your knowing, you are marooned on an island with only memories of the bygone past as your only companions. And then you become adamant about your own perceptions and thoughts. What you don't know does not exist and what you know is the only eternal truth; you are just a gestalt; no properties can be derived to guide the progress of society from any of your parts or the summation of the parts that go into your making.

Such is the state of communists today under two democracies—the richest and the largest. The communists have always been a curiosity in America, except when some Joseph McCarthy rises on the horizon to beat down all the progressives and to provide a free play to all the venal instincts or when the cold war strategists want to drum up support for the military-industrial complex. And today that motley crowd of furtive communists in their hideouts on 23rd Street in the Chelsea area of Manhattan ruminates on the fading fortunes of world communism.

Their ongoing leader Gus Hall, with a replica of the antique telephone Lenin once was supposed to have used, believes that Gorbachev has gone berserk with his crazy ideas of perestroika and glasnost. For him, the workers in Soviet Russia going on strike is anathema. "How can workers in a workers' state strike to destroy their own haven?" he asks. Hall, disconcerted by the Soviet withdrawal from Afghanistan, still insists that Soviet occupation of that country was legitimate. How can the socialist state tolerate the capitalist stooge? he asks.

They have a line to Soviet Russia but it has turned from hot to cold; messages get garbled. He is not even aware that the Soviet foreign minister Eduard Shevardnadze repudiated the Soviet invasion of Afghanistan as unethical and a blunder that Gorbachev tried to rectify. They are not wiser by the events in East Germany, Hungary, Poland, and now Bulgaria. One of their spokespersons, from the well-fortified abode in Manhattan, blames the western media for their aggressiveness. Carol Marks suggests that "the crux of the problem is that the East Germans underestimated the power of capitalist propaganda. And the East German communists did not train their youth to appreciate what they have and to prevent them from seeing what the capitalists want them to see." Asked if her comrades also hold the same views, she snaps back: "You can talk to as many people here as you like, but you are not going to get any different opinion." Yes, there is democracy but a centralised one.

These communists, twenty thousand-odd in a population of 270 million, are a comic lot. They feel that the East Europeans and the Soviets should seek their counsel. If only they had digested what the great Stalin and Lenin formulated, they would not have come to this sorry pass. At least they could have consulted Cuba's Castro who is remaining steadfast to his creed.

Gus Hall, Carol Marks and their cohorts, though bred and brought up in the affluence of a capitalist country, could be twins of our Ranadives and Namboodiripads and their other comrades both in thought and action. Indian communists are mad at Gorbachev for having let down Lenin and Stalin. They branded him a counter-revolutionary. But these comrades in two continents, separated by culture, history and traditions, think alike and in a vacuum. A Marxist, a communist is neither if he ignores that the surrounding conditions fashion his mode of thought and the perceptions of events which he is drawn into.

"A philosopher of imposing nature", said the great philosopher Alfred North Whitehead, "does not think in a vacuum. Even his most abstract ideas are, to some extent, conditioned by what is or is not known till the time when he lives." The American and Indian comrades may not be philosopher statesmen and Lenin may not philosophise, but at least they should think like those whose heritage they claim and whose creed they espouse.

Gods change when the religion changes but the religion of these communists has changed even when their Gods have not. Workers of the world, at least a part of the world, have united and disunited, but the chain which imprisoned the minds of these champions of the workers' causes has not been lost. When Trotsky drifted, he was a renegade; Bukharin was sent to the gallows, his was a treasonable act. Now, Bukharin is rehabilitated, and Trotsky is on his way back to the pantheon of twice-born communists in Russia, Poland, Yugoslavia, East Germany, Hungary. In this dispensation the geronts among the communist ranks in both countries are desperately seeking some straws to clutch so that the flag of communism can be held aloft. In these uncertain times they see a glimmer of hope in the angry China of Deng where the Tiananmen bloodbath squared the communist circle. Oh, the Chinese youth impaled the communist leaders, corrupted by surreptitiously creeping capitalism, they said. But to see the resurgence of communism in today's China is to mistake oriental despotism for the dictatorship of the proletariat. The old Chinese inscrutable character and their mysterious cultural and ethnic traits are reasserting. The only thing is that after every transfer of scene, new drapery is worn by the characters on the stage. Chinese society, even after forty years of communist rule, remained glued to its moorings. Mao Zedong, for all his communist façade, knew it better than the Indian and the American communists. When asked by Richard Nixon in 1972 whether he had changed the world, his eyes twinkled with repartee: "I have been able to change a few things in the vicinity of Beijing." That sums up what communism as a system, philosophy, and social dynamic has been able to achieve whether in the East or in the West.

And yet why, one wonders, India and America, two countries with two different cultures, should produce communists with similar mental mould? Perhaps, the historical and cultural background of both have a hidden common thread. Indians from time immemorial have an addiction to their past. Their scriptures contain prescriptions for all eventualities, for all seasons. They never age. They only mature with the passage of time. Everything therefore needs to be interpreted with reference to the written word, beliefs descended from generation to generation. To discard this is to court disaster. Though these Indian communists, when first inducted into this domain of new philosophy, look at it as a substitute for the ancestral thought, the communist philosophy remained no more than a revamped scripture on which they were brought up. Denigrating these scriptures means denying their very existence. Whatever the consequences, therefore, you have to abide by these scriptures. They have remained traditionalist, religious, while overtly debunking both tradition and religion. Did they not say that the present or the future is merely the continuation of the past?

But eastern philosophy is not the Americans' cup of tea. Then, do American communists clone the Indian communists? Perhaps. The American prospered, since the foundation of the society, by going west, conquering it, decimating the native Indian. In the fatigue that followed, they might have felt remorse for what they did. In such a weak moment, they may have felt the need to expiate by thinking of larger humanity. For those who had gone marauding to the west must have been at peace with their conscience by traversing to the east.

The time has come not only for these communists with their heads in the clouds but for all thinking men and women to realise the liberation of conscious reason, when history is made and unmade with the speed of light. If you despise "the institutions and customs which have not been consciously designed, you would thus become the destroyer of the civilisation built upon them." It is, therefore, no use setting up "'ideological agglomeration' and calling it the Holy Roman Empire because it is neither holy, nor Roman, nor an empire."

Economic and Political Weekly, 13 January 1990.

78

Consciousness precedes being

IF you say something clearly and precisely, something of common knowledge and experience, you will come a cropper. If you know what we know, then you should not come all the way to waste your time and ours. But this is not the style of the newly anointed statesmen of Eastern Europe, unshackling itself from the bear hug. Yesteryears' rebellious worker becomes today's visionary statesman in one country; in another, a playwright languishing in jail for blasphemous utterings becomes president of a new republic. Plato's philosopher king is passé; novelist prime minister or playwright president is the new fashion. This is just as well. If an old political idiom has changed with outworn clichés being junked, the new one replacing it should be sufficiently obfuscatory. It should sound sonorous and soothing but the message should be left as vague as possible.

And now comes President Vaclav Havel of Czechoslovakia with his stirring call for the consciousness of freedom, the consciousness which makes "free men reflect in human meekness and in human responsibility"—whatever that may mean. Havel invoked Tomas Garrique Masaryk, founder of the modern democratic Czechoslovakia that emerged from the ruins of the Austro-Hungarian empire. But that country of freedom vanished into thin air as quickly as it came into being. Being and non-being followed each other in quick succession. Two big nation-states, first Germany and then Russia, became the sources of nightmares for this nation and others in the hapless Europe of that period. For fifty years, the Czechs "slumbered beneath the pall of the totalitarian system."

Vaclav Havel did the most unusual thing as he held US Congressmen in his spell. He turned to Mikhail Gorbachev and paid him a tribute even his most ardent admirers had not till now. He said:

> The first act in this remarkable drama began when Gorbachev and his colleagues, faced with the sad reality of their country, initiated a policy of perestroika. Obviously, they had no idea either of what they were setting in motion or how rapidly events would unfold. We know a lot about the enormous number of growing problems that slumbered beneath the honeyed, unchanging mask of socialism.

And then Havel asked America and other western powers to help his country and others like it but help in the strangest of ways. He beseeched America that

> the best way the world can help Czechoslovakia and Eastern Europe is to help the Soviet Union on its irreversible but immensely complicated road to democracy. My request is as paradoxical as the whole of my life has been. I can only say that the sooner, the more quickly, and more peacefully the Soviet Union begins to move along the road towards genuine political pluralism, respect for the rights of the nations to their own integrity and to a working—that is a market—economy, the better it will be not just for Czechs and Slovaks but for the whole world.

Has any statesman of any country incarcerated for his beliefs and patriotism ever pleaded for his former tormentor with so much eloquence? Or was it mere drama, a contrived act for effect? Havel's message was not lucid perhaps or it was lucid but too subtle for his audience. It conveyed to his eager listeners, to Americans in particular, a much larger and prophetic message that the enemy of the past may not be the enemy of the future any more than the friend of the present would remain the benefactor of the morrow.

From his chilling survey of the experiences of East European slavery, Havel, playwright that he is, soared into the stratosphere of Becketian philosophical riddles. After having told the American lawmakers what he and his country have learnt from American history, he gave back to them something in return, drawn from "their experiences and the knowledge that has come from it." What he had to offer was epitomised in a single idea:

> The specific experience I am talking about has given me one great certainty; consciousness precedes being and not the other way round, as Marxism would have it. Without a global revolution in the

> sphere of human consciousness, nothing will change for the better in the sphere of our being as humans and the catastrophe toward which this world is headed—be it ecological, social, demographic or a general breakdown of civilisation—will be unavoidable.

And this cryptic 'one idea' left everyone, journalists, Congressmen and other cognoscenti all over America in a whirl. What Havel meant became the topic of animated discussions in this usually gossipy city. The *Washington Post* editorial was captioned "Let's Hear it for Hegel." Someone thought that the editor might have misspelt Havel's name. But could it not also be that Havel was somehow ratiocinating his understanding of Hegelian dialectics? Hegel it was who delved into the 'phenomenology of the mind' and constantly talked about consciousness or subconsciousness as penumbras of the human mind; who said that "the history of the world is none other than the progress of consciousness of freedom."

No, it couldn't have been a lapse on the part of the newspaper editors. Hegel with Havel are kindred souls born in different times and worlds. Oh, yes, Havel came from Czechoslovakia and the world knows of a Kundera film, "Unbearable Lightness of Being", on the Prague generation of rebels against the communist regime during the 'Prague spring.' Havel's reference to 'being' could have conjured up in some minds at least the delectable and sensual scenes of young Czechs salaciously photographed in the movie. Members of the US Congress could only react to the trigger word 'being' with free play given to their libidos in their mental recall of all those skinny, aquiline and voluptuous bodies. Havel may be a playwright who can occasionally take liberties with words and nudity. But Havel is President and as President surely he could not have indulged in smirky levity? "Consciousness precedes being"!—did that not remind you of Jean Paul Sartre's "existence precedes essence"? But what has 'essence' got to do with 'being' either physically, emotionally or spiritually?

Was it deliberate that the message was left without a message? Havel is 'a theatre absurdist'—like Ionesco and Becket—who could not have left what he wanted to say that unclear. The meaning is clear, but in an 'absurdist' way, like his play 'Memorandum' which, as Kundera said in his tribute to him, "shows a world where words have no meaning, or meanings differ from accepted sense or still again are scenes behind which reality has disappeared." These 'nouveau statesmen' have sprung up to the political platform without any clear perception of what is in store for them. The predatory communism which destroyed individual freedom is dead and gone. They, however, are unsure what is the shape and substance of things to come. And when you do not know what you are up against, it is better to be vague and ambiguous. If you can dress up your confusion with beautiful phrases or some lofty philosophical thoughts it is even better. People go on debating about their true meaning long enough for anyone putting out such messages to bow out of centre stage. Clearly, Havel faced this dilemma. Havel, in a separate address delivered to the Polish sejm and senate in January warned the Poles,

> But paradise on earth has not been victorious, nor can it win in future. The notion that it would win could console only the vain minds of those who were convinced that they understood everything, that there was no higher mysterious institution above them, and that they were in charge of history. Thus paradise on earth has not been victorious and there are many moments ahead.

Then he paused to clarify why paradise on earth has not been victorious. "It is difficult to imagine an undivided Europe with a divided Germany, but at the same time it is difficult to imagine a united Germany in a divided Europe..." Havel, who spoke in quizzes to the US Congress, could be the great prophet of anti-prophecy, as his admiring compatriot Jiri Grusa said of him.

Robert Mrazek, a former Czech but now a member of the US Congress, heard Havel say in Prague a few months ago, "No. The best resistance we can have is through our own people. We know what we have to do. I want to ask for your moral support." Then Mrazek walked slowly up to him. Havel urged him to say something in the Czech language. Mrazek, long torn away from his native country, remembered one six-word sentence in Czech. He responded, "Please pass the bread and butter." Havel looked at him in a puzzled sort of way before Mrazek was whisked away. For Havel, has consciousness preceded being or the other way round?

Economic and Political Weekly, 2 June 1990.

79

Flying on the wings of time

A restaurant in the side lanes, with bare tabletops; a circle of serious looking, shaggy-bearded young men in their mid-30s with dishevelled hair, measuring their life in teacups and smoking away their thoughts in a spiral of circles on historical dialectics, democratic centralism, the Stalin-Trotsky thesis and antithesis on world revolution, the decadent national bourgeoisie, and the final denouement, the raging controversy whether the Bolshevik revolution was a permanent revolution or a false alarm. And then the doubts, genuine intellectual doubts, the angst of the mind and anguish of the heart. Was the annihilation of millions in quest of the El Dorado of collectivisation of land necessary? For the beauty of living in a distant future when the State would wither away, could the ghastly killings have been avoided?

Such was the typical setting for the young in those palmy days of our childhood. Being an enslaved and a poor nation, the distance of Russia lent charm and richness to our miserable existence. We all dreamed that one day Russia—Lenin's Russia which had made a reality of Marx's utopia, his flight of fancy—would take many a hapless, poor, tyrannised country to that kingdom in heaven. We grew up in an era of imperial monarchs to be alive at the birth of national freedom and sing the thrilling national anthem composed by Tagore—that universal man who, too, enriched our dream of Stalin's Russia as the great star beckoning mankind.

From youth to middle and old age, we journeyed in timeless time. Our philosophical, ideological, intellectual universe has changed. The

Red Star has fallen from our lofty ideological sky. How do we explain it, how can we rationalise it? Were we dumb dunderheads? No, we were not a success, but we were certainly not nincompoops; we were in the vanguard of a revolution which we thought would create a new man, a new society. If Soviet Russian society has been betrayed by Khrushchev and Gorbachev and Yeltsin, it is the work of renegades and not the infirmity of the philosophy we were imbued with. Stalin may have been a bad man, but he was a great man who gave his people enough to survive on without fear of unemployment; he saved his country from the Nazi marauders. What if he butchered a few millions of his own people? The torture of the few is a sub-set of a larger set of happiness for the many. Forget Stalin, but what would you say about Lenin? He was a kind man, was he not? Do not give credence to what people like Mikhael Synyavsky, once a communist and now an ex-communist novelist, say. Didn't that great Nobel laureate, Jean-Paul Sartre, say that "an anti-communist is a dog"? Sartre was right, as we, followers of Lenin and Stalin, were right in our beliefs. Synyavsky wrote—and you must remember that he had lost his faculties and patriotism in jail where he was put for his infidelity to the doctrine—that

> it is difficult to understand Lenin because despite his all-consuming intellectuality, from his neat pen flowed seas of blood. Whereas by nature he was not an evil person, by concentrating all powers in his hands Lenin paved the way for Stalin, who erected a state church on Lenin's foundation.

Synyavsky embroiled himself in contradiction: If a kind man becomes cruel, there must be good grounds for his cruelty. The dictatorship of the proletariat must be preserved at all cost. So cruelty begets kindness which sustains a new order where man ceases to be the enemy of man.

This is how the communist groups thrash out the dialectics of the collapse of Soviet Russia and East Europe. They are supremely confident that this is a transient phase in social revolution, which will pass sooner than many gullible capitalist stooges believe. You cross the seven seas and go to France which remained home for many years for fantasizing Marxist intellectuals, who are not different from the Indian comrades. Intellectuals there have a long tradition of being rebels. Historically, they have constituted themselves into a veritable class, consulted or avoided by the ruling powers—very much like the leftist intellectuals in India—revered or reviled as the prophets of old, a symbol of France's exalted lettered self-image. Now the horizon of their ideas has been revealed to be a barren landscape. The eclipse of communism as a social philosophy has dismantled the framework of debate they had erected. What is it to be a leftist now? Bernard-Henri Levy, a leading French philosopher, gave this distraught answer: "Well, I don't know. The political system itself dies slowly, but the political culture takes even longer to die."

The French intellectuals are Sartre's children—they carry his intellectual and ideological legacy. Sartre's aphorisms fly all over in Paris and its suburbia. "The Soviet Union", he once said, "is an article of faith, is the only big country where the word progress has any meaning."

He was not defensive about Stalin's mass killings. In 1973, he said while addressing a gathering, "A revolutionary regime must rid itself of certain threatening individuals; I see no way of doing this other than death." Truly, extinction is the main plank of Sartre's existentialist philosophy. To be a person, those dissenting from you should be made non-persons. To exist, you create conditions for others to non-exist. It is equal and opposite.

But Sartre was not alone. Louis Althusser was looking towards the land of prophets in 1969: "In the Soviet Union, men are now treated without class distinction, meaning as people." André Gide echoed these lofty philosophical thoughts. But the children of Sartre, Althusser and Gide are flummoxed by events. The great walls around communist society have now crumbled, allowing these philosophers to see what was within. In communist society, the ideal of Sartre and Althusser, the communist nomenclatura were a class apart—they had privileged access to special medicines, dachas, luxury cars, holiday resorts, five-star hotels; they became the *alias* for the predatory capitalists of hated capitalist society. But the intellectual breed of France, unlike its Indian counterpart, remained true to its nature. When they saw that there was a disjunction between what they had espoused hitherto and the horrifying reality of communist society, they questioned their beliefs. Bernard-Henri Levy and his comrades launched a new movement as intellectuals to emancipate themselves from the constraints of a leftist past and to uphold new mainstream humanist moral values.

Andre Gluckmann, once a Maoist who deems himself a neutral, ruminates, "I think thought is an individual action, not one of a party. First you think and if that corresponds with the left, then you are of the left. If right, then you are of the right. But this idea of thinking left or right is a sin against the spirit and an illusion." But what about the future of intellectuals? Levy, handsome of face and compassionate at heart, has an answer, apt, pointed, and visionary.

> The ideal of intellectual is not tied to the left but to a revolution, the idea of remaking humanity. The *tabula rasa* of China and of Cambodia showed that this was a barbaric idea. The prophet must give way to another type of intellectual who can criticise the stereotype of society; they have the role of taking these ideas, concepts and reshaping them.

And see here in our country. We define an intellectual as one who does not change, who clings to his past; he lives on a different planet. He sees conspiracy everywhere. If his beliefs are challenged, he feels threatened and thinks that a counterrevolution is round the corner. They still fly on the wings of time, without knowing that their time has gone by.

Economic and Political Weekly, 25 July 1992.

80

When Karl Marx meets Indian communists

A bearded man, aged, dressed in nineteenth-century western style, a broad lapelled jacket with a crumpled necktie of faded colours, with narrow-bottomed trousers reaching up to the knees, landed at Santa Cruz airport one chilly morning in December 1989. Though a bit wan, he had a dignified mien, a sage-like look that confused the officer greeting him at the Indian immigration. "Sir, are you the great Maharshi Mahesh Yogi, the spiritual leader of Transcendental Meditation fame? What can I do for you?" Karl Marx, somewhat jaded and disoriented reaching the gateway to the Orient, quizzically looked at the officer and shrugged his shoulders. Not knowing what the officer was conveying, Marx softly replied, "I know spirits but not spiritualism. Pardon me, will you please guide me to Raj Bhavan, Sandhurst Bridge, Bombay, where Indian communists have their headquarters? I am Karl Marx, and I want to visit them as they are my disciples, preaching my doctrines in your country for the last eighty years." The officer had heard of communists but not of Karl Marx. He pottered around a bit and came back to Marx to tell him that the communists had given up Raj Bhavan long ago as it smacked of royalty, and he would have to go to the Writers' Building in Calcutta or to Trivandrum where they had formed the governments. Apparently elated that at least somewhere communists were still in power, Marx requested the officer to guide him to the domestic airport to catch an Indian Airlines plane to Calcutta. He might have figured out that the more powerful communist party functionaries reside in Calcutta. Anyone wanting to meet a minister must be a VIP and that was enough for the minions at immigration to contact all the important persons for arranging Marx's journey to Calcutta.

Messages were transmitted to the West Bengal Chief Minister, Jyoti Basu, that Guru Karl Marx was on his way to visit him and his other comrades to discuss some important matters. At first Jyoti Basu was flabbergasted. How could Marx, long dead, come back to life? Then he possibly thought that India was a land where miracles had happened. He knew many of his comrades visited temples rather covertly, asked for boons from the gods and goddesses and often consulted astrologers. Who knows, there may be life after death, as Hindu religion has dinned in their ears. Marx, having seen his whole communist universe in ruins, must have been reborn to save it, like Lord Krishna.

Comrade Basu immediately sent urgent messages to all his close comrades. He hesitated for a while. Could not his erstwhile friend and comrade Ashok Mitra also be invited, even though his acerbity and rapier-like pen denouncing renegades like Gorbachev might create an unpleasant situation? But he shrugged off the thought and brought together the phalanx of his colleagues to confront Marx. He prepared a long litany of complaints against Soviet Russia and other East European countries who had dropped their communist systems in the ocean like dead rats.

After the initial exchange of courtesies, Karl Marx started slowly but with great deliberation to explain the purpose of his visit to his Indian comrades: "I have been feeling unsafe in England for a long time. You know, the Englishmen, though they hated what I wrote and preached, immortalised me with a statue—an imposing one I must say—in High Gate cemetery. Until recently, quite a number of people used to visit me for affirming their faith. With the communist system disintegrating all round, the number of visitors has begun to dwindle. But Madam S. Pateman, a selfless and devout admirer of mine, is raising money through sale of coffee mugs, postcards and paperbacks with my pictures. But how long would this last? I am afraid my statue would be demolished as those of Lenin and Stalin in East Germany, Hungary, Poland, Romania, Czechoslovakia and even in Soviet Russia. I thought before my turn comes to be homeless, I should see some of my faithful disciples to explain what I meant to write and speak during my time, particularly because I am so misunderstood.

"I chose you, of all my other disciples, only because I am told you have remained my staunch supporters through thick and thin and held my banner high. It seems you are hopping mad about Gorbachev and the whole lot of those European communists who have betrayed my creed. I therefore felt that I should have a dialogue with you to find out where we went right and where we could have gone wrong. Mind you, I want to have a dialogue and not a dialectical discourse, which has now become old hat.

"Before I made my plan to meet you, I made a mistake, though inadvertently, in talking to Martin Jacques, editor of *Marxism Today*. I hope you have heard of him and read his writings. When he invited me to talk to him, I did not know what I had let myself in for. You know age has atrophied my brain cells and blunted the sharpness of my tongue. I am no longer the polemicist I used to be. I talked to Martin Jacques on many of the troubling issues of Marxism. I thought what passed between him and me would remain a secret with us, but after the fashion of modern journalists, he let me down by publishing the exchanges verbatim in the *Financial Times*, London, though I must admit that he did not misquote me in any of my answers to his questions.

"What I said to Martin may be unpalatable to you and you might misunderstand me. So let me state what you are likely to disagree with and then explain why I argued the way I did. First of all, Engels and I thought that a revolution in Russia might be a signal for other proletarian revolutions in the West. Unfortunately, it did not happen. When Russia went on its own, a country with a very small protelariat and no democratic traditions, it was a sure recipe for an authoritarian regime. It was socialism in the name of the people but in the hands of a small minority.

"Marxism is polymorphous and has become many traditions, but the Russian prototype became *the* Marxism. All other schools like those of the Second International were jettisoned. In our preoccupation with the laws of history and the inevitability of socialism, we became self-righteous and took pride in our elitism. Most of the repression of democracy first took place under Stalin and the world should not hold me responsible for his misdeeds. I can't be blamed for the behaviour of those whom I never met.

"While denigrating capitalism, I took care to insist that capitalism was a revolutionary system and that it had not exhausted its potential. But what I saw in the last eighty years simply dazzled me. I think Engels and I had overdrawn the picture of a collapsing capitalism and the attraction of a Utopian socialism.

"You know, comrade Martin Jacques is a smart man; he did not leave me with this answer. He rubbed it in further by referring to Eduard Bernstein, who argued that the process of reform should be seen as more important than the ultimate goal of revolution. Bernstein had warned that we must not expect to institute socialism as a result of a political and social crisis, but should build socialism by means of the progressive extension of social control and the gradual application of cooperation. We Marxists, communists, or whatever you may call us, should all have been wiser to have heeded Bernstein's prophetic pronouncements. But those were the days of intellectual intolerance and harsh language. Disagreement was treachery, honest difference of views was revisionism. I hope we all are more civil now.

"Let me explain my main mission. Much of what has happened in the communist world and most of what I said in my interview with Martin Jacques, I am sure, must have annoyed you no end, particularly in your present state of mind. Will you be shocked therefore if I disclose a little secret of mine, that much of what I have been saying was learnt from you Indian communists? I have always been hearing in my grave that you have been accused by your fellow countrymen, Nehru and all those pompous Congress leaders, that you repeat parrot-like what Lenin, Stalin and I have been saying all these years. You do not relate your positions, they said, to the situation in your own country and you always turned your ears either to the Third International in the past or to Soviet Russia or China. They even pilloried you saying that what Soviet Russia says today, Indian communists say tomorrow. I guess much of it is slander. If now communists in Eastern Europe and Russia are lamenting their vanishing empires, it is because they did not practise democracy as you did. You fought elections first in Kerala. But your prime minister, Nehru, whose synthetic socialism fooled you, dismissed you on trumped-up charges. The same trauma you went through in Bengal under Nehru's daughter. Yet you persisted and today you not only rule two states, but have also won enough seats in your national parliament to influence national policies. And all this through the democratic process. You gave democracy a chance and made achievement of socialism through democracy a reality. Engels had recognised in his preface to my *Class Struggle in France* that universal suffrage would render the insurrectionary method obsolete. You proved his prophecy right by your example. If only the communists in other countries had followed you! You sanctified Eduard Bernstein without knowing it.

"Again, Basu's communist government has grasped the real meaning of my embryonic thesis that the bourgeoisie cannot exist without constantly revolutionising the instruments of production, and thereby the relations of production, and with them the whole relations of society. I see that comrade Basu has invited the Birlas, Goenkas, Tatas, and even Ambanis, to set up industries in Bengal. He has even handed over some of the loss-making jute mills back to British capitalists. What else is this, if not rejuvenating capitalism, revolutionising its core?

"This is not all. You have gone ahead of the communists on the continent and in China. By your action you have modified the old Marxist clichés about the working class. The growing dominance of the industrial proletariat is coming unstuck. The era of the working class as an agency of change is over. Many of my comrades on the continent ignored the warning of Rosa Luxemberg that the organised working class can be as tyrannical and exploitative as the organised capitalists. Rosa may have made other mistakes, for instance in debunking Bernstein's gradualism, but on this she was dead right. Comrade Basu and one of your comrades, K.N. Raj, have now recognised the validity of Rosa's thesis. Raj has gone on record saying, "If extortion by labour does not end, more industries will shift out of Kerala." I was heartened to see that in West Bengal labour strikes have been contained effectively and organised labour has been tamed. So, you see that my point that the industrial working class can no longer remain an agency of change is validated by you here in India.

"My time is coming to an end and I would make two more points in support of your originality. You may have forgotten that amidst you was once a renowned Indian communist, Manabendra Nath Roy. Yes, he too came from this great state of yours. He, of all communists, was ahead of his times. He prophesied, and in my opinion correctly, the decline and fall of communism. He had vision, the intellectual capacity to see that social justice without democratic participation by the people would be a farce. So he first put his finger on democratic socialism, and finally ended up with radical humanism, which Gorbachev calls "communism with a humane face." But Roy was vilified in his time. Much of what is happening was what Roy had predicted long ago. This, too, is a feather in the cap of Indian communists. Then again, Roy came out with his theory of decolonisation, saying that colonial rule will end in all countries including India, and the capital invested in colonies will start yielding decreasing dividends. But we were all then inebriated with Lenin's grandiose doctrine of imperialism.

"So, my comrades, kudos to you. But before I take leave of you, I must express my puzzlement over the hiatus between what you speak and what you practise. You romanticise the communists in Soviet Russia and Eastern Europe for what they are doing. But what they are doing has been done by you long ago. Perhaps this is a cultural and sociological trait of Indians that they do not mean what they say and do not say what they mean.

"So, adieu and good luck to you. Before returning to England, I would stop briefly in China to tell comrade Deng that he should learn a bit of democracy from his Indian friends."

Marx slowly stood up and walked away without so much as shaking hands with Basu or his comrades. What would finally emerge from this unexpected visit of Karl Marx would only be known when a padded resolution passed at the next Communist party conference is released to the press.

Economic and Political Weekly, 5 May 1990.

Index

B

D

E

F

I

J

M

N

O

P

Q

R

S

Y